SAINT-MARTIN

Destabilization of the French Caribbean

5-7, rue de l'École-polytechnique ; 75005 Paris

http://www.librairieharmattan.com
diffusion.harmattan@wanadoo.fr
harmattan1@wanadoo.fr

ISBN : 978-2-296-54466-6
EAN : 9782296544666

Daniella JEFFRY

SAINT-MARTIN

Destabilization of the French Caribbean

Preface by
Fred RENO

To the memory of my father, Simon Jeffry, of my mother, Adela London Jeffry, and of my brother, Martial Jeffry,

To the memory of all those who knew how to impart to us the sense of historical continuity and who struggled to preserve our cultural heritage,

To all those who today understand that those Thirty Years of Pain are just the crossing of the desert ...

CONTENTS

LIST OF FIGURES AND DIAGRAMS

FIGURES

DIAGRAMS

ACKNOWLEDGMENTS

I could not have completed this study, without the assistance of all the journalistic sources which enabled me not only to chronologically and accurately situate all the players and events that marked this active and troubled period of the history of my native island, but also to directly reveal the opinions, thoughts, and experiences of all those who rely on the newspaper as a means of communication. I would like to thank the written press for playing this role of recording the important elements of Saint-Martin's daily life, on an island where oral expression is the most natural and privileged medium.

I wish to thank the Director of the Philipsburg Jubilee Library, Monique Alberts and in particular her assistant, Ans Koolen-Stel, and the public relations officer, Maryland Powell, who have warmly welcomed me among the staff and facilitated my access to the archived newspapers from which I extracted valuable additional information.

I thank all those with whom I have discussed and shared so many feelings, memories and experiences. There are far too many to name them individually, for fear of forgetting someone. They know who they are. Others have graciously passed on to me copies of their personal documentation, in particular, Alex Choisy, Patricia Etienne, and Omer Arrondell.

I have entrusted Oswald Francis with the critical reading of the English manuscript. I thank him for his sincere interest in this work. Professor Fred Reno of the University of the French Antilles and Guiana, who is quite knowledgeable of the situation in Saint-Martin, has agreed to write the preface and I am extremely grateful to him.

Last but not least, my son Joseph and my daughter Tiana have contributed to the fine tuning of the book's layout by instructing me on various aspects of word processing, and, in particular, on how to make diagrams, with which I had no prior practice.

PREFACE

This book, entitled *Saint-Martin: Destabilization of the French Caribbean,* is written by a daughter of the soil. It is, therefore, not surprising that the main focus is devoted to the territory of Saint-Martin, although other Caribbean societies are referenced when relevant to the subject at hand. Daniella Jeffry outlines thirty years of history in a treatise which pulls no punches. Her often biting prose, nonetheless, avoids dull controversy. Obviously, the value of the book lies in its evaluation of Saint-Martin's recent past in an effort to better grasp a complex present, especially as characterized by the choice to obtain autonomous status separated from Guadeloupe within the French nation. "Separate Status within France" - a slogan heard during the electoral campaign on the statutory condition of Saint-Martin - effectively sums up the intention and ambiguities of the island. It conveys the local desire to reconcile Saint-Martin's identity with French republican equality: two approaches deemed irreconcilable by the author. "The quest for sameness is incompatible with the quest for distinctiveness," she tells us.

This book is also a critical and forward-looking examination of Saint-Martin. It situates the primary actors of local life. Beyond that, it sheds light on a system of actors in solidarity or in conflicting interactions, depending on the stakes at play. Politicians are the first targeted. Consenting victims to the pressures from the business world and from social demands, they seem to conceive their elective function, above all, as a source of symbolic and material compensation. As for the business world, the beneficiary of tax remission, it adopts the basic ideology of liberal economy in a territory where the Welfare State seems to be failing. When a political actor does not blend with an economic actor, as exemplified by the Flemings' scenario, they are often engaged in complicit relations that produce interpersonal dependency and heavily influence the functioning of social activity. In many cases, the official decision is but a formalization of administrative arrangements, which defies the political rationale. In this game, the State, arbitrator and regulator, adapts to the system as long as its interests are preserved. Contrary to conventional wisdom, the French State is not merely the representative of the *haves* and the defender of local political elites who agree with the party line. Were this the case, one could neither explain the government's decision to impeach a mayor, who was a member of the same party as the French president and the minister of overseas departments and territories in 1976;

nor the introduction of Customs on August 1, 1990, in the face of strong local opposition. The State can, therefore, in certain circumstances, place itself above the concerns of social groups to impose its will. This is one of the lessons of political life in Saint-Martin underlying Daniella Jeffry's text.

The population of Saint-Martin, though currently multicultural and a marginalized actor, is largely unequal. Statistics are unfavorable to the *original inhabitants*. The terms used by the author to describe the forms of their exclusion, even their elimination, are varied. If the relegation evokes the social conditions of the locals of Caribbean origin, English-speaking and often unemployed who form a minority group, the *"silent genocide"* recalls the process of substitution described by Aimé Césaire. The *Friendly Island* became all too accepting of others, to the detriment of its own. The first wave of Europeans in the seventies - the most important and outstanding period of immigration - takes place almost at the same time as that from Haiti, Guadeloupe, and elsewhere. These migratory influxes, similar to those occurring in other countries, have altered the socio-ethnic composition of the territory. This happens at the expense of the original heirs of the partition of the island between the French and the Dutch, those who have never ceased being, first and foremost, the sons and daughters of Saint-Martin, and who cross the artificial border between Marigot and Philipsburg.

If one includes Saint-Martin's forced affiliation with Guadeloupe after its incorporation in 1946 into *the continent of Guadeloupe*, it becomes easy to understand the components of Saint-Martin's desire for autonomy – a clear reaction to what Michael Hechter calls *"internal colonialism."*

Similar to the case of dependent territories such as Ireland, Scotland, and Wales that were colonized by the British State, cultural differences in Saint-Martin between continental *metropolitans* and island natives overlap with economic disparities. Over time, these differences gradually become the basic criteria for the delineation of social roles. On the scale of social ranking, the highest standards originate from the European continental center, whereas the lowest are relegated to native islanders. In the case that is studied by Daniella Jeffry, a type of double colonialism emerges. On top of the control of local society by a distant French State, was added a direct administrative regulation, by the Department and Region of Guadeloupe. Just like Saint-Barthelemy, Desirade, Saintes, and Marie-Galante, Saint-Martin

---

[1] Michael Hechter, *Internal colonialism: the Celtic fringe in British national development 1536-1966*, Routledge and Kegan, London, see also J. Reele, *Internal colonialism the case of Brittany*, Ethnic and racial studies, vol. 2 no 3, July 1979, pp. 275-292

was designated to become one of the *dependencies of Guadeloupe*. This phrase felt odd by those who understand the cultural implications of the *Guadeloupean continent* versus the calls for autonomous native identity. After the French constitutional reform on March 28, 2003, the Commune of Saint-Martin chose to separate from Guadeloupe and request the status of an autonomous overseas collectivity.

By separating from Guadeloupe, Saint-Martin chose its own terms for dependency. Similar to other Caribbean countries under French jurisdiction, Marigot tried to adjust to its French connection instead of questioning the attachment. This is the trend observed in most non independent territories of the Caribbean. Martinique and French Guiana are, currently, collectivities with a special status governed by legislative regimes identical to that of France. The case of Puerto Rico is interesting for Saint-Martin, as the American territory contemplates adding its star on the banner of the United States. Saba, St. Eustatius, and Bonaire, though autonomous, have become the equivalent of provinces in the Kingdom of the Netherlands. Some of the English islands, like the Turks and Caicos are seeing their autonomy officially contested by the British government due to governance and corruption concerns. The independent island of Saint Vincent, contrary to the will of its own Prime Minister, refused to become a republic and chose, by referendum, to maintain a symbolic general governor appointed by the British Crown.

Dependency can, therefore, be conceived in some cases as a form of domination between actors functioning in solidarity, but unequal, possessing the material and symbolic means necessary for developing relational strategies between both parties. These relationships can then be based on reciprocity. For example, it can correspond to the will of the dominant to perpetuate its dominance, but also to the will of the dominated to accept it, as long as the situation concedes more advantages than disadvantages. In other words, dependency can correspond to the allocation of resources, regardless of actual constraints and correlated arguments. All the merit of this book lies in its contribution to the evolution of Caribbean societies. From this perspective, Saint-Martin exemplifies a resource-dependency,[2] whereby the French State offers public policies responsive to the socio-economic expectations of important segments of local populations within the framework of a domination which the local political nucleus cannot presently assume.

---

[2] *Fred Reno, Re-sourcing dependency: decolonization and post-colonialism in French overseas departments*, in European journal of Overseas History, vol. XV 2001 pp. 9-22, see also *Qui veut rompre avec la dépendance* in Autrement : Guadeloupe, Temps incertains, Janvier 2001 no 123 pp. 236-249

As a result, this pertinent study by Daniella Jeffry must be welcomed and regarded as an eye-witness account on the meaning of dependency in the complex society of Caribbean islands.

Fred Reno
Professor of Political Science, University of the French Antilles and Guiana
Director of the CGIA (Center of Geopolitical and International Analysis)

INTRODUCTION

This study concerns the period extending from 1977 to 2007, a period of profound upheaval in the lives and destiny of the people of Saint-Martin. The island inhabitants, with their complying elected representatives, were subjected to the forceful and rapid transformation of their rural environment into a concrete expanse of unbridled development resulting from the implementation of the 1986 Tax Exemption Law. In 1977, long-standing islanders from Saint-Martin formed the majority of the population, but by 1987 they had become a powerless minority pushed aside in the name of development and progress. Despite their resistance, the native population was reduced to a second class status through the suppression of their culture and language in conjunction with forceful pressure from external cultural forces. Without initially grasping the full implications of the profound changes occurring around them, and struggling to maintain their place in the island they loved, the life-long inhabitants witnessed the emergence of a new and alien society to which they could no longer relate.

The island first took its first fledgling steps towards modern life in 1963. The installation of electricity, the construction of an international airport, and the development of a successful tourist industry filled local inhabitants with dreams of a promising future. At last, they would be able to remain in their homeland to earn a decent living while welcoming those from neighboring Caribbean islands. This new prosperity engendered a sense of national pride as it would be no longer necessary to migrate to other countries in search of economic opportunity, as they had done for the better part of the twentieth century. Nevertheless, at the beginning of this new period, the people of Saint-Martin sensed that something beyond their control was taking place. They felt troubled by an uncertain future. What was sure, and what they clung to, was the belief in their *Friendly Island.* But how long would it remain so?

To better understand the impact these changes had on Saint-Martin's inhabitants, it is necessary to focus on a few key historical events. Despite the territory's small population, these were a people with customs, tradition and a language to which they were deeply attached – which shaped their identity and sense of personal dignity. By 2007, difficult as it may be to believe, the local people found themselves becoming virtual strangers in their own land because their way of life and traditions were smothered by external forces brought by an encroaching number of *transplants*. Now the long-term inhabitants constituted less than 20% of the population, while the recent immigrants comprised 80% of the population – the exact opposite of the percentages that prevailed in 1977. The home-grown population feels as if Saint-Martin no longer belongs to them, though they could never accept such a harsh reality in their core. Regardless, decisions about the island's future which no longer reflect the will of the local people are now determined by national relays and executed by their elected representatives. As a result, fifth of the population lives in denial and pines for the *good old days* - days when they had control of their political, economic, sporting, social, and spiritual destiny - that period prior to 1977.

Saint-Martin, with an area of 37 square miles, is certainly the smallest land mass in the world divided by two independent, national governments. Situated in the Lesser Antilles between the Caribbean Sea and the Atlantic Ocean, the southern side of the island (16 square miles) was a territory of the autonomous Federation of the Netherlands Antilles, which has become an autonomous country within the Kingdom of the Netherlands. The northern side (21 square miles) became a French Overseas Collectivity in July 2007, following the March 2003 Reform of the French Constitution, and the December 7, 2003 Consultation of the people. In 1648, the March 23 Treaty of Concordia marked the official partition of the island between the King of France, and the Prince of Orange (and the States of Holland) through their respective West Indian Companies. This treaty set the basis for peaceful cooperation and an informal border between the two territories, thereby enabling the inhabitants to enjoy the free exchange of persons, goods and capital from that day to this.

The excellent quality of the salt produced in Saint-Martin proved an economic attraction for the Dutch in the seventeenth century. The Netherlands was in need of salt for its fishing industry after it lost Brazil, where the Dutch had previously extracted salt in great quantities. After two expeditions in the Caribbean, the Dutch settled in the south of the island to extract the large quantity of salt from the Great Salt Pond of Great Bay. The first Dutch settlement was established in 1631, whereas fourteen Frenchmen, who had been chased from the island of St. Kitts by the English, sought refuge in the northeastern part of Saint-Martin and began planting tobacco in 1629. Tobacco and indigo cultivation were followed by cotton, and finally sugar-cane plantations spread all over the island by the end of the seventeenth century continuing through the mid-nineteenth century. These planters were awarded land, both in Anguilla and in Saint-Martin, and they brought in people of African ancestry to work the land on both islands. By 1838, the abolition of slavery in the British colonies – particularly in Anguilla where the slaves fled to attain freedom - led to the collapse of the sugar plantations and the transformation of the economy into one devoted to salt production. Black laborers fled Saint-Martin's plantations in great numbers as early as 1838, to reach neighboring British islands, in order to gain their freedom. Historian Jacques Adélaïde-Merlande from Guadeloupe wrote the following about these escapes:

> "In 1841, slave-owners from the French side of Saint-Martin sent a petition to the Chamber of Representatives in Paris requesting the immediate emancipation of the slaves. They were prompted by stark realities. (...) Their slaves easily escaped to English Anguilla. These escapes were encouraged: lights came on at night on both shores and *"beckoning or fleeing signals appeared from one island to the other"* (...). Several factors gave hope to the petitioners that emancipation would be granted, mainly that runaway slaves wanted to return, declaring their willingness to come back *"when the island was free."*[1]

The plantation-owners who signed this petition also cited that black people in Saint-Martin only spoke English, and offered the petition as an island-specific measure. Despite this, the Governor of Guadeloupe rejected the initiative by pointing out to the Minister of the French Navy and Colonies that out of the 142 slave-owners, 85 were English.

Victor Schœlcher, a French politician, historian and abolitionist, documented the following account which refutes the widespread belief that black people did not have strong family ties:

> "Moreover, let us leave it to a Creole gentleman nobly inspired by his contact with French democrats the burden of defending runaway slaves from similar accusations. *"I spent,"* Mr. Maurel-Duperré (from Guadeloupe) said, "*a few weeks on a small island, half French, half Dutch, the island Saint-Martin which thwarted these escape attempts. I have witnessed several, and was deeply moved by these tragic scenes, which had an overwhelming drama that broke my heart.*"[2]

It was against this backdrop of economic decline that the colonial government of Guadeloupe issued a decree on May 7, 1842, whereby it conceded control of salt production for a period of thirty years to Charles de Mery d'Arcy, who was serving as the island notary. François Auguste Perrinon, a Navy Commander, born on August 28, 1812 in Saint-Pierre, Martinique, was the great grandson of a Guinean woman. He stepped onto Saint-Martin's shores for the first time early in 1844. His purpose in coming to the island was to accept to be an associate of the notary by financing the creation of "*The Salt Manufacturing Corporation*," which was established on June 28, 1844. *Isnardon Brothers,* another company from Basse-Terre, Guadeloupe, joined them in order to produce salt in Grand-Case and Brittany. Perrinon managed the development of these work sites and by the rainy season of 1844, he had spent two months on the island organizing a work force. Perrinon employed free laborers from both sides of the island as well as slaves rented from reluctant masters. This personal experience caused him to request the immediate emancipation of the slaves. He was, by this time, able to prove to the planters that free blacks were neither lazy nor thieves, when treated with respect and consideration. Consequently, they received equal wages and corporal punishment was strictly forbidden. In May 1847, Perrinon who had by then become a navy artillery battalion commander,[3] published his findings in a work entitled, *Outcomes of Slave Labor,* in the Maritime and Colonial Annals. On March 4, 1848, he was appointed a member of the Abolition of Slavery Commission headed by Victor Schœlcher, along with three other members and two secretaries.[4] Perrinon instituted paid labor for the black people in Saint-Martin four years before the decree abolishing slavery.

The document which perfectly reflects the prevailing mood following the second official abolition of slavery in the French colonies, was the August 1, 1849 petition drafted by plantation owners from the French side of Saint-Martin and addressed to the members of the National Assembly in Paris. An extract follows:

> "... May 28, 1848 the great act was proclaimed, which marked the beginning of our downfall ... as we found ourselves deprived of our means of existence and without resources. The newly manumitted have all left the plantations, abandoned the crops to go to the Dutch side to *pick salt.* Could we blame them? Set free, they were looking for wages that we could not give them, and we were left to die from hunger for lack of workers. They all came back when the rainy season interrupted work in the salt pans; the owners welcome them with open arms and had no other choice but to associate with them. Each plantation, having its association, became a kind of Commune. Alas! We can say with regret that we went through the experience in good condition, since our workshops were already established ... The French side which once yielded 2,000 barrels of sugar only produced 160 this year. The end of the year will be terrible and next year even worse yet. All the plantations are deserted. It will be so every year. It must be stated that St. Martin finds itself in unique circumstances, and that as long as there is work in the Great Salt Pond on the Dutch side, agriculture is impossible. Our situation is horrible."

The departure of most white plantation owners, coupled with the division of plantations into smaller plots, which were bought by black laborers, fostered the growth of an economy oriented toward salt production, subsistence farming, animal husbandry and fishing. Former slaves were able to buy their parcels of land from the planters, who left Saint-Martin, with savings they amassed from selling their own garden produce, which they cultivated on Saturdays – the only day they were not forced to work. On the other hand, the white planters had obtained the land in concession during the slavery period. As there was no colonial structure in Saint-Martin to confine the new citizens, they were unrestrained to organize their own way of life and most of them became independent workers. This Saint-Martin society is described in an earlier work devoted to the so-called traditional period from 1848 to 1963. An excerpt from that book states:

> "At various times within the Traditional Period the majority of people from St. Martin worked seasonally *picking salt* in the Great Salt Pond and Grand-Case Salt Pond. Some farmed their own small *grounds* or gardens or leased smaller plots from mid- to large-sized landowners - or from government – in order to grow for basic food stuffs. Others worked for the few very large estate-owning families in agriculture and animal husbandry. The majority of the masses included fishermen, maids, market vendors, small shopkeepers, midwives, *bush doctors* (traditional healers), bakers, ironsmiths, seamstresses, teachers, and folk musicians. Often, one person worked in one or more fields according to his or her skills and the community's needs."[5]

Thus, the first half of the twentieth century was marked by successive waves of migration from Saint-Martin to the Dominican Republic, the United States, the American and British Virgin Islands, Panama, Aruba and Curaçao, and in smaller numbers to Guadeloupe, as the resources of the island were insufficient to sustain all its inhabitants. From the 1950s onwards, the return of a certain number of native islanders coincided with the birth of the tourism industry, the installation of electricity across Saint-Martin, the construction of the first international airport in 1963, and the ongoing influx of other Caribbean islanders, Americans, and later Europeans to the French side of the island beginning in the seventies.

Saint-Martin society developed throughout this period (1848-1963) without disorder or uprisings on the island, and without profound racial hostility. The French geographer, Guy Lasserre, in his 1961 doctoral thesis expounded his views on the Saint-Martin society of the period:

> "Racial problems are infinitely less severe in Saint-Martin than in Guadeloupe. Undoubtedly because issues concerning the wages of cane cutters or the price of a ton of sugarcane are nonexistent here - economic problems which are the source of social (and racial) disputes in the larger sugar producing islands. (…) As shopkeepers, whites do not have to impose

their authority over an abundant black workforce, which ensures a more tranquil existence. Even when they are plantation owners, their workforce is relatively small since they are involved mainly in cattle-raising. The domestic workers are English citizens from Anguilla who seem satisfied with their condition, living better here than on their native island. Admittedly, their status as foreigners prevents them from initiating social unrest under penalty of expulsion. It is also likely that being small landowning operators means that social and racial clashes ... do not occur as violently in Saint-Martin as they do on the sugar producing islands. Overall, there seems to be a more peaceful social mood that prevails in Saint-Martin versus Guadeloupe. (...) Peace in Saint-Martin, even during elections, is very seldom marred by racial tensions."[6]

This is quite an accurate description of social conditions in Saint-Martin, because most black people, be they farmers, fishermen, craftsmen, and laborers, were their own bosses and only a minority worked for merchants or took care of the livestock belonging to a few landowners. Locals from Saint-Martin are rather free-spirited, which is undoubtedly why they have migrated in great numbers to the surrounding Caribbean islands or to the United States to improve their living standards. There is no history of social unrest in Saint-Martin, because social structure did not engender it. Thus, other West Indians now living in Saint-Martin cannot understand why native islanders are not more belligerent and more prone to protest, considering what has happened to them over the last thirty years. It seems as if they accepted to be trampled upon.

Ever since the late seventies, when problems started with the arrival of the first wave of Europeans – right up until 1990 -, young islanders reacted strongly, at first on an individual basis, on account of their small numbers. They insisted on the right to live without domination and without discrimination, when confronted with slurs and accusations like *"racist", "xenophobic", "go back to Africa"* which were heard for the first time from a few European newcomers. It must be reiterated that the colonial administrative structure introduced in Guadeloupe and Martinique, following the abolition of slavery, never existed on the French side of Saint-Martin. And even when Saint-Martin became a sub-prefecture of Guadeloupe back in 1963, there was only one judge at the time, along with a handful of gendarmes, the Sub-Prefect and his secretary. Guadeloupe did not impose a greater presence until 1970, leaving the islanders to enjoy their uneventful lives and to figure out things on their own. This was the quality of life which attracted the first Americans and Europeans to the island in the 1950s: distinct customary laws, routine integration of the social, cultural, and economic life in the southern side of the island, as well as with the neighboring Caribbean islands. The Saint-Martin islanders were totally immersed in their immediate region. This unique climate, characterized by an uncommon hospitality and courtesy, that welcomed any stranger[7] with spontaneous friendliness, was the essential feature of the island. The first tourists that came to the island in the 1960s dubbed it the *Friendly Island.*

The inhabitants of Saint-Martin were, therefore, stunned when, in the 1980s, a second wave of Europeans, unmotivated by the ambiance that attracted their easy-going predecessors, but rather prompted by the implementation of the 1986 tax exemption law, arrived in Saint-Martin with the sole objective of making money. The social structure of the island was dramatically transformed into that of a settlement society, which erased the basic qualities that previously unified the population. A palpable disrespect for the existing way of life took hold and imposed an alien operational structure which limited the inhabitants' ability to shape the future development of the island. The clash broke out between the newcomers and the islanders, and many reacted individually and publicly to the verbal and physical aggression. This resentment was illustrated by Pierre Grenon, in his 1982 article on Saint-Martin, which he wrote for the French-language magazine, *Construire*:

> "Only the law of money seems to prevail in this Sub-Prefecture which enjoys important customs and fiscal privileges. Native residents of Saint-Martin, who are mostly black, have recently found themselves colonized once more. Their territory has been invaded by "*French Europeans*" attracted by the prospect of making a quick fortune, even though they have to indulge in all kinds of trafficking, including drugs.
> "*The air is stifling with the massive arrival of metropolitans*", the main European merchant of the town laments. "*The English-speaking Blacks are becoming tight-lipped and refusing to sell their land and houses to whites.*" ... "*Racial tension is a reality in Saint-Martin, in spite of what the whites claim*", maintains a mulatto hotel-manager. "*The reason is that the adventurers from France have one goal in mind: cheat people to get rich as fast as possible.*" Finally, we are reporting this cynical and quite revealing statement made by the young woman editor of the only [European] newspaper of Marigot, 97_1Hebdo: "*In a few years from now, we, Europeans, hope to be in majority and be able to 'kick' the Blacks out of the island.*" The future really appears troubling."

That was the article's conclusion. We are in 1982. The only inaccurate point in this quotation is that Saint-Martin islanders were not *once more colonized.* In fact, they had never experienced colonization. They lived in complete freedom on the island following the abolition of slavery, which is why they could not understand, nor even imagine what was now happening to their homeland. They were caught off guard. The situation changed rapidly, primarily because of their lack of experience with this phenomenon, which was all too commonplace on the other French-speaking islands. Being a commune of Guadeloupe, Saint-Martin and its inhabitants were assimilated historically, socially, and culturally to the same historical past. Unfortunately, this confusion played to their disadvantage, because even today, many Saint-Martin islanders are still in denial regarding this aggressive reality and are complacent in their submissive role. They have attained their state of *denial through submission*.

Unfamiliar with the effects of colonization, Saint-Martin inhabitants have endured hard knocks from a world that was out of touch with what they, as the host population, had to offer: namely, hospitality, friendliness, and most assuredly, their *naïveté*. People from Saint-Martin are not inherently racist. Quite the contrary; however, their strong reaction to racist statements and attitudes directed toward them is quite understandable. Such statements generate indignation and revolt, especially in those who recognize the extent to which human relationships have deteriorated on the island.

Saint-Martin locals, who understand the humiliating conditions that some of their ancestors suffered during slavery, are today overwhelmed by a feeling of deep anguish insofar as they are aware that their ancestors did their utmost to free themselves from the yoke of slavery so that their children and grandchildren would live life with dignity and respect. The anguish felt today results from the sense that they have lost everything, including an important part of themselves. They are confronted with the relentless fate of a dominated and threatened people. They are caught up by feelings of helplessness and hopelessness, as if transformed into abandoned orphans who are trapped, debased, and once more enslaved like their ancestors. Some retreat in anonymity, a feeling of withdrawal from reality, while others resist this degrading metamorphosis.

It is a fact that all too often human beings only appreciate what they have lost. The native population of Saint-Martin did not fully appreciate that their ancestors had already paid the price for them to inherit a free society. How to explain that after fierce resistance to such aggression during more than ten years, they gave in and acquiesced to development, which has excluded them, made them economically weak and reduced them (as early as 1989) to a mere minority on their own island? And this occurred with the willing participation of their elected representatives. Under the pressure from this kind of subjugation, a crack formed in the people's psyche and identity. This new society is thus described in an earlier treatise:

> "This society created from scratch is, with its own distinguishing features as early as the 80s, a well-structured society based on a hierarchical and stereotypic order where democracy, devoid of substance, is no longer a conscious and thoughtful principle, but merely an empty ritual.

> At the top, are the architects of the system and their agents, the propagators and servile executors of the destructive and degrading theories, whose only target is the victimized population. Afterwards, the goal is to divide the individuals in accordance with their degree of submission to the system.
> At the other end, we find all those who have resisted these theories and have refused to fall into the trap and adjust to the mold. They have been socially rejected, economically eliminated, and psychologically weakened. Because they have been vilified, categorized, and humiliated, they are the rebels, completely cast aside and often reduced to a state where they can hardly help themselves.
> All those who understood clearly what was going on but did not have the courage to bear this rejection and this quarantine, are but compliant rebels.
> Those others, who, in spite of their accurate but short-lived insight, have treated us to displays of their ever-shifting justifications, outbursts, shortsightedness, inconsistent and incoherent arguments, contradictions, even lies, these are the complicit ones. Both of these groups, which ultimately form a single whole, constitute the privileged class in the system."[8]

For clarity's sake, understand that those Saint-Martin islanders who wish to remain true to themselves, who resist such destructive assimilation, are the infidels. They are eliminated by covert means as it is never a frontal attack at this stage.

This study is concerned with the standpoint of this defiant societal core. In the current socio-economic conditions that exist in Saint-Martin, one can clearly delineate the exogenous element of the population, whose dominant language and culture is almost exclusively French European, from the endogenous element, which is further subdivided into two groups. One sub-group is faithful, submissive and ever acquiescent to all the values and dictates of the dominant culture; whereas the other sub-group is made up of the authentic resisting individuals, the so-called trouble-makers, and all those who bear the brunt of all kinds of pejorative terms from persons remaining *incognito*.

The present study will attempt to dissect this self-debasing phenomenon identified as the *silent genocide*. This decimation serves as a blessing for some but a misfortune to others. Next, similar situations in the French overseas departments of Martinique, Guadeloupe, French Guiana, and Reunion Island in the Indian Ocean, will be analyzed before expounding circumstances and the methods that prevailed in the societal disintegration of Saint-Martin. We shall inevitably propose a more beneficial alternative, taking into consideration the history of the people of Saint-Martin, who are always at the heart of their Caribbean region. Society must no longer be developed on the basis of contradictions, confusions and mental manipulations, for this harms human development. The people concerned must themselves create their own societies, prepare their future and work at it. When this does not happen, it is a guaranteed failure for any human society.

FIRST PART

THE FRENCH CARIBBEAN SOCIETY AFTER 1946

ANATOMY OF A SILENT GENOCIDE

There is a kind of genocide that while insidious and devastating is, nevertheless, devoid of bloodshed. It occurs gradually and often goes unnoticed at first, but its effects will endure for generations within the affected population. This chapter excludes the conventional sense of genocide, where bodies are destroyed, but rather focuses on cultural genocide which kills the soul, spirit, and initiative, and which promotes discrimination and devaluation of other ways of living. This form of genocide is as pernicious and detrimental as a physical onslaught. The international community expresses outrage when body counts soar to unimaginable heights in far-off lands, yet scarcely an objection is raised by these same defenders of human rights in defense of those undergoing cultural and socio-political annihilation, in so-called democratic regions closer to home. The silence on this front is shamefully deafening.

Even more sinister and disturbing is the fact that this decimation is sanctioned by double-speak which purports to bring its victims "development," "modernization," "improvement," "economic opportunity," "advancement," and other such promises of modern life. The self-serving objective is to secure the interests, with minimal force and resistance, of those possessing the power and ingenuity to initiate such change, upon the unsuspecting and defenseless populous. Their technique is especially cunning since it facilitates the process by co-opting the political process to ensure the consent and participation of those governed. Thus, long-time inhabitants are stunned to realize the full and deleterious extent of their steady disenfranchisement and ostracism.

The Process of Elimination

The actual process of elimination takes various forms depending on the peoples involved and the geographical areas and resources coveted. Though methodologies may vary, the resulting disempowerment is all too tragically the same. In some instances around the world, relocation has been forced, while in others artificial and misleading incentives – such as the promise of improved conditions elsewhere – are used to lure groups from their homeland. In the latter instance, victims do not recognize the manipulation and, therefore, do not protest their treatment. They have no incentive to object until it is much too late, and by then, they often remain silent out of shame or distress, and try to simply *make do* for years, even decades.

A group can be eliminated by imposing unfair economic, cultural or academic competition. That is how, in certain post-colonial societies, systemic inequities have emerged which disable cultural and socio-economic parity irreparably. Despite efforts to address issues of unemployment and underemployment, subjective barriers of so-called under- and over-qualification persist to prevent select communities from acquiring the necessary economic influence for self-determination. Instead, biased structures and procedures are implemented, which debilitate indigenous groups and benefit more recent arrivals who willfully manipulate the system to their advantage.

Another method of elimination involves the incapacitation of individuals through the introduction of illicit drugs, disease, forced sterilization and collective poisoning. This last example comes to mind in the use of the pesticide, *chlordecone*, in Guadeloupe and Martinique.[1] It has brought widespread calamity to these two French territories. The intended purpose of releasing such a deadly chemical on the general population of these two islands remains indiscernible. Meanwhile, its effects will ravage the environment and those dependent upon it for decades. Those who decry the irresponsible use of the pesticide are deemed *trouble-makers* and *busybodies*, because they dare to call into question the benign existence of such a phenomenon. The response is that, as such, they continue to be ignored by public authorities.

An especially malicious, yet effective, way to eliminate a specific group is to foment their own self-destruction. While this method requires extreme sophistication and complicated implementation, it remains effective since it deflects attention from the true source. In such a case, the victims participate in their own annihilation by internalization of corrosive thoughts and practices. Further examination of the *Willie Lynch method* will be explored more fully at a later point in this study as it involves a level of unconscious ignorance that ensnares the victims in a vicious cycle. If a concerted intervention, to extricate the victim from this downward spiral, is not made by those unaffected by such propensities, the resulting fall-out will psychologically impact future generations and produce many other related disorders.

The Process of Destruction

The elimination of weaker groups is inextricably linked to the destruction of their culture. This process has been perpetuated throughout the ages and is, therefore, not unique to the current era. It dates back as far as the existence of the first humans. Both civilizations and continents have been conquered by the process of elimination. The assumption and retention of power often involves the same process of elimination. It has become a hallmark of human existence on planet Earth.

Displacement and elimination go hand in hand. Violent conflict, warfare, genocide and massacres are the extreme manifestations of dehumanization which serve the objectives of the vanquisher. However, in some instances, similar results, that is to say, subjugation and control of desired resources can occasionally be achieved through psychological, economic, or emotional manipulation, as opposed to bloody confrontation. The former approach engenders a slow, and initially imperceptible, transition which sets up the sublimation of the original population by a new group of power players. It is often said that, *Nature abhors a vacuum*, and this concept helps to illustrate how a dominant group will replace those whom they have worked to displace.

This process of silent genocide disguises itself in slow, innocuous trends: displacement, transplantation, inter-mixing, and other such tactics, and will so long as the world exists. There is no outcry because those affected are powerless, and therefore weak – some would say, inherently so - and thus, worthy of elimination. This form of annihilation is not termed genocide, because the casualties are largely invisible. Without tangible corpses, the aggressors proceed to amass economic control and to impose their will upon the weaker group.

Amerindians and the other indigenous inhabitants of the New World, were decimated, and in some instances, utterly obliterated through cultural aggression. For nearly six centuries, Africans were enslaved and transported to the Caribbean and the Americas where they were forced to labor on farms and plantations. The crops from those harvests were then culled to fuel the economic engine of Europe's colonial empires. All of this was tolerated, and even sanctioned, as the natural evolution of the emerging social order.

The Process of Assimilation

While the peoples of Africa, the British West Indies, and India were striving for independence, the subjugated inhabitants of the French colonies embraced socio-political assimilation and sought to assert their presence through their communist representatives in the National Assembly. Revisiting this period, it is ironic that Communists in the French Caribbean colonies and Reunion in the Indian Ocean should formulate such claims, especially since they would later advocate self-government for these same territories. Undoubtedly, they had specific reasons, for first espousing assimilation, and then self-government, though the two approaches seem incompatible. Similarly, the colonies in the Dutch Antilles began negotiating self-government pacts with the Netherlands in 1954 in the form of the Kingdom Charter; and later, the greater part of the Pacific colonies obtained their independence.

What then is assimilation? Is it a two-edged sword? According to the historical period between the revolutionary period and the Universal Declaration of the Rights of Man, it would seem the answer is, yes. With respect to the French revolutionaries, assimilation constituted placing the territories under their guardianship. The newly emancipated would need aggressive tutelage to manage a valuable commodity like liberty. Whereas the intent of the revolutionaries was to perpetuate their dominance, the aim of the colonized was to cast off their abasement and actualize full French citizenship, with all its benefits of liberty, equality and fraternity.

To comprehend the interactions between these dominant and subordinate groups, one must highlight two distinct variations within their dynamic: dominant/subordinate. What began, in 1946, as a seemingly beneficial relationship for both, quickly transformed into one of dissatisfaction for the subordinate population. Just one year after the voting of the law (no 46-451) departmentalizing the former French colonies – Guadeloupe, Martinique, French Guiana and Réunion – was put to a vote, Aimé Césaire, a native of Martinique who was also one of the principal drafters, expressed his deep concern to the French National Assembly, where he served as a deputy. In his address to the Assembly in Paris on April 26, 1947, he states the following:

> "We, who are growing even more numerous, believe that it is time to rethink and modify the status of the overseas departments. We believe that what life and history have already left behind, and which evolution itself condemns, is in danger of being sustained out of mere superstition. When considering Black Africa - and Africa as a whole – which, along with the newly autonomous Comoro islands, is rapidly moving towards independence from colonization, it becomes irrational to believe that the current status of the

overseas departments, as the last colonial territories remaining under France's direct control, can be prolonged much further."[2]

What a sad conclusion for Césaire to reach in the apparent admission of his error: assimilation did not, in fact, produce the equality sought after by Antilleans of African descent. Rather, this misguided policy produced an unprecedented crisis of identity and social development that continues to plague contemporary French Antilleans with socio-economic and psycho-emotional dependence to this very day. These islanders yearn for equal treatment, both in society and in the workforce. However, those who espoused political and cultural assimilation in the 1940s did not foresee the subsequent state of dependence, alienation and powerlessness that would arise from this approach. Neither did they suspect it would become the main destructive element in post-slave societies, nor that its negative effects would be internalized by its adherents. The corresponding negative self-image produced a type of psycho-social regression that caused the assimilationists to adopt and revere all things French. In turn, this created a "cultural disconnect," a subconscious disdain for their own traditional culture, and a false sense of superiority over others and anything which was not "French." The Tunisian scholar, Albert Memmi, accurately describes the phenomenon as follows:

> "The stubborn attempt of the colonized individual to overcome the scorn (which his backwardness, weakness, and otherness deserve, as he is forced to admit), only generates further scorn and derision when he fawningly gives himself over to diligent attempts to replicate the colonizer's very manner of dress, speech and conduct – right down to his tics and style of lovemaking. The colonizer asserts and explains to the aspiring assimilate that his efforts will only ever gain the additional trait of ridicule; for he will never be accepted, nor even be able to correctly reproduce his role. (...)
> In fact, everything is ordered so that the colonized being is unable to breach the gap; that he understands and admits to himself that this path is a dead end, and that full assimilation utterly impossible."[3]

This insightful analysis illuminates the conflicted state in which the colonized assimilate finds himself. It is unfortunate that the new elites were unable to recognize the truth: that power is never conceded willingly. The mistake of the emancipated Antilleans was to confuse assimilation with equality. Merely adopting the customs and behaviors of the former masters would never ensure acceptance. Rather, it engendered another form of slavery - mental slavery, which proved even more debilitating than the physical form; while adopting the master's language became another form of alienating the self. Antilleans continuously speak of France as the *Metropole* and French people as *Metropolitans*; but there can be no *metropole* without a colony. Is it perhaps that, subconsciously, they still perceive themselves as colonized? Consciously, of course, they regard themselves as citizens of France, therefore, French; and by extension, European. Physically, they reside in the Caribbean, so they are Caribbean, though their mental affiliation does not extend overseas. How then, is it possible to reconcile these diverse geographical and cultural identities in one individual? This is the Antillean dilemma. Is it possible for the European Antillean to be integrated into the Caribbean region without a feeling of superiority? Conversely, can the Caribbean Antillean possibly identify with Europe without a sense of inferiority? The choice is elusive. Instead, they respond by embracing multiple identities, as their identification with the former colonizer validates their sense of self.

Invariably, the colonized individual remains proud to play the colonizer's conquering role, since it was ultimately through such individuals that France colonized parts of Africa and colonies in the Indian Ocean. Edouard Glissant, poet and cultural commentator from Martinique, recounts the situation as follows:

> "Antilleans were employed to provide the managerial and assistant managerial positions, within Africa's colonial framework, where they were treated as whites, and alas, behaved as such. The French political approach was to encourage the emergence of this assistant managerial class, which partly explains the development of a pseudo-elite which was convinced, more than any other, of their participation in national life."[4]

Similarly, the State punished rebellious French Antillean civil servants, by deporting them to other regions, if they so much as even suspected they might disturb the social order. Historian Oruno Lara elaborated on the ordinance of October 1960 in his book about Guadeloupe:

> "Ordinance 60-1101 of October 15, 1960 enables prefects to remove, within forty-eight hours, any civil servant whose behavior would be judged likely to disturb public order."[5]

The Antilleans were sent as managers to Africa to execute highly skilled functions, relative to local Africans, and thus, they assumed a sense of superiority that ultimately exacerbated their alienation even more. Their assimilated sense of self as *"French"* (in the European sense), which was nurtured for generations in the colonies, but never embraced by French Europeans, compromised the development of a genuinely Antillean identity and fostered a one-sided sense of equality. In this context, actual equality was compromised by the quest for a visible form of equality, as exemplified by the application of social privileges available in France. Thus, their internal sense of equality was sacrificed in the pursuit of external manifestations.

Equality is also, from the assimilated Antillean perspective, the desire to have the wholesale legislative benefits of the French Republic fully implemented in its distant sea-bound territories. The demand for the same rights enjoyed by continental French laborers became the battle cry for both French and Antillean communists at the time. During this period, their primary objective could be summed up in two words: assimilation and equality. This desire achieved realization through access to education and enrollment in military service. As a result, the first high school in Martinique opened in 1881 in Saint-Pierre, followed by the Preparatory Law School in Fort-de-France in 1882. The November 23 decree of 1913 allowed army recruitment in Martinique, thus fulfilling the Antillean desire to be *entirely French.* The ultimate cost of patriotism could accordingly be paid through a voluntary *blood tax*, given in service to one's country.[6]

Absolute assimilation requires blind identification with the dominant colonizer - some might call it, mindless mimicry - which, in turn, is but derided and ridiculed by the colonizer. Consequently, hypocritical expressions of scorn are inherent to all relationships born of assimilation. Such psychological blindness automatically engenders an exploitative acceptance and tolerance on the part of the dominated colonized individual. These negative elements form an integral part of the assimilation process and run counter to the liberation of an Antillean identity. The ambiguity of assimilation was not perceived by members of Antillean society in its early stages, with the exception of a select few, chief among whom was Paul Valentino. He was not only the deputy of Guadeloupe and mayor of Pointe-à-Pitre, but also one of the most outspoken adversaries of departmentalization, and a contemporary of Aimé Césaire.

II

PSYCHE OF THE ASSIMILATED

The process of assimilation can physically affect the structure of the brain and distort the perception of the five senses: sight, hearing, smell, taste, and especially touch (or feeling). The impact of assimilation on the mind induces the most serious form of alienation and can be the most difficult to cure. Recovery may be prompted by something akin to electro-shock treatments. Assimilation perpetuates a state of dependency in the colonized/assimilated, and produces a state of mistrust directed towards those of the affected individual's own group that endures for generations. The assimilated individual's language becomes the unconscious, but authentic, reflection of the extent of his alienation. Throughout the sixty-four years of department status in the French Caribbean, the language used has attained the highest degree of alienation and incoherence, becoming more ridiculous and like a caricature in the eyes of all, except the affected individuals.

Modern legend alleges that a slave-owner named William ("Willie") Lynch once gave an infamous speech, which even if the historical accuracy of the event cannot be proved, has value in terms of its insight into the power of psychological manipulation. According to the story, Lynch was from the British West Indies but came to the American colony of Virginia in 1712, where he allegedly spoke to a group of land-owners on the banks of the Jamestown River. In a fairly extensive discourse, he outlined an effective strategy for controlling the slaves. An extract from the quoted text is included below:

> "… I am here to help you solve some of your problems with slaves. Your invitation reached me on my modest plantation in the West Indies where I have experimented with some of the newest and still the oldest methods for control of slaves. Ancient Rome would envy us if my program is implemented. As our boat sailed south on the James River, …I saw enough to know that your problem is not unique. While Rome used cords of wood as crosses for standing human bodies along its old highways in great numbers, you are here using the tree and the rope on occasion.
> I caught the whiff of a dead slave hanging from a tree a couple of miles back. You are not only losing valuable stock by hangings, you are having uprisings, and slaves are running away; your crops are sometimes left in the

> fields too long for maximum profit, you suffer occasional fires, and your animals are killed. Gentlemen, you know what your problems are. ... I am not here to enumerate your problems; however, I am here to introduce you to a method of solving them. In my bag here, I have a foolproof method for controlling your black slaves. I guarantee every one of you that if installed correctly, it will control the slaves for at least 300 years [which would culminate in 2012]. My method is simple. Any member of your family or your overseer can use it.
>
> I have outlined a number of differences among the slaves, and I take these differences and make them bigger. I use fear, distrust, and envy for control purposes. These methods have worked on my modest plantation in the West Indies and it will work throughout the South. Take this simple list of differences, and think about them. On top of my list is *Age*, but it is there only because it starts with an A; the second is *Color or Shade,* there is *Intelligence*, *Size, Sex, Plantation Size, Status on plantation, Owners' Attitude, whether the slaves live in the Valley, on the Hill, East, West, North, South, have Fine Hair, Coarse Hair, or are Tall or Short.* Now that you have a list of differences, I shall give you an outline of action. But before that, I shall assure you that distrust is stronger than trust, and envy is stronger than adulation, respect, or admiration.
>
> The black slave after receiving this indoctrination shall carry on and will become self-refueling and self-generating for hundreds of years, maybe thousands.
>
> Don't forget you must pitch the old black male versus the young black male, and the young black male versus the old black male. You must use the dark skin slaves versus the light skin slaves, and the light skin slaves versus the dark skin slaves. You must use the female versus the male, and the male versus the female. You must also have your white servants and overseers distrust all blacks, but it is necessary that your slaves trust and depend on us. They must love, respect, and trust only us.
>
> Gentlemen, these kits are your keys to control. Use them. Have your wives and children use them, never miss an opportunity. If used intensively for one year, the slaves themselves will remain perpetually distrustful.
>
> I thank you, gentlemen."[7]

The use of "*continental* Guadeloupe" is at best, confounding and symptomatic of the intellectual distortion induced by the desire for cultural and political assimilation. Originally, the name "Guadeloupe" sufficed to describe the new political structure. However, thirty years later, the lack of an authentically equal sense of identity produced this implausible structure. The delineation "*continental*" was added to the name in order to assert a sense of credibility, and implied equivalence, to "continental France." But how, in actuality, could such a small cluster of islands ever constitute a continent? This type of reasoning is erroneous and confusing - especially when educating young children about the geographic distinctions between continents and islands. However, it is a clear illustration of the injurious effects of assimilation. The individual without an assimilated mindset has no compunction to validate his self-worth through identification with France, and is therefore comfortable with the relationship between Guadeloupe and its affiliated territories, as it stands. The assimilated subject, by contrast, attempts to make Guadeloupe emulate on a regional scale the role of France. This is both childishly simplistic and impractical.

There is also a tendency, among assimilated individuals, to give themselves identifying labels, or to accept the monikers created by the colonizer - as if "Guadeloupean", "Martinican", and "Guyanese" were insufficiently descriptive. Within France, Antilleans and French Guyanese are considered part of the same group - "the DOM" (or overseas departments) - and are collectively referred to as *Domians*. From the perspective of Europe, they become "ultra-peripheral" and even more far at sea. The assimilated mind only perceives itself in relation to another, who occupies the center. Therefore, it remains on the periphery, and can never assume centrality. Distance can function as a handicap, but the real question is: distance in relation to what, and from whom? When one lives on an island, distance creates a sense of *double insularity*. How can this experience be translated into another language? What does it actually express? Subjugated people do not possess an identity of their own. They remain in a perpetual state of "other" – forever dependent on something or some group more important than themselves. Their mental state of being accounts for the constant need to redefine themselves through the use of various labels. For example, Antilleans and French Guyanese living in metropolitan France cheerfully refer themselves as *Negropolitans* because they view it as analogous to *Metropolitans*. To be known as Guadeloupean, Martinican or Guyanese is insufficient somehow; yet, nowhere does the country of *Metropole* exist. Once more, the emphasis is on the relationship to France – though they would not admit such an obsession. Extensive identity confusion predominates, resulting in a permanently conflicted mental state. Those so affected constitute political leaders responsible for the future of populations – those so inconsistent that their viewpoints are in constant flux on all points. Torrents of contradictions result in their forgetting the positions that they held just a short time before. The political observer of the overseas departments is faced with a pathetic spectacle. Saint-Martin elected representatives, in their quest to obtain an autonomous status, was addressed in my previous book:

> "Those who understood clearly what was going on and did not have the courage to bear this rejection and this quarantine are the submissive rebels. Those who, in spite of their insightful, but short-lived, perception, have entertained us with displays of their ever-shifting positions, fits of anger, intellectual blindness, inconsistent and incoherent proclamations, contradictions, and even lies, are the submissive ones. Each of these groups,

> which eventually constitute one group, comprises the privileged class within the system."[8]

Psychological, economic, and political dependency is like a cancer that the policy of assimilation has spread throughout the overseas departments. Réunion, an overseas department of France in the Indian Ocean, is an extreme example of such dependency, as characterized by their refusal even to consider the Constitutional Reform of March 28, 2003. Indeed, "Réunion Island, in the Indian Ocean, had already withdrawn from this reform through an amendment. Réunion permanently waived its rights. It has requested its own exclusion."[9] The Réunionese are satisfied with their state of dependency on France. They fear abandonment. Françoise Vergès, a Réunionese historian, explains the pathological aspect of this fear in the book, *Abolish slavery: a colonial utopia*, accordingly:

> "This dependency also modeled the social ties at the precise moment when the population finally gained access to the social laws enforced in France. Family allowances, free medical assistance, and other social benefits were distributed according to the good behavior of the recipients. ... That is how a Creole pathology emerged, characterized by the absence of the father, an intrusive presence of the mother, an impossible autonomy of the self, a structural dependency ... It affects the majority of the population today, civil servants as much as the beneficiaries of the "minimum revenue of insertion" [an allowance providing a social minimum]. It affects their perspective and it has worsened these last years."[10]

The fear generated by such a situation is not a simple fear. It is a fear that immediately deconstructs and takes over the mind, reducing it to a childlike state. It is also an endless, chronic fear. Can France, a country that claims to defend human rights, still boast about achieving so-called *"civilizing"* missions when it still imposes a *new colonization* on its overseas populations even now, in the 21st century? "The new colonization", according to Françoise Vergès, "is expressed by a reinforced dependency on France and by the imitation of patterns of consumerism and other behaviors perceived as *French*. The Réunionese are expected to indulge themselves on this dependency."[11] Vergès continues, "In the end, the fear of abandonment by France awakens a deep-seated belief in their inability to make it alone, in being too distant, too external from France. Surrounded by foreigners, the neighboring Mauritians and Malagasy are perceived not as allies, nor possible historical partners, but rather as a threat."[12] This attitude is reminiscent of French Antilleans' relationship with their English-speaking counterparts in the Caribbean, or even with Haiti; and never more so than after the recent earthquake, which flattered their sense of technical and technological superiority that they enjoyed as members of the French Republic.

Although French Antilleans and Guyanese do not currently exhibit such an extreme state of alienation, no inhabitants of a colonial territory are completely immune to it. They are struggling to achieve a healthy balance, while exploring various notions, ranging from autonomy and dependency, to the complete severance of historical ties. One must wonder whether the mental state of a people so affected by this degree of extreme dependency could ever coincide with the aspirations of the French Antillean and Guyanese personality. In the present state of affairs, one should not tackle the wrong issue: it does not concern political autonomy as much as individuality. It is a question of psychological autonomy and existential responsibility. In other words, attempting to solve psychological problems with political solutions makes us fall into the trap set by those who perpetuate economic enslavement for their own interests. The damage is personal (i.e. to the psyche), not political.

Contemporary colonization no longer exerts itself as a political concept, rather it dominates through psychological manipulation and control over human development. It is a concept which accumulates all the negative aspects of the human exploitation. It is a concept contrary to the republican values of *liberty, equality, fraternity*, which emerged from the French Revolution. Modern colonization destroys the aspirations of all freedom-lovers. Nevertheless, it should not be assumed that the colonizer/dominant does not suffer from the same destructive and engulfing pathology. The relational dynamic produces a vicious circle from which it is difficult for either side to escape, and which circumvents the ability to live in true contentment. Instead, each side is constrained by the limitation of a two-tiered social construct to which they are accustomed. The impact of dependency is absolutely reciprocal. The dominant class, whose lifestyle renders them unable to function without a subjugated work force, becomes dependent on cheap and illegal labor. Their dependency is fostered by their thirst for personal enrichment, at the expense of the fundamental rights of those being exploited. Dominated individuals are desperate to find acceptance, and as a consequence, become submissive and obedient to the oppressive dictates of the dominant group. While there is a bond that connects them, there exist equally powerful divisions based on ethnicity, geography, and social class. This connection betrays the humanitarian impulses of some dominant members, because the exploitation of poverty-stricken people is a moral issue.

The dominant class has the propensity to assign identifying labels to the subordinate group, which all too often willingly accepts descriptors such as:

Domians, and *ultra-peripheral inhabitants*. At times, the relation between the word and its use is clear. In other instances, the colonizers abuse of terms, such as *Republic*, *secularity*, and *diversity*, which serve to mask their true intent. They disparagingly refer to a black person as '*un black*,' the insinuation behind which is as derogatory and pejorative for the non-assimilated Antillean as the English term *nigger*. By using the foreign term, *black*, the modern colonizer avoids the semblance of racism, which their republican ideals avoid. The dominant group directs extreme language against those who resist assimilation (or frenchification) into the dominant system. A few decades ago, such individuals were called *communists* and *independentists*. Today, they are referred as *racists* and *xenophobes*. The use of terms like *the State* and *the Republic* evoke meanings that are difficult to apprehend. Likewise, the subjective use of words like *overseas departments* and *French departments in the Americas* refer to the same thing, but with different connotations. Such phraseology inherently permits the dominant individual to manipulate the emotions and imagination of the subjugated person with whom the conversation occurs. The two-tiered environment is a world of perpetual interaction where the dominant never releases the dominated. It is never a mutually beneficial, neither equal nor a fraternal relationship between the two parties. It is often an emotional dynamic consisting of forceful and violent exchanges, which can result in the punishment and condemnation of the dominated group at the slightest departure from the dominant group's standards of conduct. When the French leave the European continent to live in an overseas department, they visibly transform and adapt their approach to dealing with the racially distinct local inhabitants. Unfortunately, the transformation can be disadvantageous to the local inhabitants, as it is often imbued with partiality, bias, exaggeration, discrimination and race-based favoritism.

III

THE RELOCATION STRATEGY

Moving individuals from their usual environment creates a void that must be filled by others. In the case of the DOM, as the French Overseas Departments are collectively known, groups were motivated to leave their homeland by promises of something better. First, for those from the Antilles, the prospect of training and jobs addressed the problem of soaring unemployment emerging from the elimination of mass agricultural production and from high population growth. Second this displacement filled a labor shortage that France was experiencing at that time. On the other side of the equation, French nationals were offered additional bonuses, including a 40% cost of living increase, isolation compensation, transportation, resettlement, subsidized vacations, and the like, as incentives to emigrate to the DOM. Even in recent years, a premium equivalent to 16 months' salary, paid in two lump sums, was granted to State functionaries who agree to work in French Guiana or in Saint-Martin for four successive years. In prior years, DOM functionaries, who were suspected of disturbing the *public order* in their home departments, were "promoted" and sent to Africa as a means of maintaining European dominance in the territories.

The BUMIDOM

How should one view the situation from afar? Was it the State, the Republic, the Government, or the Administration orchestrating these relocations? The question becomes especially relevant since such population shifts became the main strategy of France's overseas solution to achieve the desired effects of its policy-makers. Their objective served the interest of France exclusively, and thus resulted in outcomes that did not often benefit the indigenous overseas populations. From 1962 to 1981, Prime Minister Michel Debré orchestrated the migration of Antilleans from the Caribbean, and Réunionese from Réunion, under the auspices of the Office for the Development of Migrations from the Overseas (commonly known by its French acronym, BU.MI.DOM).[14] Created by ministerial decree in 1963, the purpose of this agency was "to organize emigration, relocation, vocational integration trough targeted job placement or through direct training of Caribbean and Reunionese migrants."[13] This migration corresponded to a need on both sides: rising unemployment created a social and political climate shaken by strikes and riots in the French Antilles; whereas economic prosperity in France during the *Thirty Years of Glory* created labor shortages primarily in construction, postal services, transport, domestic service, metallurgy, and hospitals. By 1983, the BUMIDOM was replaced by the National Agency for the Placement and Promotion of Overseas Workers.

The documentary film by the director Antoine Leonard-Maestrati and Michel Reinette, entitled *The Future is Elsewhere* (2007), traced the saga of this exodus from the DOM. For two decades, all the overseas departments, with the exception of French Guiana, suffered from over-population and lost the bulk of their prime population who were young and capable of the highest productivity. An estimated number of people that left during these years totaled 70,615. The territorial breakdown is as follows: Guadeloupe: 16,562; Martinique: 16,580; and Réunion: 37,473. Collectively, these figures amount to 44.7% of the 157,000 migrants from the DOM who arrived in France as desirable laborers, transferred civil servants, and those fulfilling military service.[14]

What began initially as a migration of laborers evolved into a general population transfer as early as 1970 due to the need for family reunification. Simultaneously, a campaign of persuasive propaganda aimed at French Europeans promised a prosperous future and advantageous living conditions in exotic islands, in order to encourage their resettlement in the Antilles and Réunion. On the one hand, white French settlers could readily find employment in these territories that had been depleted of their labor force; while immigrants from the DOM were relegated to the basest and least skilled employment offerings in France, regardless of their skills or educational attainments. The contrasting treatment immigrants of color received from French officials charged with solving the problems of unemployment and overpopulation in the DOM, compared to that of French emigrants, was all too stark. As a consequence, some Antilleans and Réunionese found themselves succumbing to drug use and prostitution as a means to cope with disillusionment. Compounding their problems further were the challenges they faced integrating into French society. Racial disparities limited their access to equal housing and employment, while their physical distinctiveness relegated them to treatment as second class citizens, both of which provoke fierce reactions in Antillean political leaders and intellectuals. In a 2007 interview, the filmmaker Antoine Leonard-Maestrati explained:

> "Moreover, during the Sixties, even though, technically, the Antilles were French departments, they were actually little more than colonies. Poor Blacks were considered less than nothing; yet they had been made to believe they were as French as anyone. They thought when they left for France, they were going to paradise. When the Antilleans arrived in France, they were not treated as French: they were black.
> The Bumidom was the second transatlantic voyage following slavery. What struck me, not being Antillean myself, is this continuation of human exploitation. Just as Blacks who worked in the sugar cane fields became a burden – because there was no more work, and then revolutionary movements were born - something had to be done. *As the slave trade was no longer possible, it was replaced by immigration.* What absolutely must be condemned is not that people came to France; but that they had no choice. No one abandons their country for pleasure. They leave their birthplace because they cannot afford to do otherwise. This policy of mass migration is shameful; they were even told they could earn diplomas as domestics. How dare they? [...]
> In fact, the film ends with young people from here, descendants of those who left their island due to the Bumidom. "*They say, 'I am Antillean', but over there, they are not recognized as Antilleans, and here they are told that they are black. So what are they?*"[15]

Journalist Michel Reinette dealt with the issue of identity from the French perspective:

> "Césaire termed this period one of *genocide by substitution*. It must not be forgotten that, simultaneously, they were encouraging people to inhabit the Antilles. In the islands *colonials* were invited to pick up any job they liked. […]
> As a black citizen of the French Republic, I find Sarkozy's public discourse mind-blowing and enormously upsetting. I cannot begin to understand how someone who may become president of the Republic can make such a dangerous parallel between immigration and migration. The French identity belongs to all of us! Sarkozy himself is of Hungarian ancestry. When somebody like him promotes this type of discourse, he emphasizes that the rejection is not cultural but ethnic, in nature - and that is dangerous. Where the film meets up with currents events, is that you have in front of you black citizens of the Republic who have been French for longer than Mr. Sarkozy. French identity is a conglomerate."

The issue of identity is a contemporary issue, whether in the Antilles or in France. There is the perspective of the Republic: Antilleans are French. There is the perspective of the French: Antilleans are black. Then there is the perspective of the Antilleans themselves: Antilleans are French Blacks; and this is the dilemma – being both French and black. It manifests itself differently whether one is on French soil or on an island in the Antilles.

Regardless, for many the BUMIDOM was a beneficial experience, both on a professional and social level. Furthermore, this migratory phenomenon also took place in the English-speaking Caribbean, only they went to England and North America. The successes are well known and often quite visible. Yet, the repercussions of this double migration to and from France have been shocking in Guadeloupe and in Martinique.

Migration to the French Antilles

New Caledonia serves as a well-known example of the government's intention to neutralize the nationalist claims of the local people. Unofficially, the strategy of mass migration overseas resulted in rendering the native populations minorities in their own land, thereby perpetuating the policy of domination. The 1972 letter which the French Prime Minister sent to his Secretary of State for Overseas Departments and Territories (DOM-TOM) is very explicit on this point, because it brings to light the essentially political nature of population displacements in the overseas territories and justifies the various methods used to ensure the perpetuation of the French presence in the Antilles:

> "In the short- and mid- term, mass immigration of French citizens from France or from overseas departments (such as Réunion) should make it possible to avoid this danger [the tendency towards independence], by maintaining and improving the statistical balance between both communities.
> In the long term, claims by local nationalists will only be circumvented if the expatriate communities represent a critical population majority. It therefore goes without saying that no long-term demographic shift can be maintained without the systematic immigration of women and children.
> In order to correct the imbalance of sexes in non-indigenous population, undoubtedly it would be useful to reserve employment for immigrants in the private sector. The ideal scenario would be for any employment that can be performed by women, to be reserved for them (e.g. secretarial, sales, and data processing).
> Without necessitating specific texts on the matter, the administration can oversee its implementation."[16] […]

Moreover, Jean Chatain of the newspaper *L'Humanité* observed:

> "This strategy of human asphyxiation, of statistical domination, also applied in French Guiana, inevitably brings to mind the expression coined by Aimé Césaire who, speaking from the context of the situation of Martinique, referred to a deliberate *genocide by substitution*."[17]

The effect of mass emigration of French nationals (from Europe, Réunion, and other French colonies) to New Caledonia delivered a severe blow to the indigenous Kanak people. Its repercussions caused Jean-Marie Tjibaou, leader of the Kanak Socialist National Liberation Front (FLNKS), who would later be assassinated, to say, "The worst thing is not dying, but to remain alive and feel like a complete stranger in your own country." In 1998, the ethnic distribution in the territory was as follows: Kanaks (44%), white Caledonians and French mainlanders (34%), inhabitants from the Wallis Archipelago, Tahiti, and Indonesia (11%).[18] Restoration of a Kanak majority had still not been achieved in 2009; nor was the social stability on which it depends.

Martinique and Guadeloupe have also experienced the same migratory phenomenon, coupled with surreptitious immigration, since the 1980s, from numerous Caribbean islands including Dominica, Haiti, the Dominican Republic, St. Lucia, and Jamaica. The attraction Antilleans feel for France has never ceased, even if formal migration decreased after the dissolution of the BUMIDOM. However, the arrival of many civil servants transferred to Martinique and Guadeloupe raised the alarm among unions, intellectuals, and political parties that the situation in the Antilles threatened to mirror that of New Caledonia. This development has created a pressing debate for the last ten years, but only intermittently, due to the lack of statistic documentation. On the other hand, a significant immigrant community from the Antilles and French Guiana lives in France, along with their French-born, second generation, offspring. They have become so populous that Ile-de France, a district of Paris, is considered the 5th DOM. Clearly, birthplace is no longer the sole determination of an individual's geographic or ethnic origin. Distinguishable ethnicity, which is the source of all discrimination experienced by immigrants in France, is difficult to quantify. Consequently, the issue remains a subjective topic of bitter debate that is rarely approached with dispassionate objectivity. It, therefore, is relegated to the realms of union and nationalist concerns rather than to the agendas of political parties, which rarely involve themselves in the matter.

Nevertheless, ethnic disparity remains a visible reality that is acutely evident in the employment sector. French nationals hold positions of higher level of responsibility and executive functions in the civil service (including Justice, Administration, Gendarmerie and Education - excluding the University); as well as in the private sector, whereas Antilleans occupy the lower positions. Public resentment of being invaded by French Europeans dominated the written media in 1999, following graffiti and threats. Statements still come to mind from *Sept Magazine* that were made by Jean-

François Rozan, who was described as “a white Frenchman and keen observer of the Guadeloupean society, for some thirty odd years, and who has long published warning on this issue in our magazine confirming that the invasion is a reality: ”

> “In the public sector, the invasion is even more obvious. Twenty-five years ago, the positions of responsibility were still filled by Guadeloupeans. Today, in spite of the increase in the amount of well–educated Guadeloupeans, what predominates is essentially the *whitening* of these positions, as happens in the large private sector agencies. However, at the same time, one too rapidly overlooks the extraordinary strides made in many major agencies, such as the trade and business chambers, the Social Security Administration, the Retirement Administration or the Unemployment Insurance Agency, where a massive *darkening* has occurred. In other words, where it was possible for Guadeloupeans to exert themselves, the trend has been reversed.”[19]

When the Antillean Communist parliamentarians advocated for their respective colonies to become French departments, it is abundantly clear that they only saw the situation from the perspective of elevating their overseas compatriots to be on par with their counterparts in France. Just one year after the end of the Second World War, they were far from imagining the reverse population flow, from suspecting that French mainlanders would settle the Antilles in droves. Neither could they envision that the French would abandon their colonies in Africa as well as those in the Indian and Pacific Oceans, as they achieved independence, and be drawn to the colonies – despite their departmental status - rather than toward France, for the simple fact that they would continue to enjoy the same privileges of colonial societies.

By contrast, at that time, those who opposed the departmentalization of the territories already suspected that the quest for equality and assimilation would negatively affect the predominant role of Antilleans in various positions of responsibility. They foresaw that the competition in matters of employment would disadvantage Antilleans. They remain unconvinced that a mere law could bring about a transformation of unequal human relations that were firmly established and ensconced in the colonial structure - which itself grew out of the slave society. These critics were propelled by a sense of psychological realism that was based on the history of people; for they viewed assimilation as far more than mere political ideology.

Today, Antilleans must cope with the legacy of assimilation, though they are not always psychologically prepared to confront this reality head-on, due to the complexity of their own confused, misunderstood and multi-layered identity. Upon examination of the British West Indian context, one finds that those islanders from the Crown dependencies educated in England, insisted on holding the positions due to them when they returned to their home islands. Granted, a corresponding principle of assimilation did not exist in the British historical context; and therefore accordingly, there exists no comparable crisis among English-speaking West Indians relative to a "British identity." In the past, West Indian colonies were members of the Commonwealth; whereas since 1973, they have created the Caribbean Community (or CARICOM), with both organizations possessing their own indigenous state and territorial representatives. Under these structures, there exists neither political, personal nor cultural confusion. The Dutch West Indies followed a similar pattern of representation. In neither case was there an influx of European civil servants holding governing posts in the islands concurrently alongside local civil servants.

Consequently, it is not so much a question of Antillean capacity to manage positions of responsibility, as that the advocates for assimilation did not fully grasp the implications behind the realization of the policy. They did not adequately examine its potentially nefarious consequences; for it is evident that assimilation is much more than a political framework – it is, first and foremost, a psychological framework. Hence, the resulting alienation between the two intervening groups, rather than diminishing through the years, has increased to become a source of conflict resulting in the current identity crisis and the social unrest plaguing the French Antilles today. Assimilation does not encourage leadership among the assimilated when working alongside mainlanders. It does not promote mentoring opportunities which prepare those assimilated to rise on par with their European counterparts. On the contrary, as long as this concept forms the core of the political, administrative and social setup, there will be no progress for indigenous laborers, since mainlanders give preference to their own, with no admission of ethnic bias. Yet at the same time, regional preference is absolutely forbidden and adversely perceived by privileged nationals and their supporters in positions of power. The very issue is twisted by accusations of racism and xenophobia. *Might makes right* is the law operating in Antillean society and French nationals make sure all are aware of their might. The bottom line is that the master/servant, master/slave mentality persists despite Antillean ascendance.

The desire to be considered "the same" and yet different, at the same time, is incompatible. To assert one's distinctive, or unique, nature creates dissimilarity between oneself and another. This marks the fundamental reason why the quest for sameness is incompatible with the quest for distinctiveness. Paradoxically, it seems that differentiation is not actually desired. This, then, produces a perpetual dilemma because the actual power relationship between islanders and mainlanders is that of the dominated vis-à-vis the dominant. The State's "solution" is to promote this unequal reliance in order to perpetuate the financial and economic dependence of the indigenous overseas populations. To a large degree, the State assumes the role of surrogate parent – providing care, and meeting the population's basic needs, by providing assistance that is difficult to resist. Whether in Guadeloupe, Martinique or in French Guiana, the local inhabitants have not managed to escape this deadly dependence, which inevitably enfeebles them and destroys their ability to care for themselves. Year after year, and generation after generation, their dependence and helplessness grow, until they find themselves at the mercy of their new masters – despite their expressed desire for autonomy. This paradox was recently reflected in the 2010 referenda held in Martinique and French Guiana.

The deliberate campaign of expatriation which relegated indigenous populations to minority status in their own country, such as that instituted in New Caledonia in the 1970s, has been efficiently replicated across the overseas regions of the French Republic to this very day. Such a policy, which utterly compromises the ability of indigenous people to govern themselves, constitutes a human rights violation on the part of the French Republic; and this is the debate that must be waged if all the citizens of the Republic are truly to stand on equal footing. It is unimaginable that, for example, the inhabitants of Alsace and Brittany, two culturally distinct regions of France, should accept their administrations to be managed by a majority of civil servants from other regions, under the insulting and implausible pretext that their local counterparts *"are incapable of holding executive functions and positions of responsibility, managing services, or of taking initiatives, on account of their indolence."* [20] This feeble excuse is proffered nowhere else within the continental borders of France – such claims find credence only in their application to overseas departments. In these situations, by accepting the status quo, the local populations unwittingly acquiesce to their alleged inferiority – despite its scientific implausibility, their ethnic and racial diversity, their educational attainments, and their geographic environment. People of color in other Caribbean nations and the United States absolutely refute such relegations of inferiority. Inside the French Republic, there are subdivisions, or *regions*, whose integrity must be respected without having to question the indivisibility of the Republic. Individual rights are sacred. The right of self-government provided by the French Constitution is sacred. Overseas regions are entitled to self-government without castigation or unfounded accusations of separatism, racism, and xenophobia. Thus, the expatriation strategy, with its ultimate objective of disempowering and disenfranchising native populations within their own lands, is a grave and unconstitutional infringement upon the cherished values of liberty, equality, and fraternity that lie at the core of the French Republic itself.

SECOND PART

THE SAINT-MARTIN SOCIETY
1977 - 2007

BEGINNINGS OF THE MODERN PERIOD

The Franco-Dutch island of Saint-Martin is divided into two distinct political entities: the French side which in 1946 became one of the Communes of Guadeloupe together with the neighboring island of Saint-Barthelemy through the departmentalization process; and Sint Maarten, which became an autonomous territory in the Netherlands Antilles in 1955. The island is an active, and fully integrated, participant in the surrounding Caribbean region, whose English-speaking neighbors largely gained their independence during the 1960s. Saint-Martin entered the modern era in 1963 when the Dutch side installed electricity throughout its territory and built the first international airport. There was electricity in some areas of the French side, but this side progressed more slowly, and thereby retained its rural and pastoral qualities, which the early visitors found very appealing.

Life in Saint-Martin mainly revolved around subsistence farming, cattle-raising and fishing, for the local inhabitants. Up until the 1940s and the 1950s, prominent landowners exported salt to neighboring islands during the dry season, and periodic shipments of cattle, horses, and goats. Large quantities of grass nourished livestock, and once dried, was sent to Curaçao and Aruba. Children who lived beyond the market-town of Marigot woke up early to milk cows, drive them to pasture, tend flocks of sheep and goats, and to fetch daily supplies of water from the wells. They completed these chores before walking, often long distances, to school in Marigot. Their parents, meanwhile, worked long hours tilling their grounds where they reaped great quantities of tropical produce. Common crops included banana, plantains figs, eggplants, tomatoes, corn, peas, lettuce, cabbage, callaloo, thyme, chives, yams, cassava, sweet potatoes, tania seed and a variety of other ground crops. Arrow root[1] was cultivated in great quantities and, turned into starch, was even exported in barrels to St. Kitts and other islands. Tropical fruit, such as varieties of local mango, were picked and eaten, but not sold. Youths considered mangoes no less than manna from heaven and they picked the fruit on their daily walks through the bush. Other favorites included *pomme surettes*, kenips, yellow and red plums, hog plums and with a host of other local delights.

Subsistence economies are often incapable of adequately supplying he needs of the total population, and such was the case in Saint-Martin during the twentieth century. As a result, many locals emigrated to more prosperous Caribbean islands and to the United States. However, those Saint-Martiners that remained managed to produce enough food for their personal consumption. It was only the merchants from Marigot and Great Bay who imported dry goods from Puerto Rico and the United States, as well as a few door-to-door vendors that brought clothes, beauty products, and other fashionable items from America for resale on the island. The fertile land provided sustenance for the majority of the population and, consequently their lifestyle required little in the way of imports.

When electricity was installed on the island, the first few Americans who decided to reside there permanently or who were just passing through, began importing fresh fruits, refrigerated produce (such as eggs and ice cream), and select frozen foodstuffs. Modernization also enticed a good number of Saint-Martiners to return from the Dominican Republic, the American and British Virgin Islands, Panama, the United States, Cuba, Aruba and Curaçao during the 1960s when tourism, which reached its peak early in the Seventies, began to take off on the Dutch side of the island. Prior to 1975, France had no role on the island than to ensure that its young men enlisted for military service in Guadeloupe and were conscripted to fight during the First and Second World Wars.

The Emergence of Tourism

The earliest stages of tourism began, favorably, in 1955 with the opening of the Little Bay Hotel, the first hotel to offer international accommodation. It contained 20 bungalows. Prior to that, *Passangraham*, the first government 'guesthouse' on the Dutch side, opened its doors in 1922 to accommodate official visitors to the island. Decades later, during the 1950s, the government rented *Passangraham* to Eric Lawaetz, an American from St. Croix. The ten-room guesthouse was renovated to accommodate visitors from the United States from February 1957. During the same period, he also bought the Lowlands, a large property in the southwestern part of the island. The cozy Sea View Hotel - the first hotel owned by the Hazel family - opened its five-room accommodation in 1947 on Frontstreet, in Great Bay. Just over two decades later, in 1971, it was remodeled and enlarged. Two other guesthouses, one the 4-room Lido owned by Chester Wathey and another, owned by Captain Hodge, both opened for business in 1955.[2]

On the French side Mayor Constant Fleming, made his *Hotel Beau Séjour* available to visiting officials as early as 1937. Two other guesthouses with built-in dining that were owned by Pierrot Fleming and Adela Jeffry, operated for a few years beginning in 1956. The St. Tropez, in Sandy Ground, constituted the first full-fledged French hotel, and began operations in 1973. By the end of 1974, it extended to 65 rooms. *Le Galion*, a new hotel, on the *Baie de l'Embouchure*, opened its doors at the end of the year 1975. Due to automation of the oil refineries in the early 1950s, Shell Curaçao and Lago Aruba laid off many workers from Saint-Martin; some of them emigrated to the United States, while others chose to return to their native island. With the growth of the burgeoning tourism industry, the opening of diverse businesses in various sectors, the first banks and other business-related companies, work opportunities were plentiful for those returning Saint-Martiners and other Caribbean nationals from neighboring islands, including Guadeloupe and Martinique. The car rental business also flourished as an outgrowth of the development. Figure 1, below, details significant trend.

RENTAL CARS		
Year	SOUTH	NORTH
1952	77	---
1961	400	15
1977	3,900	2,500

Note: --- indicates figure unavailable

The return of Saint-Martiners coincided with a constant influx of ever more Caribbean immigrants, including the first Haitians and Dominicanos on the island. As tourism, commercial and real estate businesses expanded, the period from 1962 to 1978 gave rise to a spectacular population increase, especially in the South, where many new residential areas were born. Work opportunities concentrated in the South, despite considerable population growth in Northern districts like St. James, Sandy Ground, *Hameau du Pont*, and French Quarter. It is during this period that the North functioned as a kind of dormitory for the island. By 1976, the illegal population numbered 4,000 individuals: 1,500 in the South and 2,500 in the North[3]. Prior to this wave, the Northern population had scarcely doubled in the twenty years between 1954 and 1974. Figure 2 below gives a more detailed breakdown.

ISLAND POPULATION		
YEAR	SOUTH	NORTH
1954	1,797	3,364
1961	2,728	4,494
1967	---	5,061
1972	9,006	---
1974	---	6,191
1977	11,371	6,950
1978	12,207	7,365

Early Infrastructure

Marigot's New Power Plant

In 1963, the small municipal power plant in Grand-Case provided electricity to Marigot and Grand-Case, followed by public lighting to French Quarter, in 1964. However, two years later, service was interrupted as the plant could not produce sufficient energy for these areas. G.E.S.M., the electrical company of Great Bay, assumed responsibility for providing electrical power to the entire island; but in 1974 SPEDEG (from Guadeloupe) installed a power plant on the French side. Nevertheless, it maintained a connection valve with G.E.S.M. in order that both plants could provide back-up in case of possible incidents on either side of the border. This arrangement is responsible for the differentiation in voltage between the French side (which remains at 60 hertz), instead of the 50 hertz cycles normally associated with 220 volts. The Lowlands were directly connected to G.E.S.M. until the completion of the new electrical plant at the end of 1975. From this period, the area received power from Marigot via an underground cable that ran from the Sandy Ground Bridge to the Bluff.[4] [See map of Saint-Martin]

In the decade between 1966 and 1975, the island's consumption of electricity increased steadily, multiplying by more than seven; but then tripled in four short years between 1975 and 1979. In 1980, to cope with the rapid increase in consumption, an initial upgrade of the plant's capacity took effect, enabling it to produce a total power supply of 6,000 kilowatts. The Albert Fleming Company performed the engineering operation without too great a delay in the construction time, despite Hurricane Frederic's arrival during the early construction phase. Five other contractors, consisting of SPEDEG engineers and technicians, contributed to the design and implementation of this work. A second upgrade to the station, to produce even more power, was launched in 1981, and a total cost of 8.8 million francs.

By 1980, electricity was nationalized across the DOM, which permitted the alignment of sale prices with those charged in France. It is important to note that SPEDEG was willing to prioritize the employment of Saint-Martiners who had training as diesel mechanics or those who possessed professional certificates in electro-mechanics, or could prove comparable work experience in the field. Beginning in January 1976, the power plant employed ten local agents.[5]

Marigot's New Sea Water Desalinization Plant

The plant produced 1,000 cubic meters of distilled water per day and a potential capacity of 1,500 cubic meters. From the outset, it contained a 25-ton boiler and two 20-ton evaporators, and became fully operational in early 1975. Moreover, with a turbo alternator, the plant was able to produce desalinated water even in the event of (electrical) current interruption.[6]

Telecommunications in Saint-Martin

By 1975, the Telecommunications buildings on the *Doigt de Gant* [a reclaimed lagoon in Marigot] were ready for installation of automatic switchboards. However, it would first be necessary to establish a large-scale expansion of the cable network, processing facilities, and connections for newly subscribed applicants. To accomplish this task, pipe work was laid to improve the existing network between St. James, the National Highway (N° 7), and the exit from Marigot towards Grand-Case. Underground pipes were installed at the Sandy Ground channel crossing, which allowed for the passage of cables that serviced the Lowlands. Certain parts of the overground network were reinforced to connect cables supporting distant areas more than twelve kilometers away from the telephone center. Lastly, existing subscribers needed to be transferred over to the new device, and their telephone sets replaced by modern, screen-equipped units. The entire operation was completed by 1976.[7]

Esperance Airfield in Grand-Case

Paved docking and maneuvering areas at the end of the air strip were completed by 1975, in addition to an asphalt-covered entry-way and parking lot for passengers. The airline company, PRINAIR, inaugurated a regular route between Guadeloupe and Saint-Martin, and AIR GUADELOUPE offered two weekly flights that same year.[8]

Saint-Martin's Roadways

The French road network was improved in 1975 and a Public Works program began repairs to Cripple Gate Road, and started construction of a bridge spanning a notorious ravine that became treacherous during heavy downpours. Beyond this, road improvements were also undertaken along the border in French Quarter, at the exit of Grand-Case to Marigot, along a section of Mount Williams [Wallawa] Hill on the National Road N°7, and along the section between the Lowlands frontier and the Bluff.[9]

II

THE SOCIETAL IMPACT OF DEVELOPMENT

The second phase of tourism development on the island - characterized, on one hand, by the continuation of the South's economic boom and the second expansion of Juliana International Airport; while on the other, by the North's involvement in competitive tourism - began forcing the inhabitants to realize that the envisioned progress was producing some serious problems, both for the island and its people. Nineteen eighty proved to be a pivotal year in this expanding economy because it already revealed the underside of development, where both the endogenous and exogenous populations exploded to unforeseen levels, and generated irreversible transformations in the environment.

During this period, Parisian governmental representatives in the North realized the undeniable social and ecological potential of this 'virgin' island, and recognized that the French side was not on a par with the economic progress made by the Dutch side, which had begun its development during the Sixties. Passions ignited and the French set out to replicate development in the North in order to reach the same, if not greater, degree of economic prosperity and, thereby, supplant the South. The harmonious cooperation between the French and Dutch sides of the island, which functioned, for a century in accordance with principles of free exchange between the two societies, had come to an end. It was replaced by a period of reckless competition and rapid development, in an effort to reduce the twenty-year advantage the South maintained over the North, which allowed the inhabitants of the North to take advantage of the South's economic prosperity as stipulated by Article 5 of the 1648 Partition Treaty[1], and agreements formulated in the early Sixties by administration heads from the two sides. Indeed, there was a fundamental divergence between those from Saint-Martin and outsiders; even if both shared the French nationality, mainlanders from France saw the French side as a mere extension of the *métropole* and took no consideration for the islanders' history, culture and traditions.

For Saint-Martiners, if the island was geographically and administratively divided into two parts, there was no cultural, linguistic, or human division. Each inhabitant maintained a sense of belonging, place and connection to the entire island, just as they did prior to the imposition of artificial borders. From 1848, when slavery was officially abolished in the North (and ended informally in the South), most of the inhabitants, regardless of their race or origin, were accorded French citizenship. This new era of freedom gave birth to an autonomous way of life for islanders from both sides, wherein their existence was not constrained by administrative protocols, but depended only on their capacity to survive, on the contingencies of the environment, nature, and their ancestral customs.

In Saint-Martin, 1980 was a year of complete upheaval, and of disillusion and confusion, a year of human and cultural confrontation, which recurred, to more or less alarming degrees, over the subsequent twenty years. Despite the impression that development "evolved" as an unplanned, "natural" phenomenon, lacking any deliberate intention or governing force, nothing could have been further from the truth. The objective did not exist to benefit the native inhabitants, but rather to take over control of the country, to displace and replace locals with European nationals, in order to perpetuate French European pre-eminence. From 1848 through the 1970s, such a system never existed previously in Saint-Martin.

Ever since the creation of the Northern Islands district in 1963, the constituents benefited from a number of practical improvements. The various Sub-Prefects respected the diversity of the habits and customs of the population who spoke their Saint-Martin English and whose children indiscriminately went to French-, Dutch- and English-speaking schools throughout the island, or were educated elsewhere - off-island. Such linguistic diversity was not unique to Saint-Martin. In Dominica and in St. Lucia, the islanders spoke French Creole even though the official language was English, as did the locals in Mauritius, in the Indian Ocean. In Saint-Martin, the situation was reversed, due to historical circumstances, in that inhabitants spoke a Creole English, though the official language was French.

By contrast, the State's control, as manifest under the municipal system, had a detrimental impact on daily life. This was especially true as decisions were driven by the personalities and whims of the Sub-Prefects, and by the nature of the missions they were responsible for implementing during their tenure on the island. From 1975 onward, the Sub-Prefects' influence on local politics resembled nothing less than overt interference, with an obvious bias for outside interests. One could only imagine the actual content of the assigned missions between 1975 and 1992, based on the appalling events that took place, and the high level of distrust that existed.

For example, the new Sub-Prefect, who took over in 1975 seemed to have a mission to unify the two opposition parties in order to defeat the incumbent Mayor, Dr. Petit. Between these two groups, one advocated the government's overseas policy, whereas the other favored self-governance and self-determination for the local inhabitants. Neither the Sub-Prefect, nor government officials in Paris showed much appreciation for the sitting Mayor, despite the fact they shared membership in the same national political organization, the R.P.R. (i.e. Rally for the Republic). So, how was it that the Sub-Prefect managed to reconcile such extremely divergent positions between the two opposing parties? Undoubtedly, through the use of intimidation, pressure, domination, and persuasion – particularly in the case of future candidates who were ensured electoral success and the support of the Paris government, which itself desired to take complete control over the electoral machinery. Recognizing they possessed weak platforms, both groups were eager to coalesce in joint opposition to the Mayor. In Saint-Martin, as in most small island communities, politics are personal, thus, people tend to vote for an individual, rather than for an ideology. As a result, it was relatively easy for the highest authority to influence and to spread doubt among the electorate regarding the dealings of the mayoral candidate, regardless of veracity. It was widely believed that the Sub-Prefect created this new party, not to serve the interests of the local inhabitants but his own designs, thus concealing governmental policies intended for overseas territories.

The controlling power dynamic that central authorities in France held over the local populations across the Antilles has already been addressed. French governments, whether of the Left or Right, have always understood, dating back to the days of political assimilation and integration into the Republic of the former colonies in the Americas, that the minds of their overseas constituents were in their control. Moreover, leverage of economic dependence meant France was able to keep these territories within the fold of the Republic, without meeting Antillean demands for access to the full benefits of liberty, equality, and fraternity, which was their political right as citizens. From a position of subjugation, one is neither as free, nor as powerful as the one in dominance, which automatically nullifies any possibility of a fraternal egalitarianism. Thus it was that beginning in 1975, this policy was openly implemented in Saint-Martin for the first time; still it possessed nuances, which for various reasons, more closely resembled conditions in New Caledonia, rather than those of the overseas departments. If the *métropole* had successfully managed to destabilize the social order in New Caledonia, with its one hundred thousand inhabitants, doing the same with six thousand Antilleans in the French controlled territory of Saint-Martin would be mere child's play.

Impeachment of the Mayor

Given his success as the incumbent, and despite his being a member of Chirac's and De Gaulle's national party, there was insufficient incentive for the two local opposition parties to oust the popular Mayor who obstructed the whims of the Sub-Prefect. In fact, during a press release, the Mayor confessed that he had entrusted the Deputy of his constituency to ask the Minister of the DOM

> "to recall the Sub-Prefect of the Northern Islands who acts like a 'Big Boss' by offering casino licenses to various hotels and, promising his cronies public beachfront property. The Minister assured me that the Sub-Prefect would leave within two months. The Prefect, who had just taken office in Guadeloupe, intervened on behalf of the Sub-Prefect so that he would not be recalled. Empowered by that support, the Sub-Prefect, immediately waged a fierce war against me."[2]

Exactly one year after Prime Minister Chirac's visit to Saint-Martin, on December 25, 1975, the decision to impeach the Mayor was pronounced by the Ministerial Council on behalf of the Ministry of the Interior. The Mayor elaborated in the same press release cited above:

> "When Chirac came to my commune, I was on the best of terms with the Administration. I had only to lift my finger to get anything that my municipality wanted; in fact, I rendered service proudly to the Administration. I had selected Guillod as the legislative candidate and managed to convince Brunon, who was then Prefect, to take him on as the majority candidate. I subsequently provided him with the votes necessary for his election.
> In terms of the presidential elections, Saint-Martin voted for Giscard, giving him 1,100 votes, in contrast to the few hundred cast for Mitterrand. Therefore, it was not surprising that there was some talk of creating a legislative constituency in my honor for Saint-Martin and Saint-Barthelemy.
> However, it was after Chirac's visit that things were going to change very rapidly."

This situation clearly illustrates the extent and nature of the Paris government's involvement in the legislative and presidential elections in that part of the Republic occupying the French Antilles. However, when it came to municipal elections and the direct intervention of the State representative who in principle was constrained by the right of reserve (i.e. the obligation forcing government officials to observe restraint in expressing their political preference during election time), the circumstances that occurred in Saint-Martin were very serious and gave evidence to a complete disregard for the democratic process, not to mention a total disregard for the people themselves. The Sub-Prefect determined that this Mayor, who dared to request his recall, would instead himself be removed; not by any legitimate, democratic process, but rather by a high-level decision which cast aspersions on both his honor and his reputation. In truth, it was highly irregular to impeach a Mayor for minor infractions, it simply is not done.

According to another statement by the Mayor in the same press release, he had alienated the Sub-Prefecture, the Prefecture, and the Ministry of Overseas Departments and Territories (DOM-TOM). In an interview with the Prefect about the problems in Saint-Martin, which the Mayor felt was used as *"blackmail"* and *"intimidation"*, he easily refuted the allegations contained in lawsuits the Prefect claimed to have been filed against him:

> "... among other things, that I permitted construction without the appropriate permits, when everyone knows that the Prefect had been signing construction permits of Saint-Martin in my place for the past five years, or that I let Guadeloupeans and Saint-Martiners become squatters on beach land in the public domain, etc ... That there would have been irregularities in the handling of the Municipal Council meetings, without specifying any facts nor giving any proof; that I would have paid 5 million to George Bernard for work that was not done, whereas I have in my possession an official report verifying final receipt of the works signed off by Bernard and the engineer of Public Works, which certified that the works were executed in accordance with the terms of the contract.
> All that would have been of little consequence had I not had to change the coil of my micro-cassette recorder that I was carrying with the intention of recording the Prefect's statements about Saint-Martin's problems, which he mentioned in his meeting summons.
> Caught by surprised, the Prefect suddenly became infuriated and threatened to sue me in Magistrates' Court. This did not stop me from continuing to record him and it is from that moment that the questioning ended, blackmailing me was no longer possible. He, however, said that I had committed a great wrong to speak ill of him."

The Mayor's 1970 speech complaining to Henri Rey, Minister of the DOM-TOM, during his visit to Saint-Martin, in which the Mayor cited Saint-Martin's referred to the inadequate administrative status, difficulties generated by the lack of equipment and insufficient financing to manage the commune, in contrast to the autonomous and prosperous Dutch side where his constituents went to find work, was not well received. The Minister was in no mood to hear about Saint-Martin's problems. The Mayor was too insistent in expressing his concerns for his commune, and by expressing himself as a concerned Saint-Martiner, his ideas *"angered"* his ministerial superiors, especially Pierre Mesmer, the new Overseas Minister, to whom he had expressed his fundamental truths.[3] The decision to impeach the Mayor little more than two months before the municipal elections of March 13, 1977, foreshadowed the tumultuous electoral battle ahead.

Moreover, the French national authorities were greatly concerned by many conditions existing in Saint-Martin at that time, namely: a) friendly relations between the administrative heads on both sides of the island in support of the total population as a whole; b) exemplification of this cohesion through the official celebration of Island's Day on November 11; c) ability of inhabitants from the French side to enter and work on the Dutch side without any formal barriers; and most troubling, d) Mayoral freedom to collaborate with the South's Chief of Government to promote island reunification and calls for independence.

The sparks of national independence already had ignited this region of the Caribbean, so it is not far-fetched to presume that fear of its influence was responsible for the furiously harsh and repressive new system imposed, not on the quiescent elected officials, but upon the unsuspecting and dismayed populous of this quiet section of the island. The apparent ease, with which the Sub-Prefect was able to get the "Black Power" advocate to submit to the R.P.R.'s ideological rallying, did not bode well for the future.

New Municipality

What follows is a detailed report of the municipal elections of March 13, 1977 as seen from the perspective of the Saint-Martiners themselves, be they supporters of the party in power, opponents, or militants. In retrospect, these elections represented (to the distress of enlightened minds) the determining factor in the process of political domination which prevailed on the French side of Saint-Martin. Young people on the island were particularly motivated to bring about the changes that would improve their situation, both in terms of their educational opportunities and their ability to contribute to their country. Unfortunately, the political authorities that controlled the destiny of the island saw the situation very differently. In their view, what mattered was not the future of the local inhabitants, but that of the French *émigrés* who came to the island to enrich themselves and who took advantage of these naïve officials and made them their main target. Having undermined the reputation of the outgoing Mayor – who was a medical doctor by profession – through dismissal from his own national party, he needed to be replaced by a more malleable elected representative who had no edifying ambitions for the island. The suitable candidate would submit to imposition without protest, because his primary allegiance would be to France and to French nationals rather than to Saint-Martin and its population. Such a successor was found in the person of the future Mayor, who emerged victorious from the municipal elections of 1977 in the first round. His party remained in power, though under various names, until 2007 when Saint-Martin took on its new status as an Overseas Collectivity.

The new Mayor, Eli Fleming, won the elections with 1,244 votes in his favor as opposed to the 1,078 cast against, which made for a total of 2,322 votes. However, 143 additional votes were included in this figure as compared to the total number of actual voters, which added up to 2,179. The number of registered voters on the books, however, totaled 3,087, plus an additional 29 voters that were enrolled by court order, bringing the total number of registered voters to 3,116. Nevertheless, no one objected to this irregularity and the results of the elections were approved by Sub-Prefect Etchegoyen. Saint-Martin's monthly publication, *Trait d'Union*, pointed out another irregularity, specifically, the fact that the Sub-Prefect's children, who lived in France, were inscribed on the electoral list and cast their votes by proxy. In a speech delivered at the victory reception on March 20, 1977, the Sub-Prefect requested to attend all future meetings of the Municipal Council.

While Saint-Martin was entering an era of arbitrary actions taken by the State representative, the municipal elections of Saint-Barthelemy (colloquially known as St. Barths), marked the end of a legend, with the defeat of the long-standing Mayor, Remy de Haenen.[4] The inhabitants of St. Barths had already expressed their frustration with the leadership back in April of 1975. They organized a huge protest at the airport against a municipal decision to shorten the road leading to one of the most beautiful beaches by 950 meters in order to accommodate the American multi-millionaire Rockefeller. Months later, the July court case - better known as, the *Trial against the people of St. Barths*, - was reported, and deemed "ridiculous" in an article entitled *"A Defender of Social Peace,"* which ran in the *Trait d'Union* journal. There were 93 defendants from St. Barths:

> "All the inhabitants of Gustavia [the capital city of St. Barths] - that is to say the entire population - were present in the Marigot Courthouse. An important strategic force of C.R.S. [the National Force of Security] was standing guard in the streets. Everything was made ready - a sad affair which would have been simply filed and done away with in any other country concerned with the maintenance of social order. Of what were the residents accused? Some for having blown their horns around 10:30 at night, and others for municipal infractions of the import tax. Every St. Barths family was charged, excepting of course, [Mayor] De Haenen who instituted the civil action. We will spare the details of the indictment and the plea,

> because you will agree with us that the facts and incriminations invoked have nothing whatsoever to do with the profound truth underlying this case."

The citizens of St. Barths would no longer tolerate being humiliated and treated like second-class citizens. They decided to ready themselves to take charge of their own destiny. Beginning with the municipal elections of 1977 onward, the younger generation of St. Barths seized control of their island (with 936 votes in favor, and 447 against)[5] and continued to steer its direction to this day.

In a 1977 interview given to *Trait d'Union*, the new Mayor of Saint-Martin illustrated his role as the elected Administration Head:

> "I am born French, which is an irreversible situation. I cannot see myself claiming a Guadeloupean nationality, much less a Caribbean one. I am proud of being French. Our integration in the department of Guadeloupe creates the number one barrier to Saint-Martin's progress. Consequently, I want Saint-Martin to separate from Guadeloupe and be established as an overseas department along with St. Barths. This can happen easily since France has already granted this status to Mayotte in the Comoros, and to other French colonies, some of which have less than 6,000 inhabitants."[6] [Here he is making reference to Saint-Pierre and Miquelon]

At this point in the interview, *Trait d'Union*, interjects the danger of such status for Saint-Martin by affirming that departmentalization was a failure in several colonies and that Guadeloupe, Martinique, and French Guiana were struggling to obtain their autonomy from that *"infamous feeding system."* The journal further added that the island was too small to adopt a status which would widen the gap between the French and Dutch sides of the island, and that rather, what was needed was a *"plan capable of unifying both sides of the island."* Such a plan would inevitably imply the abolition of the current status *"that ties us to Guadeloupe but even more so to the centralizing power of France. Becoming a department would only give the French a stronger hold on us."*

Next, the new Mayor presented the main goal of his mandate: education. He confirmed the opening of a Pre-school and Kindergarten, along with his intention to make the school canteen compulsory for all children, as it would enable them to master the French language at an early age. He also planned to build a new junior high school [middle school]. However, the *Trait d'Union* retorted that these plans only addressed one aspect of the educational problem and that it was most urgent to deal with the crucial problem of the present generation of adults by providing them with proper professional, cultural and social training because the current educational system was inadequate.

Furthermore, the new Mayor reproached Saint-Martiners for not depending on the French government for their daily sustenance, which he felt, explained their subsequent lack of national consciousness. How ironic that he should regret a sense of dependency on the part of Saint-Martiners. The following excerpt is a direct quote he gave in English:

> "Saint-Martiners seem to ignore that France owes them a debt. In other words, France is the mother country, and the duty of a mother is to provide a means of living for her children. This mentality explains why so many Saint-Martiners emigrate to Aruba, Curaçao, the Virgin Islands, and to the U.S.A. The Saint-Martiner is too accustomed of disentangling his own situation without depending on the Government."

Then he compared Saint-Martiners to Europeans:

> "We are too far behind hand, while we are still struggling for a daily bread, the Europeans have reached the point where their only concern is to secure their future."

The last point of the interview was made by Leopold Baly, the publisher of *Trait d'Union*, when he announced his intention to open a private commercial school for the 1977-1978 academic year, which would prepare young Saint-Martiners for their official examinations [CAP, BEP, Bac G2 & G3, etc.] as well as offer

> "... social promotion courses for adults. This school will meet the special needs of the Saint-Martiner. Most of our children, - when not thrown out of school at the age of 15 or 16, exactly the age when they are starting to overcome their handicap due to an unfit educational system - are transferred to domestic schools in Saint-Martin or even in Guadeloupe."

He added that,

> "the advantage for the Saint-Martiner to inherit the most universal and commercial language in the world, English, makes him more fit to succeed in Trade and Management than in domestic trainings. ... This school will rid most parents of the excessive charges involved in sending their children to Guadeloupe and create an equal opportunity for all our youth."

The Sub-Prefect's presence at the Municipal Council meetings did not augur well either for democracy or for the people of Saint-Martin. Their uneasiness increased daily and it should be recalled that the opposition parties were not yet represented in the Council. As early as May 10, 1977, the Municipal Council chaired by the Mayor - with two Deputy Mayors and 14 council members present, whereas the Second Deputy Mayor and five councilors were absent - approved the following motion:

> "SUBJECT: SHIPYARD REPAIR SITE, BAIE DE LA POTENCE
> Project: DUMOLIE
> The Mayor referred to the Prefecture's decree of April 6, 1977 concerning the authorization of private equipment with obligation to provide public service for the establishment of Mr. André Dumolie's shipyard on the *Baie de la Potence* in Saint-Martin. After deliberation, the City Council has decided to surrender its priority right to 8,000 sq. meters of public beachfront land, which will, henceforth, be leased to Mr. André DUMOLIE for a period of twenty years.
> The City Council, nevertheless, underlines the need for specific conditions to be adhered to in order to avoid pollution of the beachfront and the sea, and requests that the appropriate Public Works service to exercise constant supervision of the shipyard.
> Signed: The Mayor. Countersigned with the following notation "Witnessed in Saint-Martin on May 25, 1977" by the Sub-Prefect. Posted May 21, 1977."

This motion raised a general outcry within the population, and it would seem that the absent Second Deputy Mayor and five missing council members had boycotted this meeting, according to a June *Trait d'Union* article from 1977. It called for *"the resignation of this irresponsible City Council headed by two Mayors"*. It also opposed the Sub-Prefect's presence at the Council meetings:

> "Our Commune no longer enjoys its autonomy. Our Municipal Council only deliberates on issues submitted by the Prefect and Sub-Prefect, and the Mayor is merely there to carry out the Sub-Prefect's desires."

Another Council motion on May 10, 1977 concerned the

> "CREATION OF TOURIST AND SEASIDE RESORT ZONES
> After explanations given by the Mayor and the Sub-Prefect concerning applicable laws for the licensing of casinos, the Council deliberates and seeks annulment of a resolution passed in 1972 which made the entire municipal territory of Saint-Martin a seaside resort zone.

> The Council further decides on the creation of specific zones which will be declared touristic areas and seaside resorts: Marigot Bay, Orient Bay, Lucas Bay [Coralita].
> Each request for a casino will require a Council study."

And the newspaper commented:

> "Saint-Martin residents will therefore only have access to four beaches, rather three, for Marigot Bay is already in danger of being polluted [by the shipyard in Galisbay]. War is slowly, but surely, being prepared, isn't it?"

The unrest that was brewing, not only among the inhabitants, but also within the City Council since March 1977, would spread to the general public before the end of the year. It is preferable to present the readers – for their judgment and review - the contents of an open letter written by Councilman Felicien Maccow to his fellow Council members, which was reprinted in the *Trait d'Union* journal in November 1977. In actuality, the letter clearly explains the origins of the unrest. His dream was the same as all the young people on the island, and his sincerity, but a trademark of an authentic Saint-Martiner.

> "I've dreamed of a large family of Saint-Martiners whose future and wellbeing depended on the active role of new dynamic and responsible leaders, beyond all personal considerations and beyond all slanderous attitudes. Undoubtedly, after 8 months serving in the new Council, each and every one of us has drawn enough lessons and, as a consequence, is able to formulate an objective self-criticism. Let us then pose some hard questions which we shall attempt to answer:
> 1) Do we conduct ourselves differently from the former leaders of this community? Aren't our Mayor and deputies about to commit the same mistakes?
> 2) What is our duty as members of this new Town Council? Do we have the feeling that we form one team in which the debate is clearly and democratically organized? That is to say, one in which the free expression of every individual and their desires are fully respected? How many times have our shy interventions been stifled or rebuffed, whenever they happened to go against the Sub-Prefect's personal interests or those of his friends?
> 3) Have we forgotten all those pre-election promises?
> You may say it is still too early and that the former group took 18 years without being able to boast about one single thing done for the benefit of the people!
> But I think, from our perspective, that if we were really sincere and honest, we would concede that 8 months is ample time to have begun the debate with a view to establish a short-term socio-economic plan, with a corresponding

budget, to bring forth the Commune's resources, in order to test its limits and possibilities, and how to achieve agreed objectives.
4) If another election should come up, could we depend on the support of our voters who with 'bloodshot eyes' defended the precise objectives we clearly proposed to them?

Now that the eyes of Saint-Martin are upon us, how can we remain passive and permit the Mayor, his deputies, and a Sub-Prefect - whose only interest is that of his *metropolitan* friends - to bury the crucial problems of our community, when we have promised the people immediate solutions?
It is high time we, municipal councilors, demand that these various pre-election promises be put into concrete forms, that we seize the reins and take the lead to instigate effective action.
Do we even recall those promises that were made on April 30, 1977 at the Town-House by the Prefect of Guadeloupe in the presence of all the heads of governmental affairs? Notably:

- Building of a high school with 16 classrooms (to be opened September 1977)
- A nursery school in Marigot
- A stadium
- Setting up a preliminary vocational school
- Creating 50 affordably priced residential lots

Add to this list the promises made by our new Council:

- Electricity and public lighting in Sandy Ground, Concordia, and *Hameau-du-Pont*
- Real jobs for young people in Saint-Martin
- Construction of a market in Marigot

Up to this present moment, not even the smallest evidence of these promised projects can be seen, yet the Mayor has wiped the slate clean in order to make room for a new set of priorities. Namely:

- Saint-Martin's secession from Guadeloupe and its formal annexation to France as a department
- Creation of a '*classe de Seconde*' [1st High School class]
- Creation of a public vocational school
- Management of the airport in Grand-Case

On and on it goes! Promises, promises and more empty promises! Where are the changes promised to the people? Where is the substance?

PATERNALISM!
A Sub-Prefect who determines the management and allocation of municipal funds.
A Sub-Prefect who personally presides over Municipal Council meetings and who uses intimidation to quell opposition from Councilors during meetings.
A Sub-Prefect who interferes with employment selection of local administrative staff.

RECRUITMENT OF SAINT-MARTIN LOCALS! Of course, this is needed, but how? And in what capacity?

It is common knowledge that all Saint-Martiners employed by the Municipality are to be paid from welfare funds (pocket change), and most of those who are appointed to random jobs have not received a cent for the past four months; whereas in contrast to these remedies that have been designed to buy time and fool the masses, a large number of French nationals have been recruited and assigned to well-paying jobs. There was even an instance where a French national showed up with the receipt for his net salary in hand, and has been paid immediately from municipal funds.

WASTE!

- 3 garbage trucks
- 2 vans for the school canteen
- A van whose assignment does not seem to have been decided, if we do not retain the personal use that is made by Mr. X
- The construction of private roads
- Jobs for friends who did not need them.

Did you know that *Le SANTAL*, a European restaurant in Sandy-Ground, has just been given electricity from E.D.F., following written approval from the Mayor, whereas the Mayor withheld this same approval from Mr. Baly's Commercial School – despite the fact that the school is a public necessity within the same zone and is therefore obligated to receive electricity? (To keep it secret, the power lines to the restaurant were run underground)

Did you know that the largest room in City Hall is being used as a classroom for the so-called *classe de Seconde* urgently created for the sole purpose of providing instruction in Saint-Martin for the Sub-Prefect's daughter? A diverted way to have four private teachers for the Sub-Prefect's daughter, paid with government money.

Did you know that behind the freshly painted windows of our primary schools are classrooms, hidden from view, which are packed with more than 60 pupils in one little room, and that to make up for this overcrowding, our young pupils are subjected to a most horrific schedule?
Did you know that the word on the street is that the municipality's budget is running a deficit and that numerous civil servants are not paid?

Dear Fellow-Councilors
It is our duty to protest against the actions of our Mayor and his deputies; actions that will not fail to set the population of Saint-Martin against us. We must rise up against the interference of the Sub-Prefect in those affairs that fall within the competence of the Mayor and the Council.
We were elected by the population to safeguard our common heritage for everyone's well-being; and we must take our responsibility in hand and demand effective participation in municipal life instead of being obedient, meek, and passive spectators. We cannot allow the population to end up paying for policies with which it has nothing to do.
Our Mayor owes us an explanation regarding compromises he has made with the Sub-Prefect and these European outlaws who are taking over our country.

The Mayor has to render an account of the financial situation of the Commune.
I DARE SPEAK MY MIND AS I SEE IT."

Massive European Immigration

Everything was in place to move in full force. With the elected representatives conquered, it was possible to take complete control over this small commune, with the conviction and the weight needed to neutralize any show of resistance, even if it meant destroying the tranquility, peace, and harmony that had always prevailed on this fifty two square kilometer rock. As Saint-Martin had always been the least French among the DOM, the first phase of massive settlement from the mainland was traumatizing for the islanders. A minority of the locals supported the political leadership in power which allowed the Sub-Prefect to execute his repressive policies. The majority denounced the destructive changes to their way of life, the environment, and the disappearance of all this side of the island represented for them.

Octavia Hanna, a seventy-year old woman who once lived in Aruba, published a prophetic article in 1978 about the social situation in the northern monthly newspaper. In this article she recalled that when the first settlers decided to share the island in 1648, it was done on a peaceful basis, but that *"the new wave of Europeans who are colonizing Saint-Martin for the second time will, undoubtedly, meet with strong resistance. ... When people become aware of the bitter reality, they will stand up for their rights."* Then, she pinpointed three problems that were affecting the lives of Saint-Martiners: First, the abusive use of laws regulating land in the public domain. *"Today European colonizers are appropriating 2,700,000 square meters of public land on a little island like Saint-Martin [...] where most inhabited areas are situated between the sea and the ponds."* She added that *"every day the land grabbers are harassing the people living in these areas, even though they have possessed the legal deeds for generations." ... "The land is being distributed secretly only to Europeans."* Secondly, she addressed the influx of Europeans to Saint-Martin, *"Can you imagine"*, she wrote, *"800 European families living on a little island like Saint-Martin, without creating racial conflict? [...] When we accept a situation as inevitable, we are selling out the future of our children, by helping the white man build a white society within our own country. In this new white society, I am telling you, we and the generation after us, will be pushed aside or reduced to the mere status of shoe shine slaves for these invaders. [...] I am not saying to go around hating all Europeans indiscriminately, but what I am saying is that we must vigorously denounce their wrong doings and do everything possible to stop these abuses. Above all, we must make them understand that we are ready to use any means necessary to defend the land of our ancestors. This is the price that must be paid for our survival."* The third problem concerned *"the over-exploitation of local workers by Europeans and their deplorable work conditions"*. Lastly, she requested that the appropriate authorities put an end to these actions.[7]

The State's takeover of Saint-Martin favored European newcomers in a number of significant ways. For example, by allowing them to build the first hotels on beachfront land in the public domain, by welcoming multinational construction companies, opening the first restaurants in Grand-Case, expanding the number of businesses in Marigot – including the first controversial real estate agency on Félix Eboué Street which incensed the residents of the Marigot town center. Obviously, this development was not designed to promote tourism, nor was it intended to integrate the local population; rather it possessed all the accoutrements to support a new, colonial settlement. The islanders found themselves relegated to the role of mere spectators, for the first time, and had to ask themselves some serious questions. They had no idea what was actually happening in their country and were not prepared for such a situation. They had never experienced any system other than the comparatively benign administration, which presided over the destiny of the French half of the island since 1838. Moreover, during the previous thirty years, those few Europeans who lived on the island did so with the intention to living quietly and in harmony with the original inhabitants, and were so few as to be counted on the fingers of one hand.

From 1977 on, Saint-Martin became a type of *El Dorado*. It must be recalled that France experienced a number of great upheavals during the early 1980s: the creation of *"regions"* as new administrative divisions, the rise of the anti-racist movement SOS Racism, and problems arising around immigration, to name but a few. Saint-Martin, by contrast, was exempt from all of these problems. It was as if it lay at the ends of the earth and only attracted those in search of the exotic and the idyllic good life. Saint-Martin knew nothing of social unrest, racial conflict or labor disputes. It was an island paradise. A few investors arrived during the Seventies and the State took it upon itself to sell them prime beachfront land - at a price of one franc per square meter – which it had swindled from local landowners who were still in possession of the deeds. The State was able to achieve this under the terms of the infamous 1955 decree which came into effect as Saint-Martin was incorporated into the department of Guadeloupe in 1946, although the State's ownership of beachfront land had never before been implemented in Saint-Martin.

It was simply too bad for those who did not claim their rightful ownership within the prescribed time limit. No one in Saint-Martin, except the Mayor, was informed about the deadline, and the owners had no inkling about the law. The State confiscation of the beach properties opened the door for many such political maneuverings and enabled land speculators – including both local politicians and top French officials - to own land practically free of charge. A 1979 article in the bilingual publication *Cogito*, recounted the testimony of one young Saint-Martiner:

> "People often asked me, when I was abroad, to give some details on this marvelous island on which I am fortunate enough to reside. Several times I was tempted to reply that Saint-Martin is not a marvelous island, contrary to what people might think. I imagine that such a concise, but true, reply will not fail to make the reader wonder. Actually, how can I recognize my Saint-Martin, and the one that 'progress' is transforming day after day - and yet, I can do nothing to stop it. Soon there will be no strip of land to which our childhood memories will be attached. I do not even recognize my friends: Saint-Martiners, the real ones, those who were so attached to our native soil. All of them, one after the other, are knocked about or trampled by those who envision Saint-Martin as their Paradise. Paradise - such a grand word! Don't make me laugh - it will never be, for there is absolutely no commonality between Saint-Martiners' way of life and all those preconceived 'ideas' coming from elsewhere (Europe or America). Alas! The only 'Paradise' will be that of my childhood, embellished by my parents' and grandparents' memories. … What will it be 20 years from now? I dare not even think of it. It is true, I am young, and I do not accept easily other ideas, nor am I willing to grant the opponent the right to have his own, to take advantage of them, or to impose them. But how am I supposed to become accustomed to such savage and disorganized progress? Prevail and impose! I believe it has already happened. We are already defeated before we can even begin to fight. Now, in the street, when I look around I realize that it is useless to go on this way. For there is nothing I can do, it is too much for me."[8]

Twenty years later, that was 1999, and we will analyze then what happened in the intervening years. This was a young man who did not allow himself to be overcome by feelings of helplessness, despite the "progress" steamrolling over his island. Instead, he actively engaged in politics alongside the person who would succeed the Mayor at the time. He had understood quite well that the island had embarked on an irreversible, destructive course, which no one could stop. Nevertheless, he felt compelled to try and do something.

This chain of events provoked Saint-Martiners to the very limit. They were barraged on all fronts, including the extreme eagerness of certain French nationals who wanted to rent out everything and buy up every empty piece of land - even though none of it was for sale. Saint-Martin was on the verge of establishing its property register. Its management was assigned to a young Frenchman who was fulfilling his military obligation in the capacity of a 'Voluntary Technical Assistant.' Records were deliberately documented with critical *"errors"* that benefited French nationals and disadvantaged the rightful owners, thus widening the gap between Europeans and Saint-Martiners. There were countless examples of these occurrences. In fact, several buildings belonging to Saint-Martiners were attributed to European tenants in the cadastral register. If the owners noticed the *"errors"* and requested to have it rectified, the office would require the local, Saint-Martin owners to prove their ownership. Other buildings and empty properties belonging to Saint-Martiners were recorded in the registry under European names that were unknown on the island. The documentation of rightful ownership created an unprecedented disarray that left the door wide open to all forms of fraud.

The office responsible for the management of lands in the Public Domain, was based in Guadeloupe, and subtly exerted unlawful pressure on key landowners in Saint-Martin who possess beachfront properties, in order to force them to relinquish their land. They were informed that the beachfront was to be reserved for French Europeans who wished to invest in the DOM, though this was decided arbitrarily. As a result, French investors arrived to build hotels under the pretext that they had bought the property from the Domain, and that the local inhabitants must vacate the land. This is precisely what happened with The Grand Saint-Martin Hotel in Galisbay, and the Saint-Tropez in Sandy Ground, (later renamed P.L.M.). In both instances, French investors had the upper hand, and the administration facilitated their development of tourist zones on the island. The responsible administrators turned a deaf ear to this first wave of complaints and protests from the Saint-Martin owners. This was but the beginning of an abusive exchange of land ownership in Saint-Martin: first, during the 1960s Antillean and West Indian people from the neighboring islands in search of work squatted on Sandy Ground, followed by European laborers who arrived in the 1970s.

During subsequent years, prime beachfront land was parceled out by the Guadeloupe office to individuals coming from France and all across the Overseas Departments and Territories, in order to help them settle and build their private residences. Some were audacious enough to claim they had bought the land in Paris, believing that by citing 'Paris,' the rightful owners would readily cede their claim to the land. In fact, the former engineer of Public Works, who was on duty in Saint-Martin at that time, was so bold as to tell a local Saint-Martiner that *'the beach land area was for the metropolitans who come here.'* Thus, their intent was no secret.

Europeans profited from the municipal services that were set up to promote urbanization on the island. Within three months, at the most, they were able to buy land, draw up plans, and obtained building permits without any complications; whereas local efforts to do the same were hampered by all kinds of red tape and unwarranted objections – such as insufficient parking allotments – which, ultimately resulted in rejected permits. Yet, numerous construction projects and businesses belonging to the newcomers were granted building permits without any parking spaces whatsoever. It quickly became evident that the real objective was only to impede development opportunities for local islanders. Some Europeans, who dealt with elderly landowners that could not read French, tricked them into signing papers and falsified documents. For a few years, a climate of total distrust prevailed that forced the earlier Europeans, who had emigrated years before, to distinguish themselves from the newcomers, whom they readily referred to as *"scamps, crooks, and sharks."* Younger Saint-Martiners, who were defensive about the European take-over of the land, targeted whites to express their open hostility at their presence, and never failed to make them feel unwelcome in Saint-Martin. The racial tensions eroded the prior respect and understanding that existed between both ethnic groups on the island. In retrospect, it is clear this rift was but the prelude to the fractured and divided society that would prevail in a few short years – a ruptured society that would become the very antithesis of what had once been dubbed the *"Friendly Island."*

The March 8, 1980 Revolt

The Sub-Prefecture, having targeted Sandy Ground to become a mini *Côte d'Azur*, was preparing to expel Saint-Martin landowners, French Antilleans and other squatters that were living in the area. Consequently, their property was seized and their houses bulldozed, which brought about the intervention of the 2nd Deputy Mayor, who responded one Sunday by *bulldozing* the C.R.S. (French Security Police), barracks that had been built in the same area.

On Saturday, March 8, 1980, the Municipal Council held a meeting in the Town Hall in order to deliberate the request to transfer public beachfront land in Sandy Ground to the Commune; and also, to announce the plan to restructure the area into development allotments under the supervision of the State. The room was packed to capacity and a crowd was gathered outside.

The Sub-Prefect took the floor by appealing to the good citizenship of the inhabitants in order that *"everything takes place in a peaceful and friendly manner, thereby proving the reputation of Saint-Martin as the Friendly Island."*[10] The Mayor then spoke and, considering the crowds inside and outside, thought it best to first explain the background of the whole affair. Based on his understanding, he explained the history of land ownership in Saint-Martin, and how Sandy Ground consisted of a long piece of land wedged between the sea and the lagoon with exactly 81.20 meters of domain land from the highest waters on both sides" He stated all this to show those inhabiting the area that the terrain that they thought belonged to them, in fact, belonged to the State as a result of the 1955 decree, which *"put an end to this occupation of domain zone"*. Referring specifically to the squatters, he said, *"Sandy Ground, for those who do not know, is the result of the abuses of those people who came here to work but could not find a place to live. It was natural! They sought public land, belonging to the State, settled there, and the consequence is Sandy Ground!"* Then, he showed the plans that the Commune, as the new owner, had prepared for the public beachfront land, known as Sandy Ground. He added *"that greedy and selfish people"* would not be allowed to continue squatting in the area; and then announced that demarcation of the zone would be completed the following Monday, and threatened to take to court all those who would not yield. While assuring the population that he will do everything with great equity and secure the public interest, he closed with the following remarks:

> "The first thing I want to say to you is that Saint-Martin is in the middle of its economic evolution. On this point, I would like to make everyone aware: I have noticed that there are plenty of residents in Saint-Martin who really want progress. Unfortunately, they do not understand that to achieve progress, something must be given, sometimes you must give up your rights in order to receive something in return, for nothing can be achieved without sacrifice. You do not get anything if in return you do not give anything, if you do not make a sacrifice. […] Everybody must understand that development has disadvantages: in the first place, there will be an influx of people who will come, because as in all countries where progress occurs, everyone comes in search of opportunity. And who knows this better than Saint-Martiners who have themselves gone everywhere looking for opportunity … [Shouts from the audience]
>
> The second thing I would like to bring to your attention is that now, more than ever, we Saint-Martiners must show our common sense, our intelligence, and especially our vitality, because it's only through competition that anything can be achieved. Others will come from abroad to compete with us. Well, Saint-Martiners will get every protection from the local administration, but in no way will we give preference to anyone who pretends he was born in Saint-Martin and who does not want to come to something, or who is incapable of doing so. [Shouting and laughter from the audience]

The conclusion is that as a Mayor I am painting a picture... and everyone now must be ready to take part in the race. It is a race now. And I am convinced that many Saint-Martiners will come out as winners."

The Mayor's cynicism and insensitivity during his attempted general policy speech, gave rise to the angry protests from the audience. The following are samples of some of the most significant comments, which were interrupted by shouts and clapping:

Mrs. Berry Gumbs, a landowner in Sandy Ground immediately raised her voice [speaking French]:

> "... I live in Sandy Ground. I've endured everything that was going on there ... I've endured good and bad things. I worked and raised a child, with the help of my mother. She is dead now and she left me a piece of property. Whosoever wants this property from me, I am telling them they can take everywhere, but where they see marked Berry Jeanne and Romney, don't trespass, it belongs to us..." [Shouting, clapping]

Albert Romney-Burnett, Second Deputy Mayor, spoke in English:

> "Silence please... I would like to say a couple of words. The reason for this meeting today is to show to you all Saint-Martiners that we are going forward. We are going to make something out of Saint-Martin for Saint-Martin people. The move that was made on Sunday was neither a racial nor a political move. It was to save Saint-Martin for Saint-Martiners. ['Thank you' was heard in the audience. Applause]
> I want each and every one who is standing present here today, when they leave and go back to their homes, to understand that an important issue is to get it legalized. Anybody who is a squatter on land today that is not the legal owners of that land will have to move ... [Applause]
> ... Saint-Martin people are a very understanding people. But one thing is for sure, we are going to stand up for what is rightfully ours. I feel that Saint-Martin people have been pushed in a corner and we are going to stand up and defend ourselves ... [Applause]
> ... We in Saint-Martin are living in a country which is divided into two parts. On one side, the light shines 24 hours a day, and the next side, we are in darkness. We want light in this country. We want light, and in order to have light in this country we must go towards it together. One of the great problems that we are having in Saint-Martin, one of the great problems that we hear about in Saint-Martin, is unity. We are divided ... We must come together and fight for the benefit of Saint- Martin. [Applause]
> Today, I'm openly making two requests, and those two requests. I guarantee you, I will go to my grave, but this is for the benefit of French Saint-Martin. We have a problem on this island with foreigners. We are being taken over by foreigners.[11] We have a force in Saint-Martin that they call the C.R.S. who

supposed to be … [Comments and shouts drown out his words]. We want to make them understand today that we don't want them in Saint-Martin any more … [More comments, shouts] … not at the airport, not at the wharf, because these foreigners don't know who the foreigners are. I am asking today that these C.R.S. be replaced by local people. [Comments and supportive shouts] We are not going to stand up and leave anybody dictate for us what is going to go on in this country anymore… [Shouts and applause] … The future of Saint-Martin must be decided by Saint-Martiners …. We must join hands. … [Comments, shouts, applause] Yesterday, when I got in my car I overheard a Saint-Martiner like myself say: *"Let them go Sandy Ground to knock down houses, you'll see wha' they gon to do them"*. Now, when I took a stand on Sunday, I didn't take a stand for myself. I don't need anything. I took a stand for Saint-Martin people, but if Saint-Martin people are going to stand in the back, I am going to sit down. [Shouts and applause]

I want the people to be in the light. I don't want them to be in darkness. So I am asking you please, whatever we are going to do, we are going to protest in a peaceful way. We will never achieve anything in Saint-Martin by violence. Whatever you do, make sure you are doing it in a peaceful manner. So I am asking all of you, people of Saint-Martin, to come together and we will build the future of Saint-Martin together." [Ongoing applause]

After this speech, which reflected the disagreement surrounding the policy brought forward by the Mayor and the Sub-Prefect, the Mayor raised a question about the status of Saint-Martin. Louis Wescott, a Municipal Councilor, then took the floor to complain [in English] that "the Mayor was taking too much time [4 years] to give satisfaction to the people of Saint-Martin…" Next, some in the audience called for Mr. Alberic Richards to speak.

Alberic Richards, First Deputy Mayor and General Councilor of Saint-Martin, said in English:

"I want to say to each and every one of you how very happy I am at this moment to see that finally the people of Saint-Martin are seeking to defend themselves and their island. [Shouts and applause]

I don't want anybody to clap. I just want you to listen. I want to say that for such a long time, so many years, even before I was born, so many things have been taking place that was shameful, that was scandalous, and that nobody ever dared say or do anything about them.

Today, I realize that there is a *prise de conscience* [pang of consciousness] and I want to say this: Don't lose your cool about the matter, let us work together towards building a society in which each and every one of us is a part, and which is our society - Saint-Martin society.

But I want you to remember, dear friends, as Mrs. Jeffry-Razafin said a while ago, that Saint-Martiners even though they have been scattered all over the world, they have no bad reputation. The only thing that people will be able to

> say about us is that we do not have the instruction or the education that could push us in the right direction. But it has been proven, over and repeatedly, that the Saint-Martiner is extremely intelligent… [Shouts and applause] … I think because of this …. Let's come together… again I repeat, I don't want to make a long speech, let's get together and build the society in a harmonious manner. Thank you."[Applause]

The meeting ended in an atmosphere of general protest and indignation. The determination of the Saint-Martiners on this Saturday, March 8, 1980 triumphed over the arbitrary and repressive forces of the state representative and the Mayor of Saint-Martin. Their announced intentions to expropriate the occupants were not implemented and the residents of Sandy Ground remain in Sandy Ground up to this day. The Revolt of March 8, 1980 became a source of confidence and hope for Saint-Martin. The expropriation, domination, and contempt that characterized this first phase of imposed economic development by the public authorities, could not withstand the people's determination to live with dignity, to assert their identity, and to make others respect their culture and their history.

Municipal and Sub-Prefectural Policy

From the vantage point of the elected officials and state authorities, however, it was just a matter of time. The offensive to continue with planned development was still under way, though it might require an occasional change in tactics to meet upcoming challenges in the years ahead. Two important events were to mark this period, beginning with the sudden death of First Deputy Mayor and General Councilor of Saint-Martin, Alberic Richards, in August 1981. No less unexpected was the sudden death, a mere two and a half years later, of the Mayor of Saint-Martin, Elie Fleming, on Saturday, March 3, 1984. He died at the *Sint Rose* Hospital in Philipsburg, one year after the municipal elections of March 13, 1983.

By and large, the hostile invasion continued, and was exacerbated by acts of vandalism, aggression, robbery, burglary, murder and assassination. Caribbean immigrants were hunted down in atrocious raids that blatantly violated their human rights, and resulted in protests from local islanders. Even the Mayor objected when confronted with the negative impact these raids were having on the local economy. At the same time, social unrest in Guadeloupe and Martinique, along with terrorist acts perpetrated in the fight for Guadeloupe's liberation, cause the state authorities and the Mayor to propose Saint-Martin's political separation from Guadeloupe, as they did not want to be governed by an independent Guadeloupe. The municipality and the Sub-Prefecture used this illusory opportunity to call for a change of political status, whereby the Northern Islands would become an overseas department and, most importantly, would gain a Deputy in the French Parliament. Nevertheless, in 1981, the feasibility of such a costly and management-heavy structure that would divide the tiny half-island into three communes, inhabited by 7,000 residents, was soon brought into question. The fact that the economy was fragile and dependent on seasonal tourism did little to help the matter.

The Mayor and his delegation went to Paris to discuss the status issue, and it seemed possible that Saint-Martin would become a department. Most of the local populous objected to such a reclassification and believed their elected officials were *jumping from the frying pan into the fire.* Soon the issue dominated all aspects of island life. Local residents worried about several current matters: France's political and economic control of the municipality; large-scale European emigration that was transforming Saint-Martin society into a new European settlement; increased taxation; and widespread unemployment. Each of these matters was detrimental to Saint-Martiners – at least in the long run.

The municipal policy direction was plain to see. Its steadfast goal was to *"Frenchify"* and to *"Europeanize"* the northern half of the island. The Mayor was not intimidated by the majority's protestations because he felt strongly backed by the state representative, whose policies he was implementing. The steam roller was in motion and ready to crush anyone that stood in its way. Who would voluntarily subject themselves to that? And so it was that anyone wishing to make an appointment with the Mayor's secretary on the second floor of the Town Hall had to fill out a form, just as if they wished to see the Mayor himself. With luck, perhaps three or four Europeans who were completely ignorant of island customs and etiquette, would meet the individual instead. Similarly, any request to review the cadastral registry or the record of municipal motions would be denied as they were now sent to the Sub-Prefecture or to Guadeloupe. Island employees working in City Hall were restricted to the first floor. Besides, those possessing high qualifications, who wanted to serve on the island, were offered various posts in mainland France. At that time, it was common practice for the BUMIDOM to export young Antilleans across the French West Indies to France, but the policy was less successful in Saint-Martin.

Beginning in 1977, senior-level positions were reserved for French Europeans whether in communal or departmental management. They were given jobs in the primary and secondary schools, even if they did not possess the required qualifications. Those few Saint-Martiners with advanced degrees were considered *overqualified* by the same administrations when they returned from studying overseas. To obtain employment on their native island, required tenacity and a strong will to overcome the many obstacles. While some were successful, others gave up. In an attempt to ensure fluency in French, the Mayor planned to have local children start school as young as three years, but ultimately this plan did not succeed. One of the difficulties with this policy was that it negatively impacted the quality of education on the island and ignored efforts that were already underway, in Grand Case, to teach English at the Kindergarten level.

No High School [Lycée] existed on French Saint-Martin. Eventually the rector in charge of the Antillean Educational District (based in Martinique), approved the creation of the first class, followed successively by the two other levels of the literary section leading to the *Baccalaureate*, in affiliation with the Gerville Réache High School in Basse-Terre, Guadeloupe. This decision was the direct result of a personal request from the Sub-Prefect and was dutifully endorsed by the Mayor. It soon became apparent that this first high school class came into existence only because the Sub-Prefect's daughter, who was a Middle School [Collège] student in Marigot, was on the verge of entering high school; and *not* in response to requests from the parents and students of the last year in middle school and their Saint-Martin teacher. The fact is, parents and students on the verge of completing middle-school, had already requested the opportunity to complete their secondary instruction on the island so that they, too, could benefit from free education throughout high-school. The lack of high school education on the French side caused serious hardship, with regard to the cost of studying off-island and boarding in Guadeloupe, as numerous students and their families could attest. The Sub-Prefect managed to exploit local Saint-Martiners' needs, and gain support from the rector and the Mayor, to create this first high-school class mainly designed for the benefit of his personal family. This is undisputable, because after the Sub-Prefect completed his term of office, the three high-school classes were removed, one after the other, despite the appeals of the affected students in the second and third levels. The students expressed their earnest desire to maintain the high-school program to the new rector of the Antilles Educational District when he officially visited Saint-Martin. He, in turn, assured them that it would continue. Nevertheless, the third level was discontinued at the beginning of the 1980-1981 academic year, when the two remaining students in that class took their Baccalaureate examination in Basse-Terre.

Deliberate stress was put upon these students, and their parents, to pressure them into leaving Saint-Martin. From 1977 to 1979, at the beginning of each school year, rumors circulated that the high school program would be terminated the following year. Parents, as a precautionary measure, made preparations to send their children to Guadeloupe or Martinique, even though it meant enormous sacrifice. The majority of the students in the high school classes were from Saint-Martin, and most of their parents could not afford to send their children off-island. Airfare was expensive, the cost of boarding was equally excessive, and adjusting to the living conditions in Guadeloupe was difficult for most of the students. An inquiry into this situation revealed just how helpless and worried parents felt at the prospect of the program's discontinuation – especially as the rumors were coming from teachers themselves. Later on, some parents realized they had been misled and brought their children back as soon as they could – either later in the school year, or at the beginning of the next.

Beginning in 1980, another serious problem arose: it was the glaring inefficiency and lack of commitment on the part of some of the teachers charged with teaching in these classes. The situation produced a climate of dissatisfaction, hostility, and lack of communication between students and teachers. Given the experimental nature of the program at its inception, there was much more emphasis on the sustainability and strict requirements for the recruitment of the teaching staff. However, by the second year, those requirements were discarded. In response, concerned parents sent petitions to the rector in Martinique, requesting better consideration for students in Saint-Martin. It was to no avail, for nothing was done to quell the rumors circulating about the discontinuation of the classes. Parents drafted another petition and sent it to the rector, and to other relevant officials, requesting retention of the program. However, opposition to the program was obvious and the final class saw student enrollment severely reduced, to the point that only two students began their final year in 1979, which resulted in the discontinuation of that class at the end of the academic year. Though the remaining two classes had 15 students in each class, by 1982 with the decision to end this program, most of these students had transferred to Guadeloupe, while those who could not afford the expense of an off-island education were forced to switch to vocational studies in Saint-Martin.

The high school program in Saint-Martin offered local students hope for future socio-economic advancement and could have ensured a continuous supply of skilled and educated citizens on an island plagued by high drop-out rates. The decision to deliberately disadvantage future generations, showed a determination on the part of those in charge to undermine the growth of local youth. These detrimental actions were taken, despite the new rector's desire to create a full-fledged high school on Saint-Martin, to restructure its pre-elementary and elementary education, and to balance English language instruction with the French language instruction at the secondary level. Below are excerpts from a December 1981 letter sent to *Newsday*, the island's only daily newspaper based on the Dutch side. The letter was signed by "*A Distressed Student in Guadeloupe*:"

> "I am a student from French Saint-Martin. Actually I'm studying (if you can call it that) in Guadeloupe. Due to poor organization and poor representation I, like many others, was forced to leave my country to continue my education.
> About two years ago, a teacher, Mrs. Daniella Jeffry, fought to create a high school [Lycée] in French Saint-Martin. After a hard fought battle, it was decided to create one. This was a success for the population of French Saint-Martin because their 16 to 18 year-old children could continue their studies without going abroad. Even though the community and Mrs. Jeffry won this battle, the war was far from over.
> After two years in existence, the high school lost its final class just before the baccalaureate exam. (…)
> I am a student in my final year of a high school that should exist in French Saint-Martin. When I was first told by my teachers that the program would be discontinued, I cried, *No, not again. Why return to the old system?* At first I just wanted to drop out because I felt so bad.
> We, the affected students, have decided, with the help from our teacher, Mrs. Daniella Jeffry, to make an appeal to the Rector, because we know that going abroad - especially to Guadeloupe - to study is bad for us as Saint-Martin citizens. They ignored our request by claiming that once we get a proper high school, the next thing we'll ask for will be a university. How shameful!
> After weeks of persuasion, I decided to try going abroad.
> When I first arrived in Guadeloupe, I felt lost. I felt something was wrong, as if I wasn't in my place. The reason I am writing now is to let everyone know the conditions French Saint-Martin students live in and the problems they encounter. When you tell anyone you are from Saint-Martin, they regard you as inferior. To them you are stupid. The second problem is the place where you live. (…) [The student gives four examples] (…) Both school and classes are divided in two: between Saint-Martiners and Guadeloupeans. At times, communication is impossible, because even the teachers tend to humiliate Saint-Martiners simply because they come from Saint-Martin. Third, Saint-Martiners must constantly carry their passports to prove their French nationality. All of this is humiliating.
> When a Saint-Martiner proves to be a better athlete than a Guadeloupean, he is immediately subjected to the worst name-calling imaginable. They are even ready to fight him, if they can. (…) And I can go on and on enumerating humiliating situations that have become everyday occurrences in the life of students up in Guadeloupe.
> I do not wish to blame French Saint-Martin parents or to make them feel guilty. They are wonderful and are always willing to sacrifice themselves so that their children can study abroad. (…)

> But Saint-Martiners can avoid that. All they have to do is to open their eyes to see how the government is exploiting them. Parents and citizens of Saint-Martin have the power to stop this daily government brainwashing.
> Parents, students of French Saint-Martin, I'm appealing to you. Don't let the new year separate you from your children as this year did. Wake up, and stand up for your rights! (...) Rise up and take a stand! If not, you will lose one of your most precious possessions, your children."[12]

By July 1982, the reality of the education system in Saint-Martin had taken a serious step backwards - much to the dismay of students and parents who hoped for a healthy and peaceful society where everyone could find a place to contribute responsibly to their island's development. The situation was alarming. On the Dutch side of the border, graduation ceremonies were in full swing in the elementary and secondary schools, and the airwaves were full of encouraging speeches and congratulatory messages broadcast on the local radio. Shamefully, the situation was blatantly different in the North. There were no announcements or celebrations of student success because there were too few to mention!

One could not help questioning the purpose of the schools in French Saint-Martin. New teachers, instead of developing and optimizing their students' potentials, were quite satisfied in providing substandard levels of instruction. The vast majority of students educated on the French side of Saint-Martin attended grade school, middle school, followed by 2 years of vocational or technical instruction at the Marigot vocational school. However, vocational education was an utter failure. The newly appointed director of the vocational program encouraged parents to send their children to his school when he began his appointment, but by the end of his term – a mere two years later - he admitted that their education was little more than a scam as there was no future for them on the island after they completed their studies. Nevertheless, the vast majority of middle school aged children were attending this vocational program, while the small fraction that went abroad (after the discontinuation of the high-school classes) continued to dwindle each year. Even the middle school teachers discouraged their students from seeking a proper high-school education off-island, but rather promoted their attendance at the 2-year vocational school instead. The attrition rates were high in each of the critical middle school levels, so that by the time they were ready to enter high school, only a handful of students remained and their teachers discouraged them from pursuing the baccalaureate degree since it would be a "waste" of time, given the few employment opportunities available to them on the island. Only students from the privileged social class were advised otherwise! Meanwhile, the vocational program trained girls to work as maids and waitresses, while boys were trained in masonry and as waiters. Such were the economic opportunities that awaited them. Gone was the option to pursue a professional career as a teacher, lawyer, doctor or pharmacist. That was merely a hope from the past, unless parents had the means to remove their children from the local school system and have them educated off-island.

The fact is, less than a dozen students went on to high school, despite the fact that around 150 students had started out together in elementary school. This attrition is the main reason why parents on the French side sacrificed whatever was necessary to remove their children from middle school and had them educated on the Dutch side, in Martinique or even in France, before their fates could be doomed by the 2-year vocational school that swallowed up 95% of the students that remained on the island. These children were condemned to a limited future, and it was time someone sounded the alarm to warn of the impending crisis. At the middle school, Antillean and European teachers outnumbered local teachers ten to one. The social situation had also deteriorated to a point seemingly beyond repair. Here too, Europeans were over-represented in senior-level positions in key sectors: government, economics, education, and their interests did not coincide with the needs and interests of the general population.

Once Saint-Martiners returned from finishing their studies abroad, they did not willingly submit to the social situation at home. Against this backdrop of deliberate attempts to disadvantage the native population, an initiative gained momentum to open a private business school in Sandy Ground in 1977. This private venture was seen as the most effective way to challenge the prevailing system, but it was attacked by the Sub-Prefect and the Mayor, who rejected it on the pretext of opening the high school program, and offering additional courses at the vocational school. By September of that same year, a French leaflet began circulating throughout the island signed by *The Union of Saint-Martiners for the defense of human rights and the citizens' rights.* It read as follows:

> "Based on indications coming from the Sub-Prefecture, rumors have begun to circulate throughout Saint-Martin that Mr. Etchegoyen is doing his utmost to close down the Private Business School in Sandy-Ground, Saint-Martin, founded by Mr. Baly Léopold.
> In fact, Sub-Prefect Etchegoyen, after trying to maneuver the opening of the first high-school class, is now trying to manipulate other matters. However, Saint-Martiners have never been more alert than at this very moment. If Mr. Etchegoyen wants to close his eyes and condone the approved Agrement ghettos and the various areas across Saint-Martin that entice desperate, local youth into corruption, drugs, and debauchery; and instead spend his time and energy sabotaging an initiative to intellectually enhance Saint-Martiners and

> salvage Saint-Martin from the decay in which it is sinking, only to benefit a handful of privileged people who think they are in a conquered land, then he has another thing coming. All Saint-Martiners will join together to let him know that there is no limit to their determination to fight."

Islanders living in New York believed that the opening of the first private business school held the promise of better days for youth still living in Saint-Martin, and were therefore outraged by the Sub-Prefect's attempt to sabotage it. One of them went so far as to contact Third Deputy Mayor, Louis Constant Fleming, to get his reaction to their support for the school. The Deputy Mayor's response was that if the island needed such a business school, then it would be the responsibility of the state authorities to provide it. In other words, he was not in favor of their initiative. Moreover, he felt that the General Council of Guadeloupe was doing its part by opening a branch of AGFRMO, (the Guadeloupe association in charge of employee training), which would provide basic professional training in cooking to prepare Saint-Martin youth for work in the hospitality industry.

It was the second board president of the Youth and Cultural Center, Mrs. Jeffry-Razafin who succeeded Alberic Richards in 1977, that broke the news of the municipality's rejection of the board's request to build a new cultural center in the Spring area, next to the Marigot Middle School. She did so in a press release that was shared with all the sports and youth associations on the French side. The idea for the center was originally proposed at the end of 1978, and had been approved. Nevertheless, two years later, no steps had been taken towards its construction and, in 1980 the board once again submitted a petition to the Municipal Council. Even though the board members of the Youth Center were informed that funding for the project was available at the Prefecture of Guadeloupe, it soon became apparent that the responsible authorities had never requested any funds, nor taken any steps to file the required paper work to begin construction on the center. What was the cause for this delay? An examination of the municipal plans for the Spring area soon revealed the answer.

Locals were astonished to discover that the land which had been reserved for the Cultural Center was now designated for a housing development to be constructed by HLM, the Guadeloupe-based low-cost housing company. The 75 x 160 meter lot proved an ideal location for the proposed Cultural Center because it bordered the Marigot Middle School, now known as Concordia Mount Middle School. The fact that the project proposal had been approved by the Public Works Service (D.D.E.) back in November 1978 should have been taken into consideration, especially as there was no other suitable allotment in Marigot for such a center. Though many young and talented people from the Youth Center fought long and hard to see the project constructed, and despite the fact that architectural plans were drawn up by a public works engineer, the Marigot Cultural Center never came to fruition.

The new municipality and the authorities in the Sub-Prefecture had another agenda in mind. Their intention was to "develop a more modulated tourism than that on the Dutch side, to enhance the commune's eastern coastline, and to invigorate French Quarter to boost its independence from Philipsburg [the capital of the Dutch side]."[14] Initial real estate projects designated residential zones for individual homes to be erected around each resort hotel. This layout can be seen in The Mount Vernon project that sits around Chevrise Pond. It consists of one hotel and 150 individual lots. Similarly, the forthcoming private *Port Caraïbe* project along Orient Bay, intends to encompass 3 hotels, 77 individual homes, and a number of apartment buildings to accommodate 5,000 people within 272 acres. Oyster Pond, along the border in the east, in the east, bordering the frontier, is the site of a real estate operation comprising 120 individual lots and 200 studio apartments with kitchenettes. An American residential complex built in the Lowlands in 1955 has expanded to include 200 lots across 494 acres along Red Pond. Club Med took over the resumption of the unfinished *La Belle Créole* project, whereas construction of a hotel and residential resort at *L'Anse Marcel* was already in the pipeline, even though the area had not yet been connected to the road network. Of what use then were the local residents to the Mayor? Despite his political obligation to serve and protect the interests of his constituents, he did nothing to prevent the fate he knew was awaiting them.

In 1980, the authorities planned to set up a branch of the vocational program of the Regiment of Adapted Military Service (SMA)* on 20 acres in Marigot in order to justify lengthening and expanding the Esperance airfield in Grand-Case, and future development of the port areas. The first recruits in the Adapted Military Service were scheduled to arrive in April 1980 and expected to begin operation by the following September. Acute interest in the expansion of this airfield corresponded closely with development projects occurring on the French side of the island. In fact, the runway was extended from 900 meters to 1200 meters to accommodate the landing of the Fokker 27s and the DC3s belonging to Air Guadeloupe, and the Transall.

Improvement of the road network fell under the SMA's purview, which the Mayor acknowledged as having made considerable advancement, even above the quality of roads on the Dutch side. The routes in question included the road leading to *L'Anse Marcel;* the road between the Coralita Hotel and

Lucas Bay; the reconstruction of the road to Friars' Bay; the road to Arago Point, which was originally intended to link the National Road to the slaughter house (whose location was ultimately changed), on through the deep-water Pier; as well as the unfinished road through the hills that links Marigot to French Quarter, and still awaits completion. After the study for the deep-water Pier was completed, it marked the end of an employment boom for local businesses as there was no longer any work for them in the Public Works sector. Concomitantly, the increased numbers of law enforcement units required the construction of barracks in Marigot to house them. None of these changes escaped the local population's attention as they had witnessed the conversion of their peaceful island into one overrun by military and armed police forces in the space of two short years.

During an interview on the Dutch radio station, PJD2 in Philipsburg, the Mayor was questioned about the massive influx of French Europeans since his election as the head of the municipality, and was asked to clarify his stance on the threat they represented to the political and socio-economic well-being of the local residents. His confident retort was that it was this very "massive influx of foreigners which clearly indicated of the French side's prosperity," since in his view, "prosperity attracts foreigners." [15] Thus, progress, prosperity and French Europeans marked the three key forces driving Saint-Martin's governing policies. In reality, this was only the tip of the iceberg and the national authorities on the island concerned themselves with the massive issues submerged below the surface. In 1982, a Canadian professor from the University of Quebec spent a brief period on the island to conduct research on Saint-Martin and made the following glowing assessment:

> "After much delay, relative to the Dutch side, tourism and real estate development on the French side of Saint-Martin has benefited from planning and supervision by the national authorities. In other words, in contrast to the observable disorder on the Dutch side, the desire for a functional equilibrium is quite obvious on the French side." [16]

---

* SMA units are mandated to provide the training of young volunteers from overseas territories in a military environment. They also contribute to the fight against illiteracy and, through application projects, to the economic development of the overseas departments and territories where they operate

Beyond the simple terms of this mission, the added value of these programs is based on providing social skills derived from military habits. Volunteers of the adapted military service very often come from disadvantaged backgrounds, are often in search of a future, and sometimes they are in situations of pre-delinquency.

[Source: http://fr.wikipedia.org/wiki/Service_militaire_adapté]

By not understanding, and willfully ignoring Saint-Martin's history, Europeans and non-indigenous foreigners promulgated erroneous theories and interpretations of island life that permitted them to justify the unjustifiable. To elaborate: in 1980, it was notoriously declared in *97$_1$Hebdo*, the first local French-language journal that Haitian laborers willingly accept *"the work that Saint-Martiners refuse to do."*[17] To clarify, it was not a question of Saint-Martiners refusing to work. What they were refusing was to submit to subhuman working conditions. Most Saint-Martiners were independent workers, and skilled craftsmen and women, who had successively emigrated to the United States and other Caribbean islands as early as the beginning of the 20th century. When opportunities in tourism began to open up on the Dutch side during the 1950s, those self-employed residents who remained on the island became the first West Indians to work in the hotels, and stores, or as construction workers, taxi and bus drivers, and in other related occupations. Some emigrants to Curacao and Aruba returned to work in various businesses, banks and government positions that were available in Great Bay. By 1980, they were still in Saint-Martin. Others, who returned from abroad, did so in order to contribute to the economic development of their homeland, especially on the Dutch side, which already had opportunities for those with strong professional qualifications. A good 80% of the active population on the French side crossed the border each day to go to work on the Dutch side, and there was no problem with that. It was a normal part of life on the island. Everyone knows that *"the gale does not stop at the border"* as the late patriot, Felix Choisy,[18] was known to say. What made life on Saint-Martin unique and exceptional was that it had been shaped by the residents from both sides of the island. That is what any outsider needed to understand. The European officials and civil servants who served on the island between 1963 and 1975 did exactly that: they made an effort to understand. However, after 1975, that was no longer the case.

Beginning in 1975, a relationship was imposed to those Saint-Martiners living on the French side of the island which had nothing to do with their way of life, nor their actual aspirations. It was an error of monstrous proportions which once perpetuated, could never be undone. Following the end of a thirty-year regime, failure was evident in every sector. The central premise of this error was the following: *"Deprived of this Haitian labor means economic paralysis for the French of the island."*[19] This was grave, truly grave. To base the stability of Saint-Martin's economy on an illegal labor class was a gross and dangerous precedent. It should not be forgotten that a cheap and exploitable labor source was preferred by the European business class because it was profitable, and much easier for them to manipulate a population fearful of expulsion if it did not submit to humiliating work conditions. Few Saint-Martiners were willing to work under such miserable conditions, which is why their unemployment rates remained high on the French side, and do so even up to the current times.

Due to continuous emigration during the 20th century, a shortage of unskilled, and often unpaid, labor existed on the island. Relations between islands were based primarily on *jollification*[20] and informal labor exchanges, which promoted inter-island solidarity. The fact that the sugar cane industry was no longer viable, after the British full emancipation of enslaved Anguillians in 1838, and the French abolition of slavery in the Antilles a decade later, cannot be ignored; especially as it prompted the departure of most planters from Saint-Martin. Throughout the first half of the twentieth century, the cessation of sugar-cane cultivation fostered continued Anguillian migration to Saint-Martin where they found work as ground-keepers and domestic workers; and by the 1970s, it was the turn of Haitians and other West Indian immigrants seeking employment opportunities in that era.

A sharp distinction between the French and Dutch sides of the island did not exist in 1980. There existed only the symbiotic relationship between the two halves, which formed a unique and mutually beneficial whole. Over time, employment conditions for Saint-Martin employers and more recent European employers - with their knowledge of French labor laws - were not at all the same. French labor laws were not diligently applied to relevant cases and it was more profitable for European companies to align with the existing labor situation, in order to exploit local workers and to earn as much money as quickly as possible. Such was the hypocrisy that thinly masked the contempt and discrimination emanating from the sub-prefectural authority that imposed French law on local employers, but closed their eyes to the practices and abuses of European employers. The result was indignation on the part of local employers when they received the famous letter sent to business-owners.

Indeed, the Sub-Prefects were well aware of their mission in Saint-Martin, as conveyed in the first sub-prefectural bulletin entitled, *News from the Northern Islands*. In the January 1975 edition, the last Sub-Prefect to enjoy excellent relations with the constituents wrote the following:

> "Employment Problems in Saint-Martin
>
> In Saint-Martin like elsewhere, employment rates are an issue. It depends greatly on the world's economic circumstances, but the specific situation of Saint-Martin, which has an important influx of foreigners, requires that a certain number of measures be taken to help solve this serious problem. First, it is appropriate that priority be given to Saint-Martin workers, as much on the Dutch side as on the French side, over citizens of other countries. Instances of

discriminations having taken place, it is fitting during these troubled times to recall the terms of the Franco-Dutch Treaty which provides for the free movement of goods and all persons, whether French or Dutch, without them needing to apply for a work or resident permit."

The Sub-Prefect who took office in April 1975, after a four months' interval, revised the name of the bulletin to *The Courier of the Northern Islands District.* In the October 1976 under the heading *Letter from the Sub-Prefect*, he reminded readers:

"The tourist season is going to start. It promises to be good, perhaps even very good for Saint-Martin's hotels. We only regret that the season spreads over such a short period. ... I have reminded hotel directors that recruiting foreign personnel should be the exception as full employment for Saint-Martiners remains the priority objective. I, therefore, will not be able to issue any resident or work permits to foreigners, as long as local job applications are still pending. One hundred and fifty-six job applications are registered at the Labor Office opened at the Town Hall. Employers are requested to contact this office immediately for a list of their names and addresses, which will be furnished without delay."

In the following month's *Letter from the Sub-Prefect* he reiterated his previous points while addressing the housing problem and health insurance for foreign workers:

"At the risk of repeating myself, I will say that employment in Saint-Martin is still a matter of great concern. I do hope that many Saint-Martiners will be employed by the hotels in the coming weeks.
Upon receiving the work permit applications for foreign workers, the Director of Employment and Labor in Guadeloupe informed me how astonished he was to see that these foreigners, from countries with no particular links to France, can easily find employers to give them jobs in trades that many French workers in the department could hold.
But the problem of their housing is a major one.
However, French legislation does not permit the introduction of a foreign worker without prior verification of the quality of available housing.
Unplanned urbanization and squatting in neighborhoods primarily occupied by Guadeloupean workers seeking employment in Saint-Martin is, ultimately, a considerable burden on the commune.
It will be necessary, some day, to stabilize the situation of these occupants, by developing neighborhoods, providing sanitation systems, as well as supplying water and electricity.
In the future, we may need to establish boarding centers for young workers managed by the Department of Health and Social Action in Guadeloupe.
A study will be undertaken for this purpose."

At least that was the theory. The two consecutive Sub-Prefects between 1975 and 1980 implemented a scheme that Saint-Martiners utterly rejected. They turned a blind eye to the abuses and injustices forced upon West Indian laborers. *97_1Hebdo*, the first free newspaper published by a French European, became the unofficial replacement for the Sub-Prefecture's monthly bulletin as the source for official information. The Sub-Prefecture's bulletin ceased circulation after *97_1Hebdo*'s emergence. In that journal, the publisher stated:

> "Until July 1980, the existence of this Haitian labor force was tolerated by an administration that preferred to ignore it rather than go against the economic interests of the country, or legalize them at the risk of jeopardizing the future. Everything worked well to everyone's satisfaction."[21]

Who was *"everyone"*? It certainly was not the local population of Saint-Martin. By disregarding the relevant legislation, these two Sub-Prefects became the prime contributors to the forthcoming demographic explosion that facilitated Saint-Martin's fragile rise, and inevitable economic downfall, over the next two decades. It was an unfortunate and regrettable governing precedent. By ignoring the laws against illegal employment to the point that it became an accepted practice, employers continued to exploit a cheap and vulnerable labor force, which additionally impedes the well-being of the native population, in particular. Thus, Saint-Martin's economic prosperity was built on a foundation of exploitation and illegalities which adversely impacted population rates and tarnished the image of the island. It was therefore prudent to explain how this situation came to be, in order to understand the devastating consequences that were suffered over the long term. Who benefited from this administrative neglect?

General Dissatisfaction

The same Sub-Prefect Lacave, who found himself confronted with an angry constituency during the 1980 Town Hall meeting, over the land rights dispute in Sandy Ground, now wanted to solve the problem of illegal immigration. He drafted a letter to the local merchants, which angered many small employers, because it exemplified the biased sub-prefectural policies that favored Europeans, and exempted them from taxes, while further burdening local, small merchants and crafts people who were already heavily taxed. The Sub-Prefecture, therefore, pressured Saint-Martin workers to obtain social security cards by forcing local employers to employ only those laborers registered with the Social Security office. The same restriction did not apply to European employers, however, who did not hire workers possessing social security cards. Moreover, neither the 10% employee contribution nor the 34% employer contribution benefited immigrant workers as they were not entitled to family allowances or old age pensions, during this period. It would suffice to insure them privately. In addition, the Sub-Prefecture rarely issued work permits to foreigners that were already working on the island. As had been the practice previously, the solution consisted in admitting only those immigrants already in possession of a work contract. Only the State could control immigration in a more logical way. By 1977, more than 782 immigrants had entered Saint-Martin illegally.

Daily life became extremely tense and continued to deteriorate rapidly. Following the arrest of a young Saint-Martiner in Marigot on April 11, 1980, a newspaper stated, *"Youth and adults have had enough of being scorned, ridiculed, humiliated, tortured, deprived of their belongings, and treated like dogs."*[22] In those days, there were no local lawyers because there had never been a need for any. Therefore, the defense of even the most basic rights could not be assured. A boisterous crowd gathered in front of the *Gendarmerie* to protest the arrest, arbitrary violence, provocations and numerous injustices meted out to Saint-Martiners under the oppressive new system. Public civility, openness, and the traditional warmth of the islanders now clashed with the hostility and arrogant attitudes of the newcomers. Verbal and physical altercations between Saint-Martiners and European settlers, who enjoyed the benefit of *the gendarmes*' protection, soon became a daily occurrence. These incidents became commonplace by 1980. Peaceful coexistence in Saint-Martin was under assault and the inhabitants felt threatened.

What follows is a detailed account of the events leading to the arrest of one young Saint-Martiner, who had been imprisoned, as reported to the media by the young man's brother:

> "On Thursday, April 10, my brother Glen saw his friend fishing in a boat and decided to join him. They arrived at *Le Vieillard* Restaurant, moored their boat and went to purchase something to eat. Upon their return, they witnessed a young European boy untying the boat. Glen approached the boy to ask him what he was doing. They began arguing when, suddenly, the European boy went for a bow and arrow and shot at my brother.
> Then, they jumped in the water to recover the boat and returned to Sandy Ground to continue fishing. All of a sudden, and quite unexpectedly, they found themselves under verbal attack from the European boy's father and his friend who forced them to come ashore. Suddenly two *gendarmes* arrived, handcuffed Glen's friend and started rough handling him without any

interrogation. He began to protest and demand an explanation, but they ignored him and ordered him into the jeep. The father's friend, a civilian, attacked Glen from behind, by choking him viciously, and then the *gendarme* drove his knee viciously in his stomach. They finally forced him into the jeep as well. He was arrested and again beaten, and then shoved outside the *Gendarmerie*, at night, without his shoes and hat.

The next day, Friday, April 11, Glen went back to demand an explanation from the European civilian who had choked him. My brother was ignored, humiliated and called a '*petit con'* [real fool]. Glen retaliated by hitting him with a machete. The man ran to seek help from the *gendarmes*.

A few seconds after, a C.R.S. [national mobile police] officer and a *gendarme* arrived. They handcuffed Glen and led him like a dog to the *Gendarmerie*. A few brave individuals, who could not endure watching him being beaten, ran to assist him and succeeded in setting him free. A certified medical report delivered by a doctor confirmed that my brother was suffering from police brutality as evidenced by vomiting blood, bruises and cuts. ..."

By Saturday, April 12, 1980, bright red graffiti appeared around Marigot, including on the Town Hall, on the *Bord-de-Mer* School, and on several other buildings. The statements were obviously directed at the Mayor and the situation he had imposed upon the population. The following slogans appeared in both French and English:

We want Justice in St Martin – Warning: European crooks must go – St. Martin people can't live among Europeans – Stop flagrant government favoritism towards metropolitans – School children asking the Mayor to stop this power struggle – We have been exploited too long.[24]

It was an unprecedented historical event. Even though the graffiti was written by a few individuals, it expressed the sentiments felt in the hearts of the silent majority. In Grand-Case, observers noticed a wooden sign nailed to a tree near the wharf on the seaside, with the following inscription in French: "Construction forbidden here under penalty of prosecution. Law voted by St. Martiners." Saint-Martiners disapproved of French government policies imposed on their island. Pamphlets criticizing the repressive policies directed against Saint-Martiners were also distributed by young people calling themselves the *Youth Organization Improvement Association.* They strongly criticized the *gendarmes* for shooting out the tires on a vehicle of one, Jimmy *'Dun Dun'* Richardson, on the Dutch side on April 2, 1980 in an effort to arrest him. They suspected him of being an accomplice to a burglary that happened on the French side the previous month. The members of the *Youth Organization* accused the *gendarmes* of intimidation and of being an oppressive and brutal force. They also charged the Mayor with being a traitor to his people. In sharp contrast, these same young people praised the courage of Grand-Case residents who were fighting to retain control of their beach.

From the published articles, it became evident that the public was confronting a serious deterioration of their way of life and former social relations. There were no jobs for Saint-Martiners. Society was now structured to facilitate the settlement of European emigrants. Important loans were granted by the French banks to Europeans who frequently did not reimburse the money. The journal *97$_{1}$Hebdo* constantly referred to "...*our* St. Martin," "... *our* tourists," and to "... *our* beaches." Newly arrived Europeans began to hurl insults at Saint-Martiners they encountered in the street, saying things like, *Retournez en Afrique!* (*Go back to Africa!)* In November of 1980, a very respectful, discreet 20 year-old man was abruptly fired from the car dealership where he was employed. The reason for his dismissal by the Deputy Mayor, who also happened to be his boss and the owner, was the young man's defense of his 18 year-old sister who was arbitrarily prevented from voting in the recent cantonal elections. His firing induced a hardship because he was the family bread-winner.

The Dutch side media and young people across the island in general, defended Caribbean immigrants who suffered shameful and scandalous mistreatment at the hands of public authorities on the once *Friendly Island.* They demanded an end to the humiliation and brutality that was destroying the traditional Caribbean solidarity historically shared by Saint-Martiners. As far as the public authorities were concerned, these young people constituted a force that needed to be restrained. Coincidentally (or not), it was at this exact period, in 1980, that young European women and hard drugs arrived in Saint-Martin and infiltrated the ranks of the organization, dismantling its fringes.

A manhunt for armed assailants ensued on Thursday afternoon, April 17, 1980, following the murder of CRS officer, Henri Hervieux, during the failed hold-up of a bank on *Rue de la République* in Marigot. Subsequently, Saint-Martin was under siege for more than two months by military forces with machine guns posted along strategic points of the road network that were aimed and ready to shoot at will. An unprecedented crackdown followed, which caused panic in this formerly uneventful town that was still reeling from the hostile takeover of the island. The manhunt became more like an actual witch hunt. The locals felt as if there was one soldier for every five people in Saint-Martin. On April 22, 1980, at 5:50 in the morning, approximately 15 *gendarmes* and soldiers armed with machine-guns, kicked down the door of Glen's father's house. Ten or so days earlier, Glen had been arrested, but then freed by a group of young people. The armed enforcers dragged the occupants out of their beds and beat all of them. They shoved their machine guns up their noses and into their ears, then stomped them in their stomachs, mocked and belittled them. Three adolescents were arrested.

After 24 hours of harassment, they released two of the boys but retained Glen.[25] These teenagers never had any previous dealings with *gendarmes* before these two incidents. Prior to 1977, *gendarmes* did not attack private citizens. But times had changed. The local residents simply could not understand why European emigrants would want to leave France just to come and attack them. This was an altogether new phenomenon in Saint-Martin.

The first French presidential visit to Saint-Martin, in December of 1980, did nothing to quell the tense climate and virtual *civil war* that had overtaken the very fabric of the Saint-Martin society. This three-hour presidential visit was marked by the rapid appearance of hostile graffiti on buildings in Marigot, and by the circulation of unflattering leaflets about the President of the Republic. The authorities quickly covered the slogans over before the President could see them. Rumors abounded that his visit was connected to the upcoming landing of the Concord on the runway at the Princess Juliana International Airport, and the future realization of the *Port Caraïbe* real estate project on Orient Bay. The marvel of the Concord design enhanced the reputation of Juliana Airport and bolstered the pride of the residents who converged, en masse, on February 6th to witness this beautiful bird landing directly from Paris. The president of the research and design company developing the *Port Caraïbe* project was on board, along with other prominent personalities from the industrial world. It was an experience of a lifetime and a spectacle to behold! There were people as far as the eye could see, sitting all over the place: on top old containers, on the terminal roof, along the roadside next to the runway, and even on the surrounding hill tops. The project description did not fail to mention:

> "... Priority will be given to local construction companies. Preferential tariffs reserved for Saint-Martiners who would like to settle here.... Everything will be done to give job priority to Saint-Martiners in all sectors of construction."[26]

This was a reassuring hoax that Saint-Martiners were not going to swallow: *"creating 1,000 jobs"*... *"hiring priority"*... *"preferential tariffs"*... they had heard it all before. In light of the mounting tensions, the islanders knew these empty promises were just an attempt to ease the pressure. Politicians are experts in that art. Nevertheless, during the previous three years, they had already experienced systematic exclusion from economic development opportunities accorded to projects of lesser importance. Consequently, they were not about to depend on the *Port Caraïbe* project to improve their plight.

Impact of the New Sub-Prefectural Policy

The new Sub-Prefect arrived in July 1980 with a clear mission to restore order in Saint-Martin by reasserting French law, despite the unequal treatment Caribbean Blacks had received in the past. Nevertheless, the recent European settlers felt this policy would ruin their ability to make a profit in the island's economy. Due to the expulsion of illegal Haitian immigrants, the number of laborers from this group declined. French employers had no desire to pay the higher costs associated with local laborers for whom they would be required to pay social security contributions. Without a source of cheap (and illegal) labor, these employers complained that there was no economic viability in Saint-Martin. French business owners insisted that Haitian immigrants were essential to their ability to make a profit. Some even threatened to close due to the *"labor shortage."* Were they only *"laborers"* in their businesses? Moreover, these French business owners claimed they were disadvantaged when compared to the Dutch businesses, because the social security contributions and minimum wage they were required to pay were much higher than that required on the Dutch side. Soon after, the idea of petitioning the President of the French Republic to request a special status for Saint-Martin - while remaining French - began to gain popularity among many business owners.

For the second time in as many years, Saint-Martin's status was once again under review. The first time came about when liberation movements became active in Guadeloupe. The Mayor, who feared being connected to an independent Guadeloupe, was supported by the state representative when he requested that the island be declared a department of France. This time though, the impetus arose from the European business class' desire to have greater influence and control over socio- economic policy in Saint-Martin. They wanted the authority to remain exempt from having to pay social security contributions and company taxes. They knew it would be easy to garner mayoral endorsement because he was dependent on them to retain power, given that his policies were so unpopular among the local populous. For French entrepreneurs, it was a priority for Saint-Martin to remain a part of France in order for them to benefit from promotion of French business and social interests on the island. Would they still be able to lobby and influence municipal policies, to the point where they could bypass legal regulations and exchange covert favors, like they did when they first arrived? That is the reason why they needed to gain seats on the council. For, *if they wanted something done in their own interest, it was better to do it themselves.*

At the base of the political iceberg, the free newspaper *97₁Hebdo* revealed how the suppression of illegal labor was crippling the economy of Saint-Martin:

> "Everything changed in July 1980 with the arrival of a new Sub-Prefect and a new Captain of the *Gendarmerie.* These two, in absolute ignorance of the needs of the local economy and the damage that they will inflict, have suddenly decided to deport Haitian laborers, some of whom have worked in Saint-Martin more than 10 years, have children and possessions.
> They plan to proceed with more than 1,500 deportations, arbitrarily, unceremoniously, and with total disregard for legal regulations concerning this matter by claiming: *They are illegal aliens who have no right to protection under French law.*
> The Captain of the *Gendarmerie* organized the raids. A group of houses occupied by Haitians was surrounded at night. If the doors were not opened voluntarily, they broke them down, rounded up the suspects and drove them to the detention area in the *Gendarmerie*. The suspects were held there until 7:00 or 8:00 in the morning before their cases were addressed. They were then held in police custody until their deportation back to Haiti on the first available flight. Some remained locked up arbitrarily like this for several days.
> The suspects were denied the opportunity to sell their meager possessions, and the right to choose the border where they wish to be taken, as the law required.
> No consideration was given to the families from which they were forcibly and permanently separated.
> They were denied the right to request political asylum.
> From the many articles published in the newspapers lately, everyone today is aware of the mistreatment these unfortunate people are receiving, regardless of age or sex, upon their forced return to Haiti: imprisonment under inhumane conditions, and brutality often leading to their death."[27]

The conclusion of this investigative report referred to these deportations as a *"genuine racial pogrom"* comparable to *"methods used by the Gestapo in countries occupied by Germany."* The publisher then called for an end to such acts and requested that *"a parliamentary commission be appointed to draft an onsite report and to propose ad hoc sanctions."*[27]

This European publisher, by so defending the interests of his fellow-citizens, indirectly accused the gendarmes under the Sub-Prefect's authority of behaving like Nazis. Moreover, the treatment inflicted upon these unfortunate individuals was reminiscent of indignities suffered under slavery, he observed. It became easy to understand that, even in a country that supported human rights, authorities could indulge in tactics not unlike those used by vile dictatorships to achieve their goals, as long as such activities were hidden beneath the surface – in the underbelly of the iceberg. Even in

Saint-Martin, anything was possible. Similarly, islanders considered the new European settlers who came to Saint-Martin for self-enrichment, akin to Nazis. Who profited from *the crime*? Surely, not the unemployed islanders who were being denied a decent working wage.

For once, the Mayor and the constituents agreed on the same issue: both disapproved of Haitian expulsion, though for very different reasons. The gulf existing between the Mayor and most of his constituents was widening. The local residents objected to the ongoing mistreatment and arbitrary arrests of so many of these illegal immigrants, who had replaced for about ten years then the exodus of Saint-Martiners during the better part of the 20th century. Meanwhile, the Mayor wanted to promote French European investment and settlement on the island, and so sought to maintain their support by retaining the illegal labor supply they needed to ensure the success of their business ventures. As a consequence, the gulf between the Mayor and the people remained vast.

Once the State managed to regroup, the more recently settled Europeans decided to exert pressure on the elected Saint-Martin representatives. During the next two decades, these self-labeled *"socio-professionals"* manipulated local politicians behind the scenes, all the while claiming to be apolitical. The extent of their involvement remained concealed, but they wielded the real power behind the scenes. Blatant disregard for applicable labor laws, which the two state representatives displayed successively between 1977 and 1980, could no longer be allowed to continue. Skilful maneuvering was essential if they were to achieve success. Closer analysis of the situation revealed an interesting, if disturbing, progression. Transformation of Saint-Martin's society into one that served the interests of the new European business class, entailed an unrelenting series of compromises, trade-offs forfeited principles, and sacrifice of the native population's needs, welfare and interests. It could never have been achieved without complicit collaboration between the French State, local authorities, and the socio-professionals.

Meanwhile, responses to conditions on the island offered by State authorities did not satisfy the new Europeans. It has already been mentioned that they wanted physical and economic development on the French side to rival, if not surpass, that on the Dutch side despite the 20-year gap in starting points. Confronted with this new turn of events, the publisher of *97₁Hebdo* echoed the distress of his fellow-citizens in an editorial entitled *I don't understand* … The most relevant excerpts are included below:

> "… Everyone got down to work and then waited, resolutely, for the season. Instead, the surprise we received was of a different order. (…) Permit me to examine the problem chronologically. First, Air France increased its fares, thereby, reducing the potential for European tourism. Then, in ignorance of

> both the law and the various interventions of the Public Prosecutor in Basse-Terre, nearly all Haitians were expelled, including those working, reducing still more the irreplaceable local labor. As a consequence, we have no more workers on building sites, no more gardeners, no more domestic workers, security guards, etc. etc. The latest finding is of a fine of approximately 1,000 francs for employers hiring or providing housing to foreign workers. As a consequence, even Belgians are expelled. Relations are disintegrating. (…)
> As if this were not enough, checks on social security have gotten mixed in with other fiscal checks, fines are given out randomly, recalls occur repeatedly and over several years, a first reminder, then a second, etc. etc. to the surprise of us all. Licenses are scrutinized in turn. It is forbidden to sell alcohol without a 4th category license; inspections are then conducted on non-compliant vehicles (tires, lights, brakes, headlights, etc.) and so on, of course. So, I don't understand …"[28]

During the first four years of this regime, it was proven repeatedly to Saint-Martiners that the so-called development did not mean progress for the populace. On the contrary, it was a threat to their very way of life on the French side of the island. The new European settlers physically abused, and fired, them at will. French companies came from Guadeloupe with trucks, equipment and loads of Guadeloupean and European workers. The additional arrival of the Adapted Military Service (SMA) recruits, based in the Spring area, meant contracts were no longer accessible to local companies seeking work on construction and public works projects. Nepotism reigned and only family members and close supporters of the Mayor were granted these jobs.

In spite of silence from most of the population, this was a period fraught with displays of worker discontent as exemplified by the strike of *La Belle Creole Hotel* staff from the Bluff; the 1980 truck drivers' protest; the PLM Hotel staff strike in Sandy Ground where they demanded the immediate firing of the chief accountant/administrative manager; the 5-day strike, in 1981, at the Gourmet Shop - the first small European supermarket; not to mention the false promises of work at the *Port Caraïbe* Project in Orient Bay. Everyone knew that the main interest of the new real estate promoters was to build residential houses (for European settlers), and that the municipal management had no concern for the creation of jobs for Saint-Martiners. A good percentage of the newer European emigrants were simply individuals who settled in Saint-Martin intent on securing a prosperous lifestyle for themselves and their families. The Public Works Department counted 120 additional houses a year, between 1979 and 1980. In 1982, the South reached a record 26 hotels, comprising 1,907 rooms, as opposed to 10 hotels, and 407 rooms, in the North. By the following decade, those figures had evened out. Under the guise of development, an influx of French Europeans moved from the mainland to Saint-Martin.

In contrast, early tourism on the Dutch side reflected the political will to develop their territory in harmony with the needs of the population. This was evident in projects like the 1970 Mullet Bay Beach Hotel in the Lowlands, the 1972 Concord Hotel at Maho Reef, and the 1973 Saint-Martin Isle (later renamed the Great Bay Beach Resort) in Philipsburg, and the 1980 Bel-Air Hotel in Little Bay. Each of these establishments hired local, native workers. Others, who returned from the US Virgin Islands, following the decline in construction and tourism there in the late 1960s, as well as those returning from Curaçao and Aruba, were also hired. Even these workers were insufficient to meet the demand on the Dutch side, so Saint-Martiners from the North – in accordance with the 1648 Treaty - and immigrants from St. Kitts/Nevis and the surrounding English-speaking Caribbean islands, filled the gap. The chief of Government in the South then was able to offer Dutch and American investors, political stability, and a viable workforce. By 1981, with the South's economic boom in full swing, job vacancies numbered approximately 2,000, of which 700 were filled by workers from the North.[29] However, short-sightedness regarding the negative impact of this prosperity would generate serious problems throughout the following decades, amplified by those in the North. This study does not attempt to analyze the history of the Dutch side's economic situation as its complexity is worthy of a full study itself. Regardless, some discussion of contrasting or similar circumstances, relevant to development in the North, will occur as the lives of the residents on the island are so deeply intertwined.

Municipal Elections of March 1983

Passions ran high as the municipal elections of March 1983 approached. Clear political divisions began to emerge, ideological schisms appeared within the municipality, tentative alliances formed, campaign materials were widely disseminated, and the election process exacerbated the ongoing conflict between the local populace and European settlers. The outgoing Mayor's unpopularity forced the contesting Deputy Mayor to draw even closer to the opposing party. Three years earlier, during the revolt of 1980, this same Deputy Mayor had positioned himself directly against the Mayor's policy and had gone so far as to call for the departure of the forces of the Republican Security Company (C.R.S.) stationed on the island. The leader of the opposing party, Dr. Petit, welcomed this split believing that he would benefit from a divided support base in the upcoming elections.

Such an assumption revealed how little he knew about this municipal dissident who secretly cherished the desire to use the name of his father who did not acknowledge him. This name would identify him directly with the outgoing Mayor's political party. Perhaps he had momentary doubts about his ability to assume leadership of the municipality, given his linguistic handicap; but the fact that he had managed to distinguish himself as an entrepreneur and owner of a successful construction company on the Dutch side, coupled with his own political achievements and ambition, ultimately got the better of him. According to his campaign speeches, he was a self-made man who worked his way up from school drop-out, to learn the trade and progressed from workman-laborer to business manager and finally, company head. It was the experience he gained, and contacts he made, while working on the construction of the Mullet Bay Hotel that most helped him rise through the ranks, and become a contractor, and owner, of his own construction company on the Dutch side of the island. There, he was able to prosper and was regarded as a model of success in the eyes of his subordinates, peers and professional cohorts on the island. Once he decided to challenge the Mayor, he had two objectives: first, to legally adopt "Fleming," his father's family name, which he had been using informally all along, as a businessman on the Dutch side; and second, to create a new political party, separate from that of the outgoing Mayor. He achieved both goals masterfully and so was poised to take on all political challenges.

Campaign dealings with the opposition leader, who had been defeated in the last municipal elections, implied that the Deputy Mayor would need to position two key members of the opposing party on his ticket in order to realize the promised merger during the run-off election. The primary between the three competing parties was won by Dr. Petit, the former Mayor's party. Therefore, the merger, instead of happening with the intended, victorious opposition party, occurred with Elie Fleming, the outgoing Mayor's party. During this election the Deputy Mayor, Albert Fleming, bore the same last name as the outgoing Mayor, who had previously abandoned the race, but whose party regained a consolidated unity, because of skillful strategizing. As a result, the two opposition members on the Deputy Mayor's ticket dropped out. The outgoing Mayor's reunified party, now led by the dissident Deputy Mayor, had won the runoff, much to the chagrin of the embittered supporters of the defeated party. Europeans who supported Elie Fleming, the outgoing Mayor, joined the Deputy Mayor's ticket, which gave them confidence about their future in Saint-Martin. In his new role as head of municipal administration, his language handicap was made even worse by a managerial and legal handicap; though these were compensated, to some extent, throughout his term by support from his numerous European collaborators.

The municipal election of March 1983, with its close and disputed run-off, became the most contested election in the island's modern political history. Against a backdrop of discontent and popular anger, which had been mounting since the 1976 impeachment of Mayor Hubert Petit, the subsequent favoritism and repressive policies only served to exacerbate social tensions, which took a dramatic turn during the electoral campaign – especially when it became clear that the massive European emigration would heavily influence local politics and rumors of excluded local voters were inciting the local residents. Tensions were at an all-time high when young Saint-Martiners made known that if they could not vote in their country, then French Europeans would not be allowed to vote either. According to one observer, the decision to prevent French Europeans from voting was taken after several Saint-Martin voters complained about having been omitted from the voting lists. When they went to the Courthouse in Marigot to obtain authorization for their right to vote, the judge in charge refused to grant it to them. In stark contrast, French residents who went to the judge for the same reason were granted the authorization to vote. The judge's decision was officially motivated by the ransacking of the office furniture and equipment by a mob of some 50 enraged Saint-Martiners. They were striking out against the injustice they felt at not being allowed to vote. At several polling stations, they chanted, *'Saint-Martin belongs to Saint-Martiners'*. Their determination was such that they were able to prevent the Sub-Prefect from going to the polls. Military forces were called in from Guadeloupe to restore order, but they did not have the opportunity to intervene. The Sub-Prefect called for calm in an attempt to avoid violence, and informed the population that the irregularities during the first ballot were registered and referred to the Court in Guadeloupe. It turned out that the original opposition party had won the first ballot.

The winning opposition party from the first-round could not maintain its advantage, when the Deputy Mayor, Albert Fleming, despite pre-election promises to merge with them, returned to his original group in last minute negotiations. When the outgoing Mayor, Elie Fleming, realizing he could not retain his title alone, yielded to pressure calling for his withdrawal, and left the top of the ticket open for his dissident Deputy, who won the second-round election with a lead of 114 votes over his opponent, Hubert Petit, his ally during the first-round. The outgoing Mayor, having lost all political support and discredited by the people, retired disillusioned. The Guadeloupean daily paper, *France-Antilles* on March 11, 1983 ran the headline: *The outgoing Mayor ousted in favor of strange bedfellows*. The article asserted that, "The strange political union that hit the ground running late Tuesday night, on March 8, does not seem to appeal to members of either ticket." It was noted that the merger during the second-round made for a loss of 69 votes for the reunified party, as compared with the total votes of both parties in the first-round. In contrast, the first-round winning party increased its score by 311 votes, from 1,266 to 1,577.

Figure 3

MARCH 1983 MUNICIPAL ELECTION RESULTS		
	1st Round March 6	**2nd Round March 13**
Union for a better municipal management Hubert Petit	**1,266**	1,577
For the Progress of Saint-Martin Mayor Elie Fleming	938	1,691
Saint-Martin Unity Albert Fleming	822	

On March 9, 1983 a young woman was arrested, placed in custody, and then sent to Basse-Terre, Guadeloupe, where she was sentenced to four months' imprisonment with no possibility of remission. A few days later, two additional youths from Saint-Martin were likewise arrested on March 14, detained, and transferred to Basse-Terre. These two young people contested the charges against them, though admitted to being on the scene. The determination of their guilt was based on the testimonies of a municipal police officer, two gendarmes who were guarding the premises on the day in question, and a private citizen. Like the young woman, they were sentenced to four months' imprisonment with no possibility of remission at the March 18 hearing.[30] Despite an appeal, the sentences were upheld.[31] However, the case proved to be much more complex than it initially appeared. Indeed, witnesses, and one of the defendants in the appeal hearing, claimed that Albert Fleming's supporters had participated in ransacking the Courthouse. *Progrès Social*, a news organ in Basse-Terre, Guadeloupe, reported the following statements made by the judge on duty in Saint-Martin at the hearing in the Court of Appeals:

> "...Around 9:40 a.m. Mr. Albert Fleming, a mayoral candidate in the municipal elections, came to my office and, without giving any identifying details, informed me of his displeasure concerning two instances of rejected voting authorization. He added that such decisions could upset the crowd and that there might be incidents. ...
> While I was on the phone with the Sub-Prefect, several 'Rasta type' individuals invaded my office, and in my presence, began to engage in acts of vandalism. Desks were overturned, archives were scattered, and some documents torn. Cupboards were emptied of their contents, typewriters, and other office equipment, thrown violently on the floor and I feared for my own safety...."[32]

The convicted young people believed they had become scapegoats for the events that transpired in the Courthouse on March 6, 1983. Meanwhile, the election results were contested by the former Mayor, Dr. Petit, and rescheduled to take place the following year, on May 13, 1984. As fate would have it, Elie Fleming, the outgoing Mayor, died unexpectedly on March 3rd, 1984, two short months shy of the new date, leaving Albert Fleming, the Deputy Mayor, unopposed as head of the party, which he then reformulated as *Saint-Martin Solidarity*. It was this party that rose up to snatch victory from former Mayor, Dr. Hubert Petit, at the May 1984 re-election.

III

MIRAGE OF TOURISM DEVELOPMENT

The social and political climate deteriorated in the aftermath of the very controversial 1983 municipal elections and the 1984 reelection. The municipal team, with its very visible European representation within the Municipal Council, and a Mayor who had to be supplemented by several European collaborators, augured an intense activity of development, defying the expectations of the local followers, who were no longer in the position of control. They had been the engine, the driving force, of the party during the campaign, but they became the wagons of the party in power. After placing his closest followers in a few positions of responsibility, the political orientations went along with the projects. The prevailing role of the sub-prefectural authority continued to dominate municipal policies. The new Mayor, having achieved his dream beyond all expectations, could no longer resist the most daring ambitions of French promoters, thus betraying the initial aspirations of his faithful followers. The hope they cherished to see the situation change in favor of the islanders was surely fading.

Consolidation of the Development

At this early stage, the legal provisions offering fiscal advantages to investors in the French Antilles contained loopholes. The March 16 to April 5, 1984 issue of *The Expansion,* a national newspaper, warned French savers against their investments in three projects, *L'Anse Marcel* (Saint-Martin), *Gosier* (Guadeloupe), and *La Belle Créole* (Saint-Martin), on account of the numerous irregularities in the financial operations carried out by promoters.

> "Ownership of property under the sun in a foreign country, that old dream cherished by many French nationals, had to deal with the numerous constraints of the currency exchange regulations. However, there are still a few countries, where it is possible to invest out of France without leaving the national territory, and they are the overseas departments.

> Those distant regions actually offer specific fiscal advantages. Since 1971, companies investing in the overseas departments are exempted from paying company tax for ten years under certain conditions. And, since last year a new measure (presented in an amendment to the 1983 law of finance), has enabled individuals to deduct from their taxable income 50% - even 100% - of their investments made in overseas departments. (…) This measure is the more interesting as the investor's income is high, but this 'fiscal gift' is in total contradiction with the general philosophy of the government which consisted in replacing income deductions with tax reduction. For this purpose, the publication of the implementation decrees may have been delayed. It has actually been delayed since December 27, 1983.
> (…) This is the message promoters of touristic operations would like to pass on to wealthy investors wishing to diversify their patrimony at the expense of public funding.
> Three operations are known to be currently accessible to the public. In Saint-Martin on the French side of this Franco-Dutch island administratively incorporated into Guadeloupe, a private promoter, Socano, intends to develop an apartment-hotel resort *near the sea*. In order to increase its capital (of 40 million francs), the company requested the authorization from the Commission of Stock Exchange operations (COB) to launch a public offering After it was granted on September 6, 1983, the commission was called to order as some irregularities were committed in matter of publicity. (…) The third project, undertaken this time by Paribas was *La Belle Creole* in Saint-Martin. A real sea serpent, this operation launched around 1970 was never completed despite the intervention of the *Club Mediterranee*."[1]

In the March 21, 1984 issue of the *Quotidien de Paris*, another article clearly making reference to *L'Anse Marcel* Project was entitled *Savings: a strange operation in the French Antilles*, and sub-titled *Minister Emmanuelli discreetly managed to pass a law enabling investors to invest 60 million francs in the overseas departments, but the functionaries have been blocking its implementation under suspicion of tax evasion.*[3]

All this publicity in the national media did not contribute to reassure Saint-Martiners on the merits of these financial operations. Obviously, these laws were not intended to serve the interests of the Antillean populations. Furthermore, at the opening of the public inquiry which took place from March 19 to April 20, 1984, as announced in the March 2, 1984 issue of *France-Antilles*, the Guadeloupe daily newspaper, the Saint-Martin owner of the property concerned by L'Anse Marcel Project, a Zone of Concerted Development, invited the population to oppose this real estate project and to take a stand against the Commune and Guadeloupe administrations who intended to expropriate him *"for public purposes"*. The property on which the apartments and relevant structures were to be developed belonged to a private local company and to this Saint-Martiner. In addition, the surrounding properties - all belonging to Saint-Martin owners - were downgraded to the category of a *non constructible zone* to facilitate the installation of this French company on the site. The promoter of the project had already collected the amount of 60 million francs from 10,000 subscribers by means of publicity, strongly emphasizing tax deduction as the end result, whereas approvals for the law on tax deduction were not yet granted.

This Saint-Martin landowner accused the Municipal Council of playing a determining role in this whole affair, because it approved the creation of the L'Anse Marcel Zone of Concerted Development (Z.A.C.) and the modification of the Plan for Zone Development (P.A.Z.) in a motion voted on February 18, 1982. Therefore, the surrounding local landowners became the victims of this modification. Actually, the documents for that motion had been passed on to the councilors at the last minute, without giving them the opportunity to consult them beforehand in order to understand what they were all about. He accused also the General Councilor and the Regional Councilor of Saint-Martin to try to obtain 40 million francs from the General Council of Guadeloupe for this French private project.

This modification consisted in declaring the properties surrounding the apartments and relevant structures as a *non constructible zone*. Only the French private company had the green light for its project. The Domain administration in Guadeloupe adopted these modifying measures on the zoning plan of Saint-Martin, as approved by the Municipal Council, to allow French Europeans to install themselves, thereby blocking Saint-Martin owners from the possibility to develop their properties, as they were now *non constructible*. These owners could be tempted then to sell at a give-away price to European buyers who afterwards would obtain from the Domain administration the modification of the zoning into the *constructible* category. This was open concerted conspiracy against Saint-Martiners.

During the term of office of Mayor Elie Fleming, who was his friend, this same Saint-Martin landowner, Mr. Clair Rogers, had proposed to sell to the Commune some 32 acres of land at Mount Vernon for the price proposed then by the Domain administration, which was about 22 francs per square meter, in order to set up a housing development for the local people. He had even offered to sell the road to the beach at one franc per square meter. The Mayor had then told him that the Deposit and Consignment Office refused to grant a loan to the Commune for the purchase of the land, although it was guaranteed that the price of the land and construction of the apartments would be paid back with the rent of the apartments. Instead, preference was given to *L'Anse Marcel* Project, and the municipality agreed to expropriate him and pay him for the expropriation, and to further devaluate the surrounding properties. Europeans found their *paradise under the sun* without difficulty, thanks to the Commune and Guadeloupe authorities.

Afterwards, this measure was used whenever it was necessary. The new municipal team continued to be at the service of the State administration in implementing its policy of European settlement of the island. Could this truly be called development, when the local population was excluded from every opportunity of advancement and *progress*?

Those fiscal advantages attracted not only real estate promoters, but also professionals such as notary, land surveyor, urban planner, and numerous real estate agents. In an interview with the French magazine, *St. Martin Eco Mag*, the island notary spoke of his contribution during the early days of real estate expansion:

> "While vacationing in the French Antilles in 1976, I discovered that the islands of Saint-Martin and Saint-Barths, very different from each other, had no permanent service of a notary. By 1979, I started to visit the island professionally and I incited my clients from my office in France to invest here. (…) That is how the residential developments of Long Bay in the Lowlands and Oyster Pond came into existence (…) between 1979 and 1984, as well as the real estate developments of Marina Port-la-Royale and Grand Saint-Martin."[4]

His analysis of the administrative history of Saint-Martin already made him a staunch advocate of an institutional change for the French side, with the main purpose to bring coherence to the fiscal status which, in his eyes, was marred with *"the greatest of confusions"*. The concern was to make the texts *"coincide with the patchwork of the existing ones and with the geopolitical reality, taking into consideration the original cultural identity of the Saint-Martin people*". In retrospect, it must be observed that the consideration for cultural identity, dear to every people, has never been the concern either of the local elected representatives, or the public authorities, or those who pretended, at this early stage, to be the friends of Saint-Martiners, and later, called themselves Saint-Martiners. The following decades were a period of continuous effort on the part of the islanders to keep their heads above the water. Even while planning for the status change voted on December 7, 2003, the interests of Saint-Martiners clashed with those of the socio-professionals; with the end result that the latter's interests prevailed. During those disturbing years, the political domination of European socio-professionals emerged under the disguise of an apparent unity with the people at each electoral event. Such apparent unity has considerably weakened the elected officials' drive to obtain the appropriate status change. It created the confusion and sluggishness that were observed during the near four-year period elapsing between the Consultation of December 7, 2003 and the inauguration of the new Overseas Collectivity of Saint-Martin on July 15, 2007.

In the visible turmoil shaking the Saint-Martin society and despite the intensity of the continuous real estate development on the French side, Saint-Martiners did continue to drive across the border everyday to earn a living and thereby contribute to the economic and tourism development of the southern part of the island. The *Citizens Action committee* geared to organize what they called *Claude Wathey Day* in honor of the man that did as much for the North as for his side of the island. This group of community-minded people put together a booklet to mark this extraordinary display of affection and gratitude. The reception took place on the French side on June 30, 1985. However, this demonstration of good neighborliness from Saint-Martiners raised the concern of the French officials at the Sub-Prefecture of Marigot, who called the main organizers for questioning. Actually, the Leader of Government, Claude Wathey, delivered a rather critical speech on that occasion, referring to *"these officials on both sides as appointees, who were enforcing laws that were unfit"* for the geopolitical context of the island. He was mainly pointing out to the recent immigration laws enforced as well as the issuance of residence and work permits, which were the sole competence of the Sub-Prefect representing the State of France and the Governor representing the Kingdom of the Netherlands. Afterwards, diplomacy prevailed, and Claude Wathey received honors not only from the State representatives for his contribution to the inhabitants of the people of the North, but also from Jacques Chirac himself. *"This official rapprochement coincided with a new aviation treaty between the Netherlands Antilles and France which allows Air France to fly directly to Sint Maarten, while an agreement was also reached to permit French immigration officials to be stationed at the Juliana International Airport",* in order to check passengers going to the French side.

Saint-Martiners did not cease their undertakings to overcome the challenges which their daily circumstances placed on their path. With the arrival at the helm of the Commune of someone close to them and whom they felt proud of, they saw a glimmer of hope that their situation would improve despite the never-ending signs of an expansion which excluded them. Their leader – the one who said he *came out of the sand*, the one who said he rose *from rags to riches*, the one who said *he was the first black Mayor* –flattered their pride. In fact, at his arrival at the head of the Commune, he reinstated Saint-Martiners in some key positions around him, at the secretarial function in the Town

Hall, at the registry, at technical and urban planning departments, at the tourist office and at other administrative positions in the Commune administration. This change produced a pervading climate of ascension and responsibility around him. He represented for his closest partisans the image of success. Saint-Martiners in his surroundings radiated. They thought that if he was able to attain that goal, they too could achieve it, despite their handicaps – economic, linguistic, educational, and social. On account of the glaring prosperity assailing them, they did not think of what it took to get there and, of course, the leader could not tell them that he was shining in this position because of those who were supplementing his personal handicaps. Actually, his close European collaborators were making themselves very discreet, and all this glaring prosperity dazzling everyone was put to his credit. It is in this atmosphere that his partisans continued to work towards the upliftment of their fellow countrymen, in the shade of his prestigious ascension. An association working in that direction was the Voice of Orleans.

The Voice of Orleans brought together faithful friends and fervent partisans of the Mayor's political approach of the Seventies, and was the channel of expression for the aspirations of the Saint-Martin people. In a series of public information meetings and conferences/debates, the Voice of Orleans brought together a great number of individuals from both sides of the island representing important commercial houses, bank institutions, airline companies, promoters, hoteliers, educators, culture and sports associations, associations of community promotion, artists, teachers, taxi unions, parents, hotel employees, construction contractors, heavy equipment operators, bus owners, among others. It was a period of collective renewal for the members of this association, and they were moved by a great determination. They knew that they were on the threshold of a new era and their objective was to participate efficiently in the development of their beautiful country. With open arms, they offered their assistance in a spirit of cooperation, conscious as they were that the future was in their hands.

The members of the Voice of Orleans strongly believed that one was a better citizen when one can participate in the democratic process of government. That is why they wanted to contribute, in the best and most peaceful way possible, to the development of the social, economic, cultural and educational life of their community. At a conference on *Tourism and its Impact on Saint-Martin* it was demonstrated that certain persons sought concrete solutions to the problems facing the development of the tourism industry on the island. The awareness of local citizens was at a point where they wanted a better education system for them, as well as for their children, to enable them to assume their responsibilities and to contribute efficiently in the creation of a stable, well-planned community, beneficial to all.

Participants in the debates recommended that all information be made in English, the mother tongue of Saint-Martin people. Other recommendations emerged from these exchanges: the participants were requiring the appointment of a Planner in order to design a master plan for Saint-Martin. This Planner would be surrounded by advisors, simple local citizens, merchants, contractors, educators, restaurant-owners, hoteliers and any person interested in the shaping of this plan. Considering the many changes that had already taken place, namely the rapid sale of land and the current construction of hotel complexes, it was recommended that all citizens be informed of the laws and regulations relative to landed property and to real estate development, and that public meetings be organized for residents, landowners, investors, and business people. Recommendation was made for the drafting of a booklet, intended for tourists and drawn up with seriousness and rigor, which would include elements of cultural life, historical data, updated information of current events, and a list of sites worth visiting.

In addition, participants recommended that a training program for tourism personnel be organized to instruct them of everything pertaining to Saint-Martin, its places of interest, its characteristic sites, its road signs, its history, its geography, and activities intended for visitors. This training program could be a short course twice a year for tourist guides, taxi drivers, bus drivers, sales persons and other tourism personnel. They recommended that additional restroom services be made available to the tourists. They could be situated in Orleans, Grand-Case, and Marigot. They also suggested that a small work group be set up to gather all information relative to the carrying out of these services, who will be responsible for submitting the results of their investigation to the relevant authorities for execution.

Finally, two areas were dear to the hearts of most participants. First, they recommended that a continuous program of embellishment and cleanliness of the island be devised by a consultative committee composed of concerned citizens under the authority of the Mayor. This committee would be in charge of developing the strategy and the objectives of a plan of action to execute this program. Secondly, the Voice of Orleans recognizing the inadequate educational system and the serious consequences of analphabetism, which prevented many adults from functioning to the best of their ability on account of their rudimentary skills in reading, writing and arithmetic, started to organize night classes for adults. The association called upon the support of participants to gather funds to pay the teachers giving the courses in Basic English, French, handicraft and artwork, as well as lecturers. These recommendations truly reflected the needs of the inhabitants who cherished so much hope at the start of this new era.

What Was at Stake for the New 1983 Municipality?

How to conciliate the aspirations and future prospects of the inhabitants with the more and more visible ambitions of those who implicitly created from scratch another societal system excluding those very inhabitants? If the newcomers stayed backstage at the beginning, they would not remain there indefinitely. The Mayor of the Commune, most certainly, could not anticipate this underlying dilemma in the excitement of his achievements. He boarded a moving train and he had to submit to certain requirements, which he did not suspect how demanding they were. Boosted up by his charisma, his natural sense of business, his transcending assurance, his inborn interest in others, he faced the many obstacles standing out on the path of his successive terms of office, without being able to conciliate what could not be conciliated.

The development went on at an accelerated pace, because the French side had to catch up with the twenty-year advance of the Dutch side, in the eyes of Europeans, and essentially because Saint-Martiners had to be brought back home to the French side, in the eyes of the leader - a highly political goal, indeed. In short, Saint-Martin had to stop being the dormitory of the island. Prosperity had to be attained on both sides. This was the feeling of *French* national pride that propelled the municipal team. Inciting Saint-Martiners to return was motivated by the perspective of higher wages and better social insurance coverage. This perspective exactly matched the ambitions of those crossing the border every day. Two hotel projects were opening their doors in October 1986, the ninth and the tenth: La Belle Creole Hotel with 170 rooms at the Bluff for a cost of 8,5 million dollars, and L'Habitation de Lonvilliers with 253 rooms at L'Anse Marcel, nestled behind the hills of Grand-Case and Cul-de-Sac for a cost of 27 million dollars. These hotels intended to employ about 500 persons.

In the months prior to their opening, the general manager of the two hotels diligently interviewed Saint-Martiners and professionals locally. However, the Mayor disclosed that the hiring operation was not as satisfactory as he expected: Saint-Martiners were not applying for the *"primary posts"*. In an interview with the daily newspaper in the South, he declared that the reason was that most Saint-Martiners worked in the South and did not want to give up their jobs there. He added *"young people are not aggressive when looking for a job"* and was blaming the educational system for failing to properly motivate them.[6] This was the first serious criticism he made against his people, which met an immediate reaction. A French Quarter resident, member of the Voice of Orleans, retorted to these statements:

> "Saint-Martiners are not being told about these hotel jobs. There is no advertisement in the newspapers, and I didn't hear any on the radio. How are people supposed to know, if they don't see it in print, especially if most Saint-Martiners work on the Dutch side."[7]

One Saint-James unemployed youth strongly reacted as follows:

> "But they know they were building these hotels, so what nonsense are they coming up with? That only 110 Saint-Martiners applied, and not enough for top positions?
> They're fooling people, man. Why didn't they send a bunch of Saint-Martin youth to study for these high positions? Because they know already that only Europeans and Americans would be getting them."[7]

Nevertheless, Pierre Verdier, the general manager of L'Habitation de Lonvilliers, engaged in recruiting young Saint-Martiners at all levels of employment with determination and sincerity, which enabled this hotel, even during its difficult moments, to remain the flagstaff of the hotel industry on the French side. So far, L'Habitation de Lonvilliers is a model of stability and performance, thanks to the noble nature of this executive. We imagine that it is with deep satisfaction that when he came back, twenty years after around 2005, he saw the advancement of the young people that he had hired at the opening.

The local administration had to prepare itself for its own expansion. It was rumored that SOCOMAR, the Municipal Company of Saint-Martin, was quietly and without fuss taking charge of the planning, decision-making, administrative organization of the Commune, and the drafting of the budget. It was, in fact, making the municipal policies rather than executing them. Everything to be undertaken in Saint-Martin from now on passed through this company and not through the elected officials. This company ran the affairs, decided and approved, and the Municipal Council just confirmed. The offices of this company were located in the area where the library was built. It was said to be the real power-house behind the development of Saint-Martin carried out by French developers. In the eyes of the island population, this development continued and intensified the practices of domination, making Saint-Martiners second-class citizens in their own country. Few people knew the existence of this company and its functioning. Rumors circulated that its director was sent by the President of the General Council of Guadeloupe who had just lost her position at the recent 1986 cantonal elections and was appointed Minister in the government of Prime Minister Chirac. The director had held the position of General Secretary of the former President's Cabinet. The Mayor never announced to the population the existence of this new organization and the discretion of this director, who was not seen in public, seem to be the accepted norm at this early stage. His start in the political life of Saint-Martin occurred stealthily.

The year 1986 began and was marked by events mobilizing Saint-Martiners for the defense of the image of their island and for their own defense. The development was showing its ugly face with the escalation of insecurity, the assault on the environment, the emergence of new infrastructures, transforming the landscape into a vast building site. The environmental look was changing with the constructions rising out of the ground, which negatively affected the presence of tourists in the streets of Marigot. All this took place without the participation of the inhabitants. However, they answered the call of the young people who organized the protest against the landing of the two Heineken kidnappers on their island, as France deported them to Saint-Martin. They heard this news from the Netherlands and not from France, and that is the reason why they were able to intercept this operation. Through their contacts on the Dutch side, the organizers learned that Corv van Hout and Willem Holleeder, the two kidnappers of Alfred Heineken in 1983 were to be flown to Saint-Martin under the protection of the French authorities on Thursday, February 13, 1986. In fact, after receiving the 2,5 million dollars of the 10-million dollar ransom which they requested for the release of the Heineken magnate, Hout and Holleeder fled from Holland to France where they hid in a Paris apartment. One year later, they were arrested by French police, and spent 18 months in prison. Meanwhile, extradition talks failed due to judicial complication between the two countries. The Netherlands media not letting go its pressure and France not finding a country who would accept to take them, the decision was taken to transfer the fugitives to a distant Franco-Dutch territory, which was Saint-Martin. The native population already knew that France was secretly dumping its former convicts on Saint-Martin, *laundering* them in the island's economy. They, therefore, gave special attention to this news. Everyone, except for the elected officials and Europeans, got ready to stop Saint-Martin from becoming the human dumping ground of France. The distribution of a flyer alerted all the inhabitants of what was going on. The radio on the Dutch side did likewise. Saint-Martiners were furious. Curaçao, alerted, sent the public prosecutor to arrest the two kidnappers at their landing on the Juliana Airport runway. The other alternative was to make them land on the Esperance airfield in Grand-Case.

On Saturday, February 15, 1986 the Sub-Prefect published a French press release in the *Newsday* of the Dutch side, confirming the departure of these criminals:

> "I the undersigned, Jean-Pierre Hubert, Sub-Prefect, Deputy Commissary of the Republic for the District of Saint-Martin and Saint-Barthelemy, hereby declare that I had the two foreigners who were assigned to forced residence in Saint-Martin (French side) leave the island by boat for the French territory, and such, in order to guarantee the protection of persons and goods.
> I must add that these two foreigners are escorted by police forces. (…)"[8]

On that same day, the inhabitants of Saint-Martin marched in the streets in a massive protest against the *"dumping of two criminals"* in Saint-Martin by French authorities, which was the reason for the Sub-Prefect's press release. The elected officials, who without any doubt knew all about this deportation, kept silent. They were, therefore, surprised by the reaction of the people. Some tried to intimidate the organizers; others stated that they could not take part in the demonstration because the streets were blocked. The people were convinced that their elected representatives were not on their side. They could not defend Saint-Martin against France.

The March 1986 cantonal elections were an opportunity for the Youth Organization to call for the boycott of these elections by voting blank. They distributed all over the island a flyer which pictured the three candidates as follows. They considered that the First Deputy Mayor *"contributed to put Saint-Martin in this deplorable condition, where our land is stolen by French Europeans. (...) and he has never defended Saint-Martin or Saint-Martiners;"* the second candidate, a newcomer in politics, *"has to go among the people more. He has to work for our votes, and not just around election time;"* and the third candidate was the representative of the National Front, *"the racist party of Jean-Marie Le Pen, the most offensive and insulting of all the choices. How dare the National Front come here to solicit votes when it does not want Saint-Martiners, Blacks, Arabs, etc. in France?"*

Reactions of the People

For some time, Saint-Martiners have disapproved of the inhuman brutality with which the Immigration officers were unjustly treating immigrants from the Dominican Republic and from Haiti, men and women, young and old. Accounts of such treatments were heard everywhere in the streets of Marigot. But when, on a certain Tuesday, June 17, 1986, they ill-treated one of theirs, the incident turned into riot and fire. The atrocities of the PAF were rumored to be perpetrated by Inspector Khaelin and his assistant Amédée. The incident, resulting from the campaign to fight illegal immigration, hit the headlines of the local, Guadeloupe and France newspapers. A flyer signed by the *Saint-Martin Committee of Defense* related the incident as follows:

> "The customary brutal operation conducted by the Air Frontier Police (PAF) logically directed against foreigners took a bad turn this time. On Tuesday, June 17, 1986 in the fore day, the man hunt started, first in Sandy Ground, and then proceeded to *Hameau du Pont* where the terrible 'blunder' was committed. At about seven o'clock that morning shots were heard. A local lady, busy at her daily chores in front of her house, was grabbed by two PAF police who asked for her residence permit. Her children, relatives and neighbors alerted by the screaming, rushed to her. Her nephew, a local person also, inquired in English, and not Haitian Creole, what happened. For an answer, he was given a good slap by one of the PAF police. Since he was resisting, two other PAF police overpowered him, and a third one, Amédée Santenac, seized the opportunity to pound his face with the butt of his revolver. Meanwhile, a 69 year-old Saint-Martiner was beaten up, especially in his head, and had to be taken to hospital. The injured nephew ran home to alert his parents while the PAF police drove back to their Headquarters in the center of Marigot, on the first floor of a building with two classrooms underneath, which are the annex of the *Bord-de-Mer* Primary School across the street. The wounded young man's father arrived on the spot with the firm intention of revenging his son.
>
> Rapidly informed of the incident, the population arrived in numbers in front of the PAF office, clamoring for Amédée Santenac. At that moment the PAF police tear-gassed the crowd. They took no heed of the presence of school children on the first floor of the building and in the school across the street. The frightened children took to the street screeching and crying, trying to escape through a lane leading to the seaside. The children's eyes were burning; other children in a panic ran to the sea. Coincidentally, the employees of the Sub-Prefecture next door to the PAF office had been informed the day before to keep the office closed. During that time, the PAF police barricaded and armed themselves. A young PAF police even shot his own leg while trying to pull out his revolver. He was taken to hospital after the crowd agreed to let him pass. The suspicious crowd searched the car before he left to make sure that Amédée Santenac was not on board.
>
> The heat of anger rose in the street. PAF cars and vans were put on fire. Military reinforcements from Guadeloupe were requested. Two Twin-Otters, chartered by Air Guadeloupe, landed on the airport in Grand-Case. The imminent arrival of these reinforcements on Marigot and the increasing pressure of the crowd clamoring to get Amédée or exacting that he leaves the island immediately, forced the concerned parties, that is, the representatives of the Municipal Council and the PAF, and the young man's father, to facilitate the escape of the PAF officers and their chief Khaelin to the Grand-Case Airport, where a special aircraft was waiting for them. A line of fully armed

policemen blocked the entrance of the airport in order to keep away the crowd that had already gathered on the spot. The aircraft took off immediately.
In Marigot, a few uncontrolled elements plundered Amédée Santenac's apartment as they were disappointed for not being able to get Amédée. Saint-Martiners were much surprised to find about ten fans, five television sets, three refrigerators, several mattresses, a bag with jewels, cases of champagne and whisky, etc... in his apartment. Amédée Santenac was well-known in Saint-Martin for his weird practices, namely, abuse of women after arrest, physical violence, granting of favors in exchange for money (in fact, this man went so far as to extract money from people residing illegally on the island to allow them to stay here, etc...). As for Inspector Khaelin, he was well-known in the drug world.
France doesn't want Khaelin. Guadeloupe doesn't want Amédée Santenac. And we don't want them either. We don't want any *Tonton Macoute* in Saint-Martin."

The local newspaper, *Newsday*, of June 20, 1986 published three articles about the incident with the picture of 21 year-old Jacques Hamlet on front page, one of the victims of the brutal raid, showing a scar under his swollen right eye. He was brutalized by Inspector Khaelin and his assistant Amédée, when he inquired about his aunt Genia Piper, who was arrested. She had no papers to prove that she was not illegal on the island. The article entitled *Priest calls Authorities Actions on Tuesday Barbarous* [It was the priest of the Dutch side] disclosed other cases of brutality:

"(...) That woman from the Dominican Republic who was terribly beaten by the immigration forces showed her wounds to the people. (...) A young man was there with a bruised-up face, beaten the day before because he could not prove that he was *legal*. It happened that he was a native of Saint-Martin. That was his *crime*. Since when do you have to walk with your passport in your own country? And I saw another lady, released on that infamous June 17 afternoon: two men had to hold her up because she was so ill-treated in prison that she could not walk. (...)"[9]

In the same issue, the incident inspired a young man to write a poem entitled, *June 17, 1986*. It can be read in Appendix 3. Another article reported how the vehicles were put on fire and the PAF officer's apartment ransacked:

"(...) In the street five vehicles were torched in the morning hours. Another vehicle on the waterfront was also torched. A man came walking down the street with a pan of kerosene, with the intention to burn down the building. He then proceeded upstairs on the porch of the Immigration Department, and threw the kerosene on the wall. Thereafter it was in flames. The people then started to run down the street to get away from the flames. The fire didn't last long as it was put out by the fire truck. Up the road, another car was set ablaze

> right next to the government apartments where one immigration officer lived. His apartment was looted by a group of people. One lady came out of the house with his picture and she told one of the Haitians to carry it back to Haiti and work Voodoo on it. The officer whose picture the woman displayed was reportedly that of assistant PAF Chief Amédée. The people then started to throw out everything he had in the streets. The police did not intervene. Minutes later the *National Guard* was brought in from Guadeloupe. They came to the immigration building where they cleared the street and then proceeded down the street to the Sub-Prefect residence."

It was the squad of the Mobile Guard from Arras, France, detached in Guadeloupe. The *France-Antilles* reported the incidents in Saint-Martin in an article entitled, *The inhabitants obtained the departure of two police officers*:

> "Following a whole day of protest, marked by incidents resulting in four wounded among the policemen and three among the population, the inhabitants of the island of Saint-Martin (…) obtained the temporary departure of two police officers assigned to Air and Frontier Police (PAF) on Tuesday, June 17. They participated in an abusive police operation that same morning. The Mayor of Saint-Martin, Mr. Albert Fleming, declared that during an administrative police operation, some of his fellow citizens have been *"treated like animals"*.
> Pointe-à-Pitre. – According to a reliable source, some *five thousand* illegal foreigners live mainly on the French side of the island and work on the Dutch side. The island of Saint-Martin has a population of *thirty thousand* inhabitants and an area of 96 square kilometers [blown up figures]. It is important to note that in 1985 out of the *three hundred and ninety nine births* registered at the local hospital, only *35%* represented the French population. The national Gendarmerie by itself processes more than *four hundred cases of expulsion* per year. To this troubling demographic situation, one can add the presence of members of the Antillean and metropolitan underworld attracted by the official use of the American dollar. (…)
> Immediately, the merchants closed their stores, and nearly four hundred protesters, according to official sources, set on fire vehicles and the apartment of a police officer. They were demanding the immediate departure of a police sergeant, a Guadeloupean, and a chief inspector, Mr. Gilles Khaelin, a metropolitan. Inspector Khaelin, considered on the island as a *"cow-boy"*, had already a bone to pick with the population on several occasions. His altercation with a prominent figure of the island, a presumed informant of the CIA, two years ago had resulted in a three months' forced leave of absence.
> On Tuesday, a source from the Sub-Prefecture explained that the departure of the two police officers was out of the question. (…) On the other hand, the violent incidents which shook this tiny island last February at the arrival of the two presumed kidnappers of the Dutch beer magnate, Mr. Freddy Heineken, were still stuck in people's minds. (…) In a telex sent to the new Prefect of Guadeloupe, Mr. Yves Bonnet, later that morning, the Mayor of Saint-Martin demanded that *"the officers responsible for such brutality be*

sanctioned", and he joined the population in *"their wishes for the immediate departure of these officers."*[10]

Another article in the same issue of France-Antilles, showing pictures of Amédée Santenac's apartment, of his furniture thrown in the street, of the van rented by the P.A.F on fire, and of Chief Inspector Khaelin's overturned car in flames, was entitled, *After the events of Saint-Martin: a coroner's inquest has been conducted.* The following day, Wednesday, June 18, the First Deputy Mayor of Saint-Martin and Regional Councilor, Louis Constant Fleming, in mission in Paris, communicated to the Minister of Overseas Departments and Territories, Mr. Bernard Pons, the following message:

> "Have the honor to inform you that I:
> - Deplore the incidents that have just occurred on the island of Saint-Martin between the Air and Frontier Police and the population.
> - Deplore that Mr. Sub-Prefect and those responsible for public order undertake control operation of immigrants without consulting the elected officials of the island.
> - Denounce the brutality with which certain representatives of the Air and Frontier Police perform their duties. On several occasions, we have informed the Public Prosecutor of such brutality.
> - Reiterate my request of the immediate replacement of the Air and Frontier Police Officers and the Sub-Prefect of the District."[11]

One week after the events, Louis Hamlet, Jacques Hamlet's father, and the arrested young woman Genia Piper's brother-in-law, published in the *Newsday* of the Dutch side the following message entitled, *Long live the determination of the people of Saint-Martin*:

> "June 17, 1986, I believe that day should be remembered by all Saint-Martiners. It was definitely the day when all natives and residents got together to defend a just cause. (…)
> I believe that the best way to take care of incoming strangers is at the airport and the dock. On the contrary, the PAF permits the overflow of strangers, and then suddenly PAF forces raid the villages, breaking open people's homes, but worse than all, they beat the people, women and men, maybe because they are a little reluctant. (…)
> On that June 17, their forces were reinforced by new PAF forces who didn't know who were natives or who were strangers. However, the one called Amédée was there and he knows the difference, but he turned out to be the brutish animal. (…) It was only normal and fair that an explosion of human reaction in the population would take that incident to the extent that it reached.
> I would like to let the elected people of this community know that I lived through that day and that they should also be aware of a terrible tension that is

> alive in this country; and every possible thing in their power should be done in an urgent way in order to help stop what may be the ruin of the economy of this island.
> On behalf of my neighbors, family, and myself I would like to express a great deal of thanks to the population for their support on that Day which ended in a great victory of getting those two barbarians off this land. (...)"[12]

In addition, the school children suffered from the tear-gas. Those that panicked ran to the sea nearby. One child nearly drowned. Many children had to be treated at the hospital. The parents' committee of the *Bord-de-Mer* School "*organized a silent protest march with many parents, walking through the streets of the town, holding up signs bearing hostile slogans at the police. They stopped at the Town Hall and were received by the Mayor.*"[13] Parents complained that prior to the arrival of the forces from Guadeloupe, Sub-Prefect Hubert ordered his employees not to open to the public, but he did not say a word to the headmistress of the 350-student school, just opposite, about the security of the children, so classes were going on while PAF offices were closed when the incidents occurred. The committee handed to the Mayor a protest letter, which was also sent to the Prefect of Guadeloupe and to several ministries in Paris. The Mayor left for Guadeloupe the following day to discuss the events with the Prefect and to decide what will be done with the Sub-Prefect with regard not only to the June 17 incidents, but also to the two Heineken kidnappers in February. The Mayor called for the removal of Sub-Prefect Hubert as soon as possible. His term of office was up in August.

The relations between the national law enforcement forces and the municipal police were not at their very best. The demographic explosion put a strain upon the population, reinforcing the antagonisms at all levels of society. The national newspapers had also their say on the situation in Saint-Martin in general and on the incidents in particular. *Liberation* in its June 30, 1986 issue focused on *The anti-French blues of Saint-Martin* illustrated by a street picture and two maps locating the island. Apart from the generalities, the following remarks were brought to the fore:

> "It must be noted that the tremendous leap made by the island these last years, transformed this vast free zone into a real Eldorado bringing about, it is true, a serious economic as well as social and racial imbalance.
> However, there is no or almost no unemployment in Saint-Martin. Hardly four unemployed persons were recorded last year out of a total population evaluated between 10,000 and 12,000 inhabitants. The massive arrival of citizens from Santo Domingo and Haiti in search of a job is really a good thing for many people. Primarily, the metropolitan contractors who can use this docile and relatively cheap workforce (there is no labor union in Saint-Martin). But also Saint-Martiners who make things meet by renting them

shacks in the Sandy Ground area. Only Sub-Prefect Jean-Pierre Hubert is concerned about this *"wild immigration impossible to control"*.
The State representative suspects the Dutch side (only in private) of willfully closing their eyes on this massive arrival of foreigners, hoping that it will destabilize the French side because the economic boom there, it seems, was starting to be in competition with the Dutch side.
This immigration does not seem to worry the Mayor of Saint-Martin most, even if he does admit that *"the girls from Santo Domingo create family problems because they take Saint-Martin women's husbands"*. No, what worries Albert Fleming, is the invasion of the white people *"who come to make money without trying to integrate"*.
Today, this former contractor (...) feels that things have gotten out of hand. He decided to slow down the speed of the development by cutting down on the granting of building permits. According to his detractors (and they are numerous), that was not always the case. However, today he admits that *"Saint-Martiners are not benefiting from the development of their island"*. He even drops in at the hotels, with his Municipal Councilors, to strongly urge the metropolitan employers to employ locals. (...) On both sides of [Port-La-Royale] this white enclave, the cement mixers, the backhoes, and the cranes are busy on the seaside because the Marina is expanding.
The inflow of metropolitan capital representing 85% of the investments made on the island generated a real frenzy in the field of construction. Hotels and buildings, with stores on the first floor, are popping up like mushrooms. With 400 rooms in 1984, the hotel capacity increased to 1,200 in 1986 and was expected to reach 1,600 the following year. (...)"

Two months later in August, the prestigious Paris newspaper *Le Monde* still wrote about Saint-Martin in an article entitled *Scuffle in Saint-Martin*. It referred to the usual generalities on the fight against illegal immigration in Guadeloupe. It, however, commented on remarks pertaining to the activity of the municipal police:

"The PAF officers accuse their colleagues of the Municipal Police of Saint-Martin of indulging in *"racketeering"* with *"illegal foreigners"*. So, on September 4, 1985 two illegal women who were selling lottery tickets on the street (in violation of the regulations) had their handbags snatched away by municipal officers. The two concerned municipal officers explained that they wanted to discourage illegal gambling. (...) The methods used are *"worthy of a banana republic, and discredit all law enforcement representatives,"* commented Gilles Khaelin, the Immigration chief inspector (...)
Other areas of interest handled by immigration functionaries concerned situations where elected officials employed illegal foreigners as domestics and chauffeurs. (...)
Illegal immigrants backed by Saint-Martiners react more and more violently to bust operations conducted by the immigration police. On June 5, 1986, these immigration officers were compelled under threats to release illegal workers arrested on the building site of La Belle Creole real estate complex,

> during a mission carried out at the request of the Sub-Prefect of Saint-Martin, Mr. Jean-Pierre Hubert, a former officer of the National Headquarters of Exterior Security.
> Such violent scenes already yielded results. Two immigration police officers (...) were since transferred out of Saint-Martin. (...) *Mr. Security* of Guadeloupe is presently trying to install the air and frontier police at the Dutch airport of Juliana, following an agreement between the Governor General of the Netherlands Antilles and the Prefecture of Guadeloupe."

The June 17 incident was the incident of the year, and an overview of the press coverage indicated that the social context was much more complex than it appeared. The diverse populations involved were steadily increasing, except for the native population who was developing at a normal pace. This diversity on such a tiny territory where conflicting interests were visibly brought into play, greatly inflamed human contacts. *No longer was there a community of destiny within the population*, because each group of population coexisted with absolutely different, even opposite, prospects; and on every occasion, the positions of each group clashed. In the case of the Dutch kidnappers, the native population was opposed to the French authorities, and the elected representatives did not side with their population. Four months later, an incident of simple police routine turned into a riot because Saint-Martiners were taken for foreigners, a mistake never admitted as such by French authorities, which highly shocked Saint-Martiners, widening even more the gap between Saint-Martiners and national law enforcement agents. Furthermore, one could sense an antagonistic rapport between the Mayor and French authorities, because the Mayor did not seem to favor the invasion of *metropolitans,* which he considered to be a social threat, whereas he tolerated the invasion of illegal *Caribbean* people whom he seemed to protect. Nevertheless, Europeans with the support of French civil servants heavily voted for this Mayor. They tilted the scale on his side despite the unpopular policies of that political clan. This produced a perfect imbroglio which neither side could disentangle. The native population was in almost daily conflict with various populations from abroad at all levels of contact.

Immediately after, in the month of August 1986, the villagers of Colombier opposed the project of a 92-bungalow hotel to be built in their village. Colombier with its lush vegetation was the most picturesque and quietest village of the island, cozily nested between two hills along a dry ravine which could become a torrent in time of heavy rains. The 200 villagers led a traditional life perpetuating the agricultural activities of their ancestors. Arrow-root was still cultivated and transformed into *farine* and *cassava bread.* All kinds of fruit and ground food were reaped in season. Fowls, sheep and goats, hogs were still raised. Then, one day, the villagers learnt that a French promoter wanted to build a 92-room hotel there. Immediately they wrote a letter to the Mayor, to the general councilor, to the regional councilor and to the Sub-Prefect to let them know that they were absolutely against this project in their village, because they wanted to preserve the beauty of their environment and their way of life. Besides, this project that would cover an area of 4950 square meters will increase the risk of flooding by obstructing the natural flow of rain waters. The promoter of the project answered the villagers in a letter dated August 17, 1986. He described the project in detail: 92 wooden bungalows, a grocery store, a restaurant and swimming-pool, an automatic laundry, a tennis court. He would also build a sewage system to accommodate 400 persons and a 300 cubic meter cistern. This hotel would be situated opposite *La Rhumerie* restaurant. The promoter did not fail to praise the benefits this project would bring to the village, as he begged the villagers to accept it. Those benefits were summed up as follows: attract tourists, employment reserved for the villagers, of course, 15 housekeepers, 4 male and 4 female security guards, 6 employees for the laundry, 4 maintenance men, and two bilingual (English/French) telephone operators, among others. He admitted that the road will be congested, but that the villagers had to keep their yards and their properties clean *"to accommodate the tourists"*. The villagers were not impressed by that letter. This project never saw the light in Colombier on account of the villagers' determination and tenacity.

In a press release, Roland Richardson, the famous Saint-Martin painter, deplored the nature of the development that was causing anxiety and tension. After demonstrating that history repeated itself, he indicated that it was the actors who had to determine their role, and the hope of change depended on them. Then, he lamented about the rapidity with which the island's heritage was destroyed these last years:

> "Development on St. Martin has been accelerating at a dizzying, exhilarating pace for the last twenty years or so. At first only one side of this progress was seen: the good it was doing to the country. Little or no attention was or has ever been paid to the other side: the gradual, but also accelerating, tearing down, erasing and covering up of the heritage of the people of this land. It reached to the point where we have so few old buildings that they can be counted on the fingers of our hands. (...) So less is left of the history, heritage and culture of St. Martin that nothing will remain if we do not actively protect it. If we do not bridle our run-away development immediately, tourism will be lost with the last building we tear down, with the last field and hill we cover with cement.
>
> If we continue to give over our heritage to the bulldozer, the rubble we are left with is that of our past and our future. And we will be no more than dust particles blown from tumbling walls. What made us who and what we are

> today, our identity, is all that we truly have between us and the conqueror. That we continue to allow, unchecked and unquestioned, such callous and wanton destruction is shameful, revolting and extremely dangerous. Such destruction should be seen as the criminal barbaric act that it is and it should be stopped. Whoever the perpetrators may be, from here or elsewhere, we are the ones who are allowing it; we are the ones who will lose and suffer. We have taken tremendous risks at high cost, now we should see the necessity to pay and risk just as much, and be willing to do so, in order to keep what we have."[14]

This almost apocalyptic description certainly seemed exaggerated to some, but crafted by an artist so sensitive to the beauty of his island's landscapes, it reflected the depth of the anxiety of most islanders in 1986. By destroying our environment, our landscapes, our ponds, our identity was deeply affected. Those who managed to stop some of this destruction feel today a great sense of satisfaction, because Colombier remained that tiny part of Saint-Martin which we are all proud of. And those who have tried and did not succeed feel exactly like our artist, who had tried to save a lovely old building in Marigot and to whom the various elected officials gave the assurance that *"no way could it be destroyed"*. For a time, work was stopped, but when he travelled to America for three weeks he learned that the building was torn down:

> "I am ashamed to walk in the town where I was born. I failed utterly. In the depth of my shock I realize that we, St. Martiners, have all lost forever something irreplaceable: a part of ourselves was removed and ceased to exist. ... When a community refuses to passively accept the destruction of what they hold dear, when they actively undertake preventive action, the outcome and their struggle take on a new character and a new level of meaning not only to those directly concerned but to all men."[14]

He ended by praising the efforts of the Grand-Case villagers and parish who had rebuilt their church from charred ruins into a new structure which harmoniously emerged from the past into the future. He found encouraging the decision of the government of the Netherlands Antilles to finance the restoration of Fort Amsterdam in Philipsburg. It was a glimmer of hope that the work was done by Saint-Martiners themselves. Finally, he acknowledged with satisfaction the struggle waged by the villagers of Colombier to preserve their precious heritage.

Intensification of Real Estate Activity

Despite the admonitions made in the local press, the general deterioration went on steadily. The Cultural and Educational Association of Saint-Martin, SMECO, echoed the disastrous consequences of this rapid and uncontrolled development: the population was sacrificed on the altar of progress. In fact, the members of this association acknowledged that Europeans owned all the business places at Port-La-Royale Marina in Marigot and that Saint-Martiners were losing their preeminence in the business world, as they became second-class citizens. SMECO saw that the development of the territory was undertaken without consideration of the population's aspirations and needs. With all these constructions and all these populations invading the island, the road network was unchanged; the drainage of waste water did not improve. No parking areas were created in Marigot, as it was becoming a saturated little town with congested streets. They believed that we were ready neither politically nor socially to face this unbridled development. The Caribbean tourists who visited the island to have a taste of our culture and way of life were offered a disguised European way of life. As a result, the escalation of hard drugs, criminal activity, armed scuffles between drug traffickers, and high day thefts of vehicles and two-wheelers were daily occurrences. The SMECO members were begging to change the course of events *"immediately"* and to restrain the arrival of the "*out-laws*" by freezing building permits.[15]

At the beginning of the year 1987, the local press disclosed the municipality plans to make the capital Marigot a *tax haven* for French multinationals. It included the construction of the Galisbay deep water pier to handle the transshipment of merchandise out of Europe, particularly France, to Latin America, the United States, and Canada. This plan was allegedly supported by the Baron de Rothschild who hosted the private visit of the St. Maarten/St. Martin political delegation to Paris, where it was reported of a supposed confrontation between the Ambassador of the Netherlands and Senator Claude Wathey. This delegation left for Paris to be part of the officials who took the inaugural Paris/St. Maarten flight on January 7, 1987. This flight returned on January 14. It was also planned that a variety of international banks would offer their services locally. The ultimate goal was not to supplant Philipsburg, but to be a complementary commercial port. No elected representative or opposition politician informed the population about the preparation of this commercial project. Furthermore, it seemed that this project would be beneficial neither to the population in terms of employment, nor to the municipality who would not be able to tax the financial transactions in transit. Those operations could very well minimize the importance of the island's tourism industry. But then, who would benefit from this project? The objective was actually to give these multinational companies, banks, and powerful consortiums a 10-year tax holiday.[16]

The Port de Plaisance and Casino project in Cole Bay and six new hotels in the North emerged in the wake of this economic planification. The property bordering the Simpsonbay Lagoon, south of Marigot, was bought in 1986 for 10 million dollars and was controlled by French interests. Situated on the Dutch side where the laws on the opening of casinos were less strict, the Port de Plaisance Resort, close to the border, would attract many tourists from France. The Air France Paris/St. Maarten direct line was opening at the end of the year and the prospects of optimal tourism prosperity were under way in perfect symbiosis with the authorities of the Dutch side, yet in direct competition with the Dutch side's hoteliers whose activity has started since 1955. In the North, the construction of two hotels totaling 400 rooms was in the pipeline. The promoter of the 250 room hotel was Sheraton, an important international chain, who had formerly managed Mullet Bay Resort. The project would be implanted in Friars' Bay and would open between April and May. However, it never broke ground. The second one of 150 rooms would be situated in Oyster Pound and four others of 50 and 60 rooms would be constructed at Nettle Bay, close to the Lowlands. This brought the number of hotels to a total of 20 in the North with an increase of 8 hotels during the two last years. The whole island numbered over 40 hotels, with 22 in the South, including townhouses and condominiums, in addition to 80 hotel-type apartments available. The tourism industry dated back to over thirty years on the island, and less than one per cent of the larger hotels and about 14 guesthouses and motels were managed by local owners. Restaurants were already flourishing in Grand-Case for a few years, with international signs on their fronts along the Main Street and local restaurants were concentrated in the open air close to the pier.

This economic plan was connected with the launching, for the third time since 1977, of the idea of an institutional change designed to link Saint-Martin and Saint-Barthelemy directly with France, without the input of the population. It aimed at achieving a form of autonomy which would facilitate Monaco-type financial operations. The Mayor gave an interview to the local daily newspaper *Newsday* on the ins and outs of this possible institutional change, published on March 2, 1987. He was presenting to the population an autonomous status which would restrain the political and economic domination of Europeans on the island and give more control to Saint-Martin and the elected officials over its social, political and economic destiny. This was pure demagogy since Europeans would never allow that, even though those aspirations were politically legitimate and the solutions sought politically correct. The Mayor wanted to control the movement of people to Saint-Martin, and then have the investors bear the additional fiscal burden, which was visibly dreamland. Even in Paris, this type of status, explained to the concerned ministries during the recent visit of the Saint-Martin delegation, was not seen favorably. However, he persisted in saying that the situation required some serious adjustments:

> "The gap between local Saint-Martiners and French metropolitans is very wide and the situation is very explosive. If this situation continues to deteriorate, it will have a very negative effect on the progress of this island. As a loyal citizen first and then as a responsible politician, it is my responsibility to do everything possible to avoid any revolution in this country. To avoid this calamity we are seeking to control the movement of people to Saint-Martin. We are proposing that any person not born on Saint-Martin should be required to have residence and working permits in order to work on the island."[18]

He mentioned the difference with the system on the Dutch side where Saint-Martiners themselves were controlling their economic affairs and, with the symbolic border between both sides, he was dreaming of the autonomy enjoyed by the South since December 1954. But the Paris authorities judged this desire for autonomy differently. The Mayor naively contradicted all those who said that this type of status would link Saint-Martin directly to France, which will make it a colony or a department. He then gave the characteristics of this status that did not exist anywhere in the French colonies. *"It was a bastard type of status which will permit us to be in full control of our destiny."* The idea was to have control of the financial situation, of immigration and other advantages which can benefit Saint-Martiners, because he said *"At the moment we have no benefits at all because French metropolitans are not giving the population an opportunity to participate in the economic affairs of the island."* That was, indeed, the reality which he acknowledged at that moment, and not the contrary, namely, that Saint-Martiners did not participate in the economy on account of their indolence. Then, he continued with his initial accusation that Saint-Martiners had a *laisser-faire* attitude. The contradictions in his statements were blatant. He was exposing his own limits: he could not stop metropolitans from hiring their country fellow people, more qualified than Saint-Martiners, and who *"in addition were aggressive money makers."* The Mayor considered this situation *"chaotic."* In reality, he could not stop metropolitans from controlling any aspect of life in Saint-Martin. Faced with such manifest handicap, the question was: What about the status then? Was it just a fairy tale or was it a means to keep in suspense all those who could believe in it? Afterwards, he placed this handicap on the backs of Saint-Martiners who, he said, had no motivation, whereas he was fully aware of the number of Saint-Martiners' projects which his administration constantly rejected, giving the preference to Europeans often for similar projects. The standard procedure was the following: Saint-Martiners were asked to deposit their projects at the

Town Hall, and then nothing else happened. Now, the approval of the Commune administration was necessary to start. Many Saint-Martiners conceived projects in many fields, for example on the Simpsonbay Lagoon, but to no avail. In addition, the Mayor outlined that his major achievements, first in the field of education. He built 24 classrooms and planned to build 170 apartments to ensure *"the stability of the teachers as they would be able to perform better"* for teachers who, for the most part, came from Guadeloupe. Secondly, through his administration's policies he was able to stimulate economic growth on the island. Thirdly, *"scheduled to begin in March we will be having cruise ships coming in Marigot on a daily basis,"* a great advantage for the merchants of the capital. Finally, promoters had joined him *"to sponsor scholarships for students attending institutions in Guadeloupe, Martinique, and France. Because French educational system is free, these scholarships amounting to 500 dollars were to cover boarding and study material expenses."* The following year, he would add 5 more students. His goal *was "to equip our people with the necessary skills so that they would be able to contribute towards the development of the island."* Was it once more crumbles or was he daydreaming? Did the effort, somewhat laudable, measure up to the reality pictured in this interview?

By then, the labor market was already saturated by foreign workers' cheap labor. It was more and more difficult for Sint Maarteners, in the South more than in the North, to organize and demand better working conditions and better wages. In fact, the increasing cost of living affected them negatively. Many foreign workers, we have said it previously, worked in the South and lived in the North. The situation of illegal labor was very different in the South. Problems loomed on account of the cheap labor offered by these foreign workers. The leader of government did not accept to bear the entire responsibility of this situation. He threw the ball in the court of the business community by saying, *"If you look at the wages certain business people are paying their staff after 15 years of service, they pay them the bare minimum that government specifies by law,... it is caused by greedy business people."*[19] So his opposition was demanding that minimum salary be adjusted at least to the growing cost of living, which was the responsibility of government. Many employers paid their employees at the bare minimum wage rate, which stopped Sint Maarteners and many cheap laborers from neighboring islands from earning a decent livelihood. Moreover, on account of the increasing intensity of the raids and the forced departure of illegal foreigners, the shopkeepers, beauty salon owners, and grocers in the countryside all over the island complained about the drop in their turnover. Actually, *"these people buy from us,"* they said. *"Even after the raids the Dominicanos who remain look like they shop less, because they are afraid to walk the streets in the day and at night. By the time they start coming out again, or others get back to the island, there is another raid.*" Another small grocer added: *"If there was no work in Sint Maarten for people from Santo Domingo or Haitians, they wouldn't come here. I'm barely making it as it is, so what do you think happens when they raid and take a chunk out of my shop."* A local small grocers' association is needed to take these grievances to the government and so put pressure for solutions to be found to alleviate the constant fluctuation of their income. They did agree with immigration control, but they believed that better policy should be implemented so that these raids do not affect the local base of the economy negatively.[20]

It should be noted that in other countries, illegal immigrants were a threat to nationals because they were taking away low-paying jobs from nationals and even sending considerable amounts of money out of the country to their home country. In Sint Maarten, illegal Caribbean people actually appear to fill a vacuum at the bottom rungs of the economic ladder and often as skilled or semi skilled workers, such as electricians, carpenters, hair dressers, construction workers. Their employers were often Saint-Martiners affected by these raids, which sometimes gave rise – even temporarily – to a complete halt of business activities. As for the money sent back to their countries, nothing much remained after paying out the price of food and the excessive rent of their shacks. It was no longer the case on the French side from 1993 when the State of France brought in its welfare system to provide for the legalization of the numerous foreigners. We will deal further with the abuses deriving from such a system, which were one of the destabilizing factors of the Saint-Martin society.

At Happy Bay Hotel, management was undergoing financial hardships. It was a French-style luxury hotel with 60 superb rooms and a breathtaking view on the Caribbean Sea. Early in May 1987, some 25 employees, mostly Saint-Martiners, planned to take action to get paid for their work: they had not been paid for about one month. They complained that the hotel manager told them on several occasions *"to go and come back next week"* and they were tired of the lying. He even told them that those who want to leave can leave. The employees accused the former bosses of ripping off the hotel, so they were ready to stand up for their rights. There was no labor union on the French side and they decided to see the Mayor to put some order in this affair, to enable them to get their wages. Most workers had families to support, some with children studying abroad.

At the start of his term of office, the Mayor urged the new Europeans to hire Saint-Martiners. A certain number worked in the North, but soon problems developed between Saint-Martin employees and European employers on account of the oppressive nature of employment and the bad working conditions: workers were not respected, pay not in adequacy with work done, no social security, wages often not paid. These conditions were largely stripping the local labor force of their motivation, and not, as some official reports or studies made believe, their lack of qualification, their lack of motivation, or their indolence. Apart from rare exceptions, those generalities could not apply. A labor union to defend the rights of the workers was needed on the French side, and a group of young people got together to organize the first local labor union. Labor unions were already established on the Dutch side and were very active.

The Mayor's wishes for the year 1987 were paved with good intentions. The tax exemption law was already in full swing on the island. The Mayor gave himself good conscience considering the scope of the phenomenon, by making Saint-Martiners believe that they should not sit back, but take the responsibility of *"pooling their resources together, working together, and trusting each other to make matters work."* But how to do all that, when he, as their representative, was only making them promises. In fact, he was fully aware that this vast operation of *development* was excluding them completely. He was fully aware that his role was to promote this vast operation of *development* in order to stay in power. He, therefore, had to make them feel guilty to discharge himself from the moral responsibility, at least, of the fate falling upon them. He knew their aspirations. These aspirations were publicly expressed. He constantly told them to seek other means to minimize the effects of the economy being in the hands of Europeans, but he did not tell them that the Europeans had the stranglehold of the administrative and political machinery, and that his opinions, his good will to direct the course of events to better integrate his people - even to direct the social and economic future of the country – did not suffice to overcome that control. He was granted only a few concessions. Nevertheless, he did not stop preaching *"unity and solidarity."* He even asked them *"to have patience to wait and see things develop"* for them. He, therefore, encouraged long-term planning. He certainly had in mind institutional change. To conclude, he insisted that parents must teach their children *"the values of life to avoid falling prey to drugs."* He reassured them that *"his government will do what it takes to eliminate this evil that is destroying the future of our country."*[22] Throughout the year 1987, the population let him know that they were not dupes.

As early as October 1986, the general public learned that the municipality planned to create a housing development at *La Batterie*, Friars' Bay, for the benefit of Saint-Martiners under a program of landownership. Land speculation in connection with the *development* caused the cost of land to multiply exponentially. He wanted to stop people from squatting at Nettle Bay, from filling the Galisbay Lagoon, the Simpsonbay Lagoon in Saint-

James, and the lagoon in Grand-Case. Now, it was only an 80-lot housing development ranging from 400 to 900 square meters. The goal was to limit the devastating effects of a rapid development on the islanders. They needed to get something out of it. The Mayor, therefore, showed some kind of concern for the well-being of his population with this project. The Commune development society, which became since, SEMSAMAR, a semi-private company was entrusted to put in place this housing venture and install the necessary infrastructure: water, roads, electricity, telephone, and a sewage system. The attribution of lots was handled at the Town Hall by selection. For a maximum of 150 applicants registered to participate in this selection, a committee had to assess the attribution requirements. In fact, this housing development was intended for the benefit of the neediest. The Mayor had contacted two government banks based in Guadeloupe to provide financing for the land and the building. The conditions were as follows: 10% of the cost of the house, the land had to be paid to the Commune, and the balance mortgaged over a 15 to 20-year period. Financing was granted up to 80% of the cost of the project. When the selection was made, a 30-day grace period was granted for applicants to come up with the 10% in order to gain title of the land. Building permits would be issued without difficulty. House plans were chosen among four Caribbean-style models available, and the drafting was the responsibility of the owner. Two other projects intended for Saint-Martiners were proposed. One of 250 lots in French Quarter attributed with serious issues concerning the ownership of the land, and a small 30-lot housing development in Sandy Ground which did not materialize. This was the Mayor's contribution to the participation of the population to the progress of Saint-Martin[23].

The applicants were, however, astonished when they confronted another reality: a higher price for the land starting at 90 000 francs; the term of the loan over six years with 12% interest; obligation to complete the construction within five years with penalty; obligation to pay notary's fees of 12,000 francs within 30 days under penalty of not receiving he title-deed! In addition, if the construction was not completed within the five years, the balance of the loan should be paid in full. A press release from the SMECO organization entitled, *Has Mayor Fleming lied to us about housing for Saint-Martiners?* seriously questioned the first magistrate's credibility and concluded, *"We must realize that Mayor Fleming has misled us and failed us once more on a matter that is very important to all Saint-Martiners."*[24]

Saint-Martiners were entrepreneurs in many areas. What they had lost, was their preeminence, and consequently, their importance in their own country. No one was interested in them. It was easier to generalize and stigmatize everyone as lazy and without ambition. Yet, parents continued to sacrifice to send their children to study in Guadeloupe, Martinique, France, the Netherlands, England and the United States, even without any municipal assistance as it was seemingly rather reserved to family and partisans. It was clearly observed that since the beginning of the famous *development* during the 1980s, the local administration did not hire educated Saint-Martiners, except for relatives and partisans. They were making things difficult for educated locals because room was made for the new Europeans. Unskilled therefore underpaid employment, favoritism with regard to Europeans or the Mayor's partisans and family members were standard occurrence in the 1980s. Those who came home after their studies had to go back, and the others did not come. One can easily talk now about a new Saint-Martin Diaspora in a certain number of foreign countries, where they are welcome on account of their professional qualifications, especially in the U.S. Virgin Islands, the United States, Canada, France and England.

We find one of the Mayor's friends, a municipal Councilor, working as a fireman, who saw the necessity to create a private ambulance business. The ambulance service which was operated by the Fire Department of Saint-Martin was congested and could not meet the needs of an unexpectedly increasing population. The first private ambulance company, the Saint-Martin Ambulance Company, was operational on January 18, 1985 after obtaining the ambulance license. This company also serviced the inhabitants of the Dutch side, when they happened to come over to the North, and has established good working relations with its counterpart in the South, as the Marigot Fire Department also did. Its services were, nevertheless, limited to domestic emergencies, and the assistance to vehicle accidents.[25]

It was obvious that two forces opposed each other, one coming from elsewhere, stronger, conquering, destroying, eliminating, and pushing aside everything in its way, and another one, displaying a certain amount of energy, but not enough to resist the destructive effects of the stronger force. We were at that time in this first phase. The Nettle Hill incident in Sandy Ground in April 1987, when the Sub-Prefecture administration ordered the destruction of houses belonging to young Saint-Martiners, gave rise to the indignation of the population who openly expressed their anger in a protest march. In fact, it was the second attempt to move out the inhabitants of this St-Tropez-like part of the island, the first having failed in March 1980. At that time, the first magistrate was Second Deputy Mayor and nurtured the ambition to replace the Mayor. It was then necessary for him to be on the people's side. In 1987, on the contrary, he was compelled to secretly approve the policy of destruction implemented by the Sub-Prefecture. He played for time rather than try to solve the Saint-Martiners' problems.

The Lowlands was another zone which suffered from the assault of the *development*. It was a vacation residential area belonging to rich Americans created in 1963. The residences, in the owners' absence, were secured by Saint-Martiners who took care of maintenance and security. The development specifications stipulated that the area of each parcel must cover a minimum of 2.47 acres with one main one floor-residential structure, and when the topography made it possible, a partial basement intended for service purposes. The main structure had to be constructed at 15 meters minimum from the property limits and 25 meters from the public road. The outhouses, garages and domestics' quarters were tolerated on condition that the previous isolation distances were observed. Any additional floor should be subject to a derogation granted by the Prefect of Guadeloupe.[26]

In February 1987, the extremely threatening insecurity in this zone prompted the gendarmes and the Sint Maarten police to carry out a joint plan of action. In fact, it became dangerous to drive through Lowlands after sunset, since armed highway gangs operated there by robbing tourists on the road at the border. Even though the security guards at the Cupecoy Hotel tracked and chased them, they were not armed. They barely escaped alive with their car riddled with bullets, forcing them to beat a fast retreat. According to reliable sources, the gangs were not only persons from surrounding islands, but most were reportedly French Europeans operating out of the Dutch Lowlands district called *Côte d'Azur*. One of them had already been captured by the Marigot gendarmes and left the island. This Lowlands district had the reputation of a drug haven for bandits. Law enforcement officers from both sides of the island were tight-lipped about their plan of action to neutralize these highway bandits, and about their progress with the criminal cases, in order not to negatively affect a newly emerging economy. They only told the press that arrests were made. One of the measures used was to intensify the patrols in this zone in unidentifiable cars. Insecurity in the Lowlands was a hot topic of discussion during the routine meetings between Lt. Governor Richardson and Sub-Prefect Hubert.[27]

The hardcore criminal gangs who made this Lowlands road a *stick-up* zone operated in two cars on the French as well as the Dutch Lowlands, according to the victims who were also native islanders. They sandwiched the targeted car, then armed and masked, came out of their cars approaching the victim's car at gun-point. They robbed the driver and passengers of their money and valuables. They also burglarized and vandalized the residences which were often the vacation homes of fairly wealthy Americans. During the day, most of the rental cars with registration plate identified by the letter R plus a number were broken into while their occupants were on the beach. However, the most alarming incidents were the increase of rapes on Bay Rouge, one of the most beautiful beaches in that Lowlands area. [28] Within more than a month, the catch was some 18 suspects and accomplices arrested in the Lowlands. The search of the robbers' homes disclosed an extensive cache of weapons, including machine guns, ammunitions, and stolen merchandise, but also cocaine and a precision scale. European businessmen were also involved in this drug trafficking.[29] As a result, a certain number of American victims, who had come to the island to enjoy its quietness, sold their properties and left, leaving room for the new European settlers.

Paradoxically, the Association of the Resident Merchants and Craftsmen of Saint-Martin, ACASM, who came to the island with the recent development of the French side, made a disastrous account of the implementation of the tax exemption law in these early beginnings. It revealed their *"concern at the general deterioration of the economic, social, and cultural climate of the island"* as follows:

> "... Until recently, Saint-Martin was one of the most beautiful Caribbean successes in terms of tourism. But this year, the tourists deserted Saint-Martin. The occupancy rate of the French side hotels, as much as the Dutch side hotels, dropped by 40% compared to last year, according to the figures communicated by various associations. This drop is not felt in the neighboring islands because the hotels are full for the season in Anguilla, Puerto Rico, St. Thomas, Antigua, and Aruba. ... Every tourist guide and every travel consultant say that Saint-Martin is too congested, over-built, not quiet, not relaxing. Saint-Martin is losing its attractive image on account of the real estate frenzy that is overtaking the island, as a result of the tax exemption law program.
>
> ... What are the consequences of the tax exemption law program in Saint-Martin?
>
> A great quantity of apartments is built to be rented out as main residence for their tenants; their number predicts that they will exceed the needs of the well-off people, even though they are increasing steadily. The builders will not be able to keep their promises with regard to the rent. They are creating an artificial market which will only bring a lot of trouble.
>
> ... In Saint-Martin large capital is essentially invested in the hospitality and related sectors. But here again the results are disappointing because many realizations are the result of hazardous legal montage intended to provide fiscal advantages at any cost to metropolitan investors who do not care about the needs of tourism on the island. ... Other buildings will operate as real hotels, but they do not match the international standards and will only offer a low-cost accommodation on account of the poorly manner in which they were conceived and built.
>
> Many other projects consist of the construction of new boutiques, and even commercial centers. We have 6 times more stores than in Nassau, Bahamas, but we only have 500,000 tourists per year when Nassau receives 5 times more.
>
> ... The excessive, inadequate, and anarchic construction boom is destroying both the economy of the island and employment in the long run.

… The labor demand on these building sites generates an influx of metropolitans that are just transiting, together with an uncontrolled immigration from the neighboring islands. …
A short time ago, income tax was not levied in Saint-Martin or in Saint-Barths. … Saint-Martiners themselves are now taxed without moderation, without any transitory measure from a system where hardly anything was taxed to another where everything is taxed.
(…) The charm of this island consisting of its old-time houses, its beautiful and quiet landscapes, the style and culture of a well-balanced and peaceful population, must be preserved."[30]

Incredible but true! This was an extract of an open letter dated May 4, 1988, sent to the President of the Republic, intended only to plead in favor of maintaining the additional law enforcement forces during the high season. Prime Minister Chirac's answer was the following: *"On my request, the Government decided to reinforce the maintenance of public order and devised a plan to upgrade State services in Saint-Martin, which are insufficient represented."* In a letter dated on April 25, 1988 written prior to the open letter, the General Director of National Gendarmerie stated: *"... that concerning the situation referred to, the necessary measures have already been taken. Since the month of August 1986 a detachment of mobile gendarmes from France has helped the local Gendarmerie with this situation and this measure will be maintained as often as possible. It has further been decided recently, despite present budgetary constraints, to send to the island 9 additional non-commissioned officers in reinforcement of the existing deployment, permitting the creation of a squad in French Quarter and a command unit."*[31] Both the business association and the Mayor were pleased and happy.

Incredible but true! Administrative situations were used to solve economic and social problems!

Premonitory Signs of General Deterioration

The intensification of European investment resulted in exacerbating the negative aspects of this prosperity: the Air France Paris/St. Maarten direct flight increases, the growing arrival of dangerous elements, the amplification of drug and arms trafficking and use, the unsatisfactory working conditions and employers' abuse of power, the permanent transformation of illegal immigration into settlement immigration, the visibility of exogenous prostitution, the escalation of insecurity and criminality, the constant sabotage of Saint-Martiners' initiatives and the deterioration of social climate. All these problems were of great concern to the entire island. Yet, it was difficult for non-Saint-Martiners to apprehend them when seeking the proper solutions, because the principle of communicating vessels, one of the characteristics of the Saint-Martin experience, was totally overlooked. In fact, problems do not exist on one side without effects on the other side. Likewise, solutions should not be sought for without consideration of the other side. In this particular case, raising the point of which national side you belong to was a motive of stagnation and exacerbation of the challenges. Human issues on the island of Saint-Martin must be dealt with jointly because it is actually one people and one island. In the February 1989 *Letter of the Regional Councilor*, as a potential candidate for the upcoming municipal elections, the Regional Councilor admitted Saint-Martiners' minority status and the new social climate no longer reflective of the islanders' traditional friendliness, without taking responsibility for this situation, although he was the currently First Deputy Mayor. He rejected the entire responsibility of this policy on the Mayor:

> "Between October 1988 when the census revealed the count of 24,869 inhabitants and today, it is most likely that 500 additional persons have freely come to establish their residence in our collectivity.
> If we do not immediately change our attitude, it is likely, and even certain, that we will be a smaller minority for the 1995 municipal elections, and we will lose our most precious possession, that is our Identity."[32]

In the first article of this *Letter,* he continued as follows:

> "Saint-Martin has always been a haven of peace and tolerance, where the most elementary form of racism had no grip. One of us once said jokingly that Saint-Martiners are *of pure stock but in the plural* ... It is just normal that, with this open and friendly frame of mind, Saint-Martiners never demonstrated any form of hostility towards people coming from abroad. (...) Yet, signs of xenophobia, not to say racism, have been visible for the last two to three years. The massive and rapid influx of communities, as different as they could be one from the other, is surely the reason for that change. But we also think that nothing was done to acquaint the newcomers with our customs and traditions, and therefore to promote their harmonious integration. The various communities now present in Saint-Martin must find some balance in participating and not dominating each other."

Unfortunately, this *"domination"* has prevailed so far and generated the chaotic evolution witnessed on our *Sweet Saint-Martin Land.*

The year 1989 was decisive for the municipal team, whose popularity was measured by the overwhelming victory over two adversaries. The former first Deputy Mayor, who advocated an institutional change, a project of the municipality did not find favor with the voters of the majority. The former Mayor, the physician, who tried to rehabilitate himself in the eyes of his electorate after struggling with national authorities and the justice system for over ten years, focused his platform on the increasing insecurity crippling the tourism industry of the island. The outgoing Mayor blamed his former first Deputy Mayor for personalizing the status project. One could easily perceive an underlying rivalry between two European clans who chose their separate candidate within the majority party. One could detect that the change of status wanted by Europeans and supported by the municipality was pushed in the background, when it was necessary to emphasize the positive aspects of this *economic revolution*, and reappeared, when the negative aspects prevailed. Moreover, it was noted that the change of status wanted by Saint-Martiners did not have the same contents as the one advocated by Europeans. There was a sharp difference between administrative and economic status on one hand, and fiscal and social status on the other hand. In prosperous times, it was better not to rock the boat. Therefore, the Mayor distanced himself from the status that his former First Deputy Mayor proposed.

The Europeans' satisfaction was tangible after the outgoing Mayor's reelection in one round. They knew that their votes weighed heavily in that reelection. Their objective was reached. Their preeminence was established. A decisive step was made. In addition, having somewhat gotten rid of his too ambitious former first Deputy, the Mayor felt more at ease with his new first Deputy with whom he shared common affinities: he was a young man whose ascension he had contributed to when he was in business. This second term of office was characterized by the Mayor's desire to bring together partisans and political adversaries. He strengthened his base, and reinforced the Municipal Council with municipal commissions, where civilians and elected representatives met. The contagious euphoria of victory generated a more peaceful climate which resulted in the popular demonstrations of October 1990 against the introduction of customs in Saint-Martin, organized by the Mayor and the municipal team. The Mayor opposed this imposition by the Paris government and got the unconditional support of the population. This imposition was perceived as an assault on the historical rights of free port enjoyed by the island of Saint-Martin since October 1848 and by the island of Saint-Barthelemy since December 1879, both by virtue of a gubernatorial decree. But after the showdown with the Director of Customs based in Guadeloupe, when he addressed the population in Saint-Martin, limiting the customs control to illicit trafficking, as well as the visit of a Paris minister, the Paris decision prevailed. The Mayor distanced himself from his population. Was he called to order by the Paris authorities? In any case, it was rumored that he did. Thereafter, national and Guadeloupe press published displeasing accounts on the Mayor of Saint-Martin.

Measures in favor of Europeans quickly materialized with the extension of the urban zone of Marigot to include Sandy Ground which became a constructible zone by virtue of a decision of the Municipal Council voted unanimously in July 1989. We can remember that in this same area, exactly at Nettle Hill in April 1987, two years before, the Sub-Prefecture ordered the demolition of houses belonging to young Saint-Martiners because they allegedly violated zoning regulations, which was never brought to their knowledge. They addressed their grievances to the Mayor in order for him to find a solution to help them, but his response was mere promises. Since, a wealthy Frenchman acquired land in Sandy Ground, and as soon as he was reelected, the Mayor undertook to change the zoning provisions of Sandy Ground. Later on, the *St. Martin's Week* noticed changes in the Lowlands specifications in an article published in 1991.[34] The concerned architect afterwards refuted those *"breaches to the specifications"* by indicating that the building permit for the two floor house, referred to by the newspaper, dated back to August 18, 1989, when it was *"signed by Mayor Albert Fleming and granted without any reservation."* Furthermore, he confessed, *"having considered the development regulations obsolete and rigid"* and he thought that *"they had to be more flexible, especially considering the great freedom enjoyed by our neighbors on the Dutch side in this field."*[35]

The year 1989 stood out as a year of great discontent among the entire population of the island about decisions taken by the political leaders to meet the demands of a development, which, they were now convinced, fell short of their expectations. The commemoration of the bicentenary of the French Revolution, symbolized by a gallows erected on the *Bayside* in Marigot, was a shock to most Saint-Martiners. On the other hand, the local press on the Dutch side also echoed the protests of the Simpsonbay inhabitants against the filling of the lagoon banks, which they have managed to stop. The inhabitants of the entire island could no longer bear to see their island gradually destroyed as new structures were rising out of the ground. The July 1987 Single European Act of Twelve, which was coming into effect on January 1, 1993, weighed heavily on the people's minds on the eve of the June 18, 1989 European elections, on account of the continuous invasion of European workers on the island, the deployment of military forces, the free circulation of hard drugs and weapons in such strategic points as L'Anse Marcel, Port la Royale, Oyster Pond, the gradual disappearance of upscale tourism for the benefit of a vacationing tourism coming from Europe, the revolting exploitation of Caribbean workers, land speculation and the fraudulent use of public funds. Above all, the European threat was real for Saint-Martiners who had become second-class citizens in their own island in a span of eight years. Already, most Saint-Martiners were in favor of an association with Europe just like their neighbors in the South. They expressed that desire with the force of their ballots on September 20, 1992 representing 80% of the votes cast against the Maastricht Treaty, with the support of their elected representatives.

If the political climate improved, following the outgoing Mayor's overwhelming victory, the social climate continued to deteriorate. Economic progress, the persistent European and illegal demographic explosion, the real estate explosion, the rapid increase of hotels on this tiny 54 square kilometer-half island, very rapidly showed signs of a chronic social and security breakdown. The publication of a beautifully colored large format booklet distributed during the 1989 political campaign, not only revealed all the innovations realized during the Mayor's first term of office, but also disclosed the new projects of this real estate expansion, despite the visible decline of tourism activity. Already, during the electoral campaign in February 1989, the first signs of this expansion were reflected in the filling of the southern part of the Galisbay Lagoon. This vast 48,000 square meter basin collecting the rain waters from the surrounding hills spreading out in a semi-circle was linked to the sea in its southeastern part. The owners around the lagoon, in a state of stupefaction at hearing the noise of the dump trucks pouring their loads of tuft into the water, formed a Defense Committee of the Galisbay Lagoon with concerned inhabitants of *Hameau du Pont* and Agrement in order to communicate their deep concerns to the Mayor. It took several meetings to alert the local authorities about the damages that were already affecting their properties on the western part of the lagoon: a swampy mud was pushed on their properties from the filling.

The filling of the natural mouth of the lagoon to the sea, bordering the northern part of the Grand Saint-Martin Hotel, represented a real danger of flooding for the neighboring owners. The committee, in several press releases, communicated their opposition to the destruction of their environment. After completing the first phase of the filling project covering an area of 15,000 square meters, the filling was resumed in 1996 after the devastating passing of Hurricane Luis in September 1995. At that time, the inhabited zones in the east, on a lower level than the filled part, collected the waters which normally would have flown into the lagoon. For this second phase of the filling, they pumped the sand from the nearby sea-bottom, which was a fatal blow to the beach, as all the sand was drawn down to the sea-bottom. This second phase covering 20 000 square meters and the third phase the remaining 13,000 square meters rang the knell of the Galisbay Lagoon [See photograph on book cover]. Finally, a public inquiry was carried out from June 26 to July 26, 2000, eleven years later, in order to declare the public benefit of a future road passing over the filled lagoon, intended to service the nearby future marina, Fort Louis, in the making. Throughout this lengthy period, the committee had alerted the public, the political, administrative, environmental authorities, on the local, departmental, or national levels, about the consequences of this ecological disaster, by means of graphic press releases and correspondence, but to no avail. Summary proceedings were instituted before the County Court of Basse-Terre, the administrative capital, but the claim was given no consideration. Despite the violations to applicable laws in matter of lake, pond and lagoon protection,[37] might was right: the lagoon disappeared replaced by a narrow channel taking the waters to the sea under a bridge to be built. Actually, as the State owned no land reserve on the island, it was a project of the Sub-Prefecture, executed by the Commune, as announced in an interview of the Sub-Prefect with the *St. Martin's Week* in 1988:

> "Mr. Seners, however, mentioned a project in the making with the Commune that will consist in filling the Galisbay pond [State maritime Domain] in order to create 3 distinct zones: 1) an inner harbor zone reserved for craftsmen with the development of small and medium-sized enterprises and warehouse activities; 2) an administrative zone (Post Office, Gendarmerie, …; 3) a social housing zone where the S.I.G. [a State-subsidized housing company] will build individual small houses with garden to be rented at about 1,500 francs monthly."[38]

This did not really materialize as planned.

ADICASM, the Association of Saint-Martin Merchants and Craftsmen, created in September 1988, held several meetings with the Mayor and the Sub-Prefect to explain the difficulties they were facing in their sector. Their survival was threatened by the uncontrolled proliferation of European businesses and multinationals. The unfair competition of a second wave of Indian and Chinese businesses gave rise to some concerns among the local merchants. A new supermarket in the center of Marigot built without any parking facility created total discouragement for the 17 local businesses in Marigot.[39] ADICASM deplored the insensitiveness of the Commune authority for small local businesses which represented the driving force of the economy, because their profits, unlike the outside investors, stayed locally and refueled local employment. A letter dated July 5, 1989 sent to the new Sub-Prefect Seners, was a follow-up to the promises made previously by the public authorities to have the regulations in matter of illegal employment enforced. It did not produce the expected effects, in spite of the aggravating circumstances of local business.

The opening of the *House of St. Martin* in Paris, an initiative of *"private enterprises around the real estate engine of Port de Plaisance"* presented itself as a center of great promotion for both sides of the island. *"A split with the Tourism Office of Guadeloupe"* was then contemplated. At the same time, both political leaders of Saint-Martin and Sint-Maarten persuaded *"the Mayor of Paris, Jacques Chirac, to hasten the administrative procedures leading to the presence of French immigration officers at Juliana Airport."* Meanwhile, from May 3 to May 10, 1989, 25 journalists from France visited Saint-Martin on an observation trip. The announcement of the golf project for Port de Plaisance in Cole Bay, spreading around the symbolic border between both sides, challenged the inhabitants of the entire island and hit the headlines of the local press on the French and Dutch sides. A vast movement took shape and a silent protest march was organized against this project for the November 11, 1989 celebration of St. Martin's Day. This project consisted in the displacement of the National Road in Bellevue and the Union Road in Cole Bay, as well as the historical frontier monument at the foot of the central chain of hills to make room for the Port de Plaisance Golf Course. It would also entail the removal of the none the less historical rock walls. The Committee to Save the Frontier Road from the French side joined with the *We for We* Foundation of the Dutch side to organize the logistics of the *March on the Frontier*.

Under the pressure of the population and the local press of the Dutch side, the investors as well as the owners and directors of Port de Plaisance accused the political leaders in a press release of not taking their responsibility towards the population, and making them believe that they had informed the public of the project. Both political leaders, Albert Fleming and Claude Wathey, after denying the existence of this project, and following the publication in the *Newsday* of the project plan, had no other choice than to withdraw from the public's eyes. [41] On that Saturday November 11, 1989, demonstrators from the north with placards and banners bearing such inscriptions as *"Save St. Martin"*, *"No to the destruction of the road"*, and chanting patriotic slogans, marched to the Frontier Monument. There, at around 9 o'clock they were met by demonstrators from the South marching on one side of the Union Road. At the Monument, the organizers addressed the crowd. The official ceremony for St. Martin's Day with laying of wreaths at the monument did not take place as usual, and had been transferred to the other frontier monument recently built in French Quarter, far from the presence of the demonstrators. [42] Two months earlier, an open letter to the President of the French Republic published in *Newsday* of September 13, 1989 authored by one of the three opposition Municipal Councilors, expressed the native people's distress at the figures of the intermediary 1986 and 1988 census counts revealing that the population had tripled in six years. The Municipal Councilor saw looming the threat of *"re-colonization"*, of *"a wipe out by substitution"* where *"democracy would have no meaning"* if nothing was done to control this invasion.

IV

DEMOGRAPHIC EXCESS

The environmental project making Marigot *"the prettiest capital in Sint-Maarten/Saint-Martin"* continued in high gear during the decade of the nineties, in accordance with the Mayor's plan widely publicized in a brochure distributed at the 1989 municipal election campaign. The development of the Marigot *Bayside* with a name change to *Waterfront* and the sea-filling of the Marigot Bay were completed. The transformation of the shoreline made room for the construction of a covered market in replacement of the picturesque open-air market between the two several-century-old sandbox trees (which were destroyed), for modern shelters for fishermen, souvenirs and handicraft vendors, restaurants, public restrooms, a recreational area for young people and sunset strollers, reserved parking areas for taxis and tourist buses, and a pier accommodating passengers commuting on the Anguilla and Saint-Barths boats. This new development confirmed Saint-Martin as a tourism-oriented island. In addition, between the market and the future beach along the cemetery there would be public gardens with lawns and walkways, a circular pond for model sailboats, a giant chess board, games for children, and a giant aquarium, all of which have not materialized.[1]

The inhabitants on both sides of the island felt more and more excluded from this rapid growth. They vividly perceived the threat of the upcoming 1992 integration of Europe, as it would impact the entire island, even though only the French side was an integral part of Europe. At the beginning of the year 1990, the association SMECO organized a two day forum at the Cultural Center in Sandy Ground, attended by many Saint-Martiners from both sides of the island. The effect of voting rights granted to citizens of the European Union in municipal elections, and essentially the direct consequences in matter of economic opportunities for Saint-Martiners, were considered, among others, as serious dangers for Saint-Martin. It was already obvious that the islanders could not compete either with French Europeans or citizens from other member countries of the Union, especially as the local administration favored their establishment on the island. The continuous European influx and massive illegal laborers, had devastating effects on local employment, and the hope for an improved situation for the islanders was shattered. In the manner of the opposition municipal councilor who had expressed his concerns in an open letter to the President of the French Republic, SMECO inferred that *"genocide by substitution"* was in the making in Saint-Martin.[2]

Blockade on January 15, 1990

The atmosphere was tense on the island. The St. Maarten Business Association, SMBA, and the heavy equipment owners and operators, sporting yellow T-shirts with the inscription *No More* decided to express their anger publicly on Monday, January 15, 1990. They parked some twenty pieces of heavy construction equipment, with their engines droning, - flatbed trailers, 930 and 966D caterpillars, cement mixers, dump trucks – in front of the Government Administration Building in Philipsburg at about 5:30 a.m., waiting for the arrival at work of government authorities. Then, at about one o'clock in the afternoon, they blocked the Simpsonbay Bridge on the Airport Boulevard with heavy equipment. It was removed by 5:30 p.m. under police escort. The ongoing development on the Dutch side did not cause any public unrest until Bobo York, a taxi driver, disclosed the presence of imported equipment on the three new building sites, belonging to the Italian company in charge of the execution and financing of the projects. They were deeply concerned by the fact that no public bidding was organized. The current projects, namely the Philipsburg Harbor expansion, the construction of the new Hospital, and the Juliana International Airport expansion served as catalysts for the anger of the protesters. Actually, by November 1989, the Executive Council had made promises to the SMBA and the local heavy equipment owners as to their participation in these projects. However, so far they had not received answers from the Airport Board to their requests for information about the opening of the public bidding, and the removal of the Italian heavy equipment from the island.

These actions, together with widely distributed *No More* and *Charity begins at home* protest flyers, received the support of several members of the opposition party[4] wearing the yellow T-shirts of the *We for We* foundation, of the taxi and bus driver organizations, of the Workers' Unions, as well as the heavy equipment owners from the French side. The traditional solidarity was on the agenda once more. Just as the Union Road symbolized the unity and fraternity of the inhabitants of St. Maarten/St. Martin up to this day, a fair solution, without bidding, put an end to this major conflict, to the satisfaction of the organizers. The Union Road was the road leading from the historic Monument to both capitals and, in the words of the St. Martin poet Lasana Sekou, it represented *"the spine and the navel"* of the island. This demonstration of solidarity and strong unity boosted the organizers of a Conference on National Symbols on August 31, 1990 sponsored by ICONS, an ad hoc Information Committee on National Symbols. ICONS also worked on a proposed flag to represent the traditional unity of the Saint-Martin people.[5] The Unity flag was present among the four other flags of the island of Saint-Martin at the ceremonious celebration of three anniversaries on the Concord Mount on March 23, 1998 namely, the 350 years of the 1648 Treaty of Concordia, the 150 years of the 1848 Decree of Abolition of Slavery, and the 50 years of the 1948 Frontier Monument.

The 1990 Census

The greatest concern on the French side centered on the new population figures, on the number of foreigners who, at that time, saturated the only public clinic providing free pre- and post-natal care and child vaccinations, on the *gypsy* taxis and buses, on the increasing number of school drop-outs, on the Paris government's decision to introduce customs on the island without prior consultation of the elected representatives. The 1990 census projected a disconcerting and frightening reality for some, and a comforting and encouraging hope for others. Some experienced the continuation of the social difficulties that the recent population explosion generated as a compressive, stifling limitation, and others sensed the prospect of an evolution that would offer them new opportunities. Still others felt mixed feelings since their responsibility was publicly engaged in this state of affairs. Nevertheless, no one was prepared to give up, and both groups separately, sometimes together, vigorously voiced their diverging goals. Following the census findings for the entire department of Guadeloupe, Saint-Martin emerged as the second Commune of Guadeloupe after Abymes with regard to the number of inhabitants, and as the Commune with the highest increase percentage of 350% since the previous general census in 1982. This demographic explosion was extremely pleasing to the elected representatives who anticipated a proportionate increase of the operating funds allocated on the Commune's budget, as well as more finances allocated by Guadeloupe's general and regional councils to meet the island's needs in matter of additional constructions of middle and high schools, of a hospital, and of public clinics. However, with the subsequent creation of a second *canton* [political division], these additional funds would hardly be sufficient to solve the latent social problems arising from this runaway population increase. The population count was 8,072 in 1982. It was estimated at 12,000 in 1986, then it increased to 24,000 two years later, following the implementation of the 1986 tax exemption law, at the 1988 official intermediate evaluation. It reached an alarming peak of 28,524 at the 1990 general census. This count naturally excluded the illegal population evaluated at about 10,000 for the entire island.

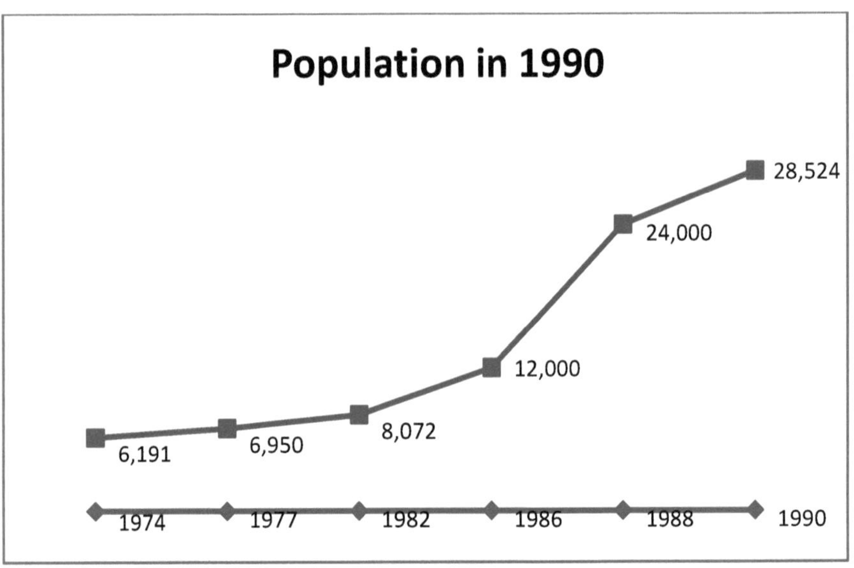

The Union of Transportation Contractors and the Taxi and Bus Association were the first to publicly denounce the illegal practices in transportation, following a similar action undertaken on the Dutch side. Public transportation was the activity in which both sides were most involved. The two respective presidents, Raymond Helligar and Monique Emmanuel, invited their members to participate in a protest rally starting at the *Belle Creole* Hotel, situated in the northern limit of the Lowlands. It headed slowly through Marigot towards the Gendarmerie. The purpose of the rally was to identify the illegal buses and to urge the Commune and national authorities to solve the problem. At this early stage, the owners were Saint-Martiners and the drivers Haitians. The first bus identified was parked in Saint-James doing transportation for hotel employees, but also tourists and people picked up on the road, as the driver explained. This bus was not registered at the Chamber of Commerce, and had no authorization from the Commune to engage in public transportation. Next, a non-registered vehicle was spotted in front of Marigot ball-park, while a *Gendarmes'* van passed by. The van stopped, the gendarmes did their job, and the union representatives explained the driver what he had to do to legalize his job and his bus. Finally, the union delegation went to the *Gendarmerie* and handed the authorities a list of all the identified illegal buses on the French side. In a cooperating manner, the *gendarmes* promised they would take action to solve the problem. To this day it has not been solved. The bus owners considered that they were victims of unfair competition because being legally registered they have to bear all the charges of the profession: special insurance, technical inspection of their vehicle, medical examination twice a year, and purchase of special equipment for their vehicles. Their desire to see only registered buses and taxis on the roads was never fulfilled.

Introduction of Customs

This exogenous development affected the very fabric of the Saint-Martin society, generating a distressful atmosphere which was reflected in the Mayor's speech during the festivities of Bastille Day on July 14, 1990. The Mayor had just voiced his disagreement with the imposition of customs on his Commune, effective immediately on the first of August 1990, *"without any previous consultation"*. In his opinion, such an important issue – the island's historic situation as a free port – should be treated by the Paris government with more consideration of the representatives of the people, especially as this decision could negatively impact the island's already fragile tourism economy. The following was reported in the French side paper, the *St. Martin's Week*:

> "The news came as a thunderbolt: Customs is coming to St. Martin! Many thought it was another joke intended to inflame the many rumors that excited (or more often pestered) daily life in Saint-Martin. Yet this one was everything but a joke and it can be fairly said that it raised hell as if it were a declaration of war."[6]

The following week, an extraordinary meeting of the Municipal Council was held before a full house. A ten-point motion was presented to the Municipal Council reaffirming, among other things, *"its complete support for the fight against drugs, especially with the reinforcement of the Gendarme squad, the Immigration Force, and a branch of the Judicial Police"*, and requesting *"the postponement at a later date of the Customs services on the territory of the Commune of Saint-Martin."* The motion was voted unanimously. Nevertheless, by September 6, 1990, the General Director of Customs, together with the Prefect, came from Guadeloupe to explain to the population the exclusive mission assigned to Customs in Saint-Martin. Actually, it would focus only on the fight against illegal immigration, drug traffickers, and money-laundering from drugs. For that purpose, the gendarme forces would be increased by 7 auxiliary gendarmes, a squad would be based in the Lowlands and a branch of the Regional Judicial Police would be created. It was clear that the General Director of Customs did not intend to give in to the pressure of the municipality or the wishes of the population. Meanwhile, strongly disagreeing with the manner in which the Paris government imposed Customs on Saint-Martin, the Mayor openly supported a vast protest march held in October 1990 to say *No to Customs*. Two years later, in August 1992, Minister Michel Charasse travelled to Saint-Martin from Paris to check with the new Customs officers on the activities of the service and on the patrol boat put at their disposal. Everything went smoothly as to his relations with the Mayor, because never again did the latter lead a public demonstration.

In a pro-active manner, immediately after the October protest march, the Mayor convened association leaders and active civilians to a meeting to form a workgroup whose mission was to draft a report on the best change of status adapted to the situation of Saint-Martin. The *Saint-Martin People's Consensus* was born, an eleven member committee that lost two of its appointed members at the very first meeting. Saint-Martiners were truly seeking a new status to preserve all their historic specificities, in particular, the free movement between the two sides of the island, the cultural identity of and the integrity of the Saint-Martin people. However, the European merchants sought a fiscal and social status to preserve their economic interests on the island. This fiscal and social status was drafted informally at the same time as the *Consensus* work and was presented to the president of the Region of Guadeloupe as their main agenda, at a later date.

Situation in the Schools in 1990

During the 1989-1990 school year, in the only Middle School of Saint-Martin, there were 530 students in the academic classes: 200 in the 6th grade, 187 in the 7th grade, a total of 387, 75 in the 8th grade and 68 in the 9th grade, a total of 143 students. About one third of the 68 students in the 9th grade were Saint-Martiners, among whom only 4 were eligible to the 10th grade, and had to continue their studies abroad. The others were transferred locally to the Vocational School. The school situation in Saint-Martin was, therefore, alarming: in July 1990 there were only four girls to continue to High School level abroad, what happened to the boys? This number of students continuing to High School was too small to ever cherish the hope that the educational system locally worked for the betterment of the future generations. How many among these four girls would choose to become teachers, for example, considering how difficult it was then for our students at the completion of their college studies to find an employment on their return to their native island. Whereas, it was easier for a European living on a boat in the Marigot Bay to obtain a teaching post at the Marigot Middle or Vocational Schools.

The educational setback was foreseeable, considering the assault directed at the advancement of Saint-Martiners since the year 1978. The previous pages attest to the relentless efforts exerted a few years ago to kill all local initiative in the bud. Reference can be made of two sentences in a young Saint-Martin graduate's article published in 1979, on his return from studying abroad, on page 78: *"They are all, one after the other, being bullied or trampled by those who are planning to make Saint-Martin their Paradise";* then at the end: *"We are defeated before we ever waged the battle."* The possibility of educating oneself locally under favorable conditions became a mountain difficult to climb to the top. The circumstances leading to the suppression of the first high school classes and the private commercial school, when all the students were Saint-Martiners, were a perfect illustration of such obstruction.

Fortunately, from 1975 many parents chose to take their children out of this school system. These children attended school elsewhere, in the South, at the Methodist Agogic Centre, at the secondary schools of Milton Peters College where Dutch was the language of instruction, the St. Maarten Academy preparing the Caribbean GCE or CXC, as well as in Guadeloupe, Martinique and France. The progress or continued *'development'* in the North was undoubtedly taken place in parallel with a growing school failure. Before, in the 50s, 60s, and beginning of the 70s a greater number of students were successful, at a time when French was hardly heard outside the classroom. There were no French television and no French newspapers. Why was it that an increased use of the French language in the latter part of the 80s did not enable Saint-Martiners to improve their usage of French and motivate them in their studies? Was it due to the climate of oppression and rejection they suffered then? Saint-Martiners, however, are known for their ability to pick up languages easily and to adjust to various multicultural and multilingual societies. They had proven it throughout the twentieth century, when they migrated in successive waves all over the region. Those who returned from the Dominican Republic in the 30s and 40s spoke three languages currently: English, Spanish, and French. Those who returned from the Netherlands Antilles as early as the 50s spoke English, Papiamento, and Dutch. Did the events marking the recent development in Saint-Martin and the accompanying circumstances reducing the local people to a minority in their own country hinder the natural sense of adaptation and openness of the islanders to others? The Principal of the Vocational School stated the following in an article published in the *St. Martin's Week*:

> "If all the measures taken lately were taken ten years earlier, the growth of Saint-Martin would not have encountered the problems that we are facing

> today. The use of English as the mother tongue, a better educational supervision, better institutions, would have yielded better results. Years of school failure cannot be erased by waiving a magic wand."[7]

The school drop-outs in Saint-Martin was not due to any flaw in the learning ability of the young population, but ten years earlier, in 1980, the authorities' sole objective was to eliminate those who were the most engaged in taking initiatives. During those ten intervening years, in matter of education, the objective had not changed. It was, therefore, not surprising that *"school failure"* was the theme of the second forum organized on August 2, 1991 by ASMIS, the Saint-Martin Student Association in the French Antilles and France created in Paris in 1985. This *"association that is working hard to ensure a better future for Saint-Martin students"* attracted a numerous attendance of parents for the most part. The speakers were all experienced teachers with a maximum of thirty years' service. For example, Frantz Gumbs, the assistant principal of the Vocational School and a Maths teacher, before tackling the measures proposed to solve the school failure, identified the problem as follows:

> "School failure is generally the inability for the learner to reach the goals set by the institution, by society or by oneself. Therefore, the 5th grade student who does not go over to the 6th grade is facing failure; a student in the 12th grade who failed his final exam is also facing failure. However, failure can be temporary or permanent. The causes are multiple, and can be identified in two main categories, either the educational system is not beneficial to the individual, or the individual is not adapted to the system."

Then, he added that schooling 3-year olds and even 2-year olds was not sufficient to avoid failure, other factors were equally important:

> "The educational system must function properly; teachers should be of quality, school equipment adequate, and it is necessary that the community supports its school. (…) [Yet] (…) lately, the schools [in Saint-Martin] has functioned with a high number of inexperienced young teachers, without specific training, without motivation, whose only desire when landing on Juliana Airport is to return to Guadeloupe. (…) The entire class of graduates from the Teachers' Training School should not be sent to Saint-Martin every year. (…) The school staff should be stable, and for that purpose Saint-Martiners should be recruited."[8]

All these beautiful ideas have gone unheeded, because *progress* had to continue in spite of the school failure of Saint-Martiners, of their uselessness on the job market since foreign workers cost much less and were at the bosses' beck and call. On account of their illegal status, foreign workers could not report their grievances to the Labor Inspector - if he was still on duty. The minority that did not accept to be exploited, as a result, became the outcasts of society. And as they were the natives, who cared? *"They were backward, illiterate, could not speak French. They need to go back to Africa!"* Shocking, isn't it? Not at all. This viewpoint was also heard in Saint-Martin. Meanwhile, the revelation of the disproportionate figures of foreigners finally became a serious concern for the Commune, the Department of Guadeloupe, and for national administrations. Illegal labor and an economy entirely dependent on it were placed at the forefront of the State's actions in Saint-Martin.

Foreigners in Saint-Martin

Depending on which side - French or Dutch -, the circumstances determining the presence of foreigners were not necessarily similar. They correlated as much with the economic demands of each side as with the legislations enforced and practices used locally. Concurrently, the mobility of the illegal population hardly permitted an approximate evaluation of a separate clandestinity on either side, even though the demographic services on the island would produce distinct statistics. Taking into consideration the nature of this clandestinity and the unique characteristic of the island of Saint-Martin, statistics relative to clandestinity could not be limited to one side. As it was in transportation, interconnection was truly a reality in this field. Therefore, these statistics based on assumptions are questionable. The figures in the table below are those of the French side.

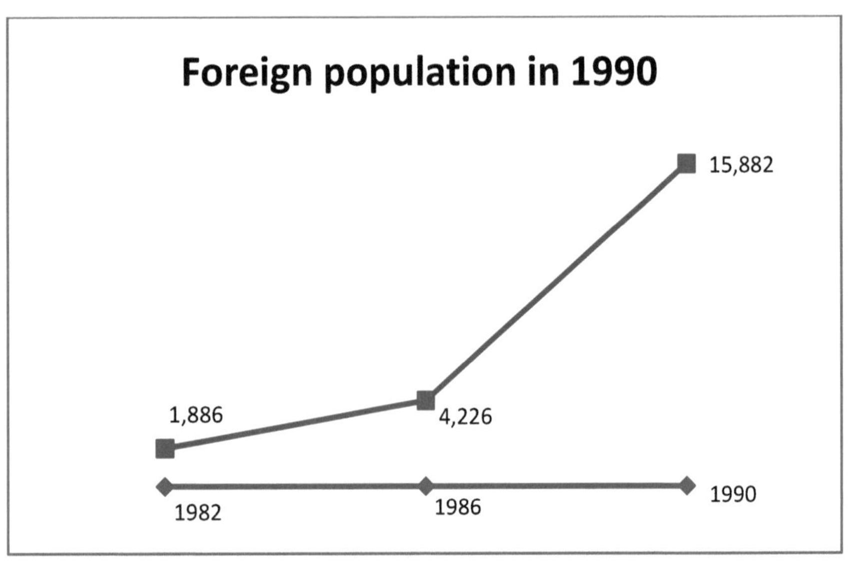

The above figures published by the National Institute of Statistics, INSEE, very sharply revealed the demographic excesses in the wake of the unbridled development beginning in 1986. They indicated how the outrageous labor immigration was transformed into settlement immigration, equaled nowhere else on the planet, not even in French Guiana. Yet, when foreigners formed 55% of the Saint-Martin population, national authorities often ignored the extent of the phenomenon, only speaking about French Guiana and Mayotte in the Indian Ocean. Saint-Martin evaporated in the global figures of Guadeloupe. The findings of a mission inquiry carried out in October 1991 indicated that the Prefecture of Basse-Terre revealed that the foreigners residing in Saint-Martin *"were less than 2,100 documented by December 31, 1990 and that 1,276 others were being processed (...). At the same date the rates for foreigners were established at 3% in Guadeloupe and less than 1% in Martinique...,"*[9] compared to 55% in Saint-Martin.

Those figures confirmed the public statements made by the Director of the National Employment Branch in Saint-Martin during meetings of associations and administrations organized by the municipality, that the restaurants in Saint-Martin recorded zero employee. All sectors of activity were involved in illegal employment: public works and construction, hospitality, restaurants, business, transportation, and household jobs, whether large companies or individuals such as executives, civil servants and merchants. Only 400 jobs were declared from 1985 to 1991, of which 100 in public works and construction, which made the author of this study state:

"From the small task to the hiring of undocumented foreigners, from bargaining wages to sub-contracting illegal laborers (even by European companies), false craftsmen and unregistered workers, nothing is left out of the series of violations of labor laws observed in Saint-Martin. From the most traditional to the most sophisticated, the island offers a wide range of illegal forms of economic activities and employment."[10]

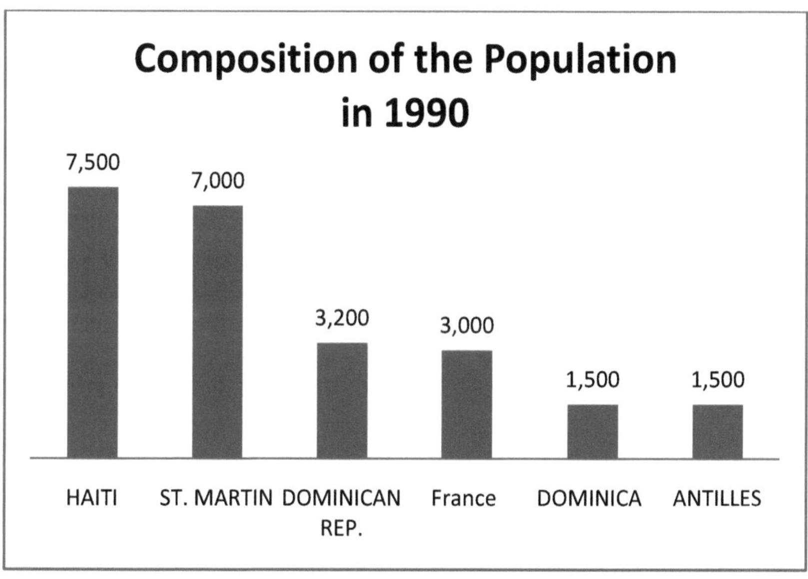

Structural Difficulties

On account of the fulgurous popularity of Saint-Martin, the island was the subject-matter of many articles in the national press and special reports in the Guadeloupe press. Nice things were said like, *"In the eyes of everybody, Saint-Martin represents an oasis of prosperity: high standard of living, no unemployment, no minimum revenue of insertion R.M.I."*. This was, however, partly true since the minimum revenue of insertion and unemployment benefits were granted shortly after. Less nice things were also said, such as, *"A metropolitan lady living for years on the island confirms to me that it is impossible to associate with most of those metropolitans. They want to impose everything, to control everything without any respect for the natives and for their way of life."* The Gulf War kept American tourists from travelling out of their country, thereby causing a drop in the occupancy rates of the hotel industry, 35% in 1990 and 30% in 1991. The Public Prosecutor of Basse-Terre who came to Saint-Martin twice a month considered the island as *"the paradise of good bargaining and drug traffickers", "the little far-west made in the Caribbean.* This notorious reputation disquieted the president of the hotel association who lamented, *"It's not enough to build hotels. When hotels are built, rooms need to be filled, and what if there are too many hotels?* A young schoolmaster from Guadeloupe, living on the island for several years in contact with the children, also gave his opinion, "*With the tax exemption law a lot of Europeans fell on us like grasshoppers, and with them came drugs, prostitution, and delinquency. Before, it was one island. Now, you can clearly see two parts. This island was a paradise and in six years, it changed completely."*[11]

Structures were bursting. At the Grand-Case Airport another building was added to the existing terminal and a longer runway was built. The total cost amounted to 1,3 million francs divided between the Commune and the General Council of Guadeloupe. A shed for the fire-truck was also in the planning. The condition of the road network leading from French Quarter through Oyster Pond down to the eastern border with the Dutch side was in deplorable condition. In the West, the only used water-processing station at Plum Bay in the Lowlands was built in 1974 and received the sewage drain recently put in service from Agrement, *Hameau-du-Pont*, Concordia, all of Marigot, Sandy Ground, Nettle Bay. The station was saturated for the last two years and a pipe system in very bad condition ran through the Lowlands. Untreated water overflowed into the sea at Long Bay. This resulted in a complete sanitary and ecological disaster. The eight-generator electric plant that consumed ten tons of gasoil a day each, had two broken down generators. This caused frequent power outages at the slightest incident, because one generator had to be switched off in order to repair the incident. This plant produced 14 megawatts and 36 were needed for it to function efficiently. A new plant was planned for 1995[12]. Altogether, the infrastructures were in bad shape, and the price of water skyrocketed to 81 francs per cubic meter for the hospitality industry.

Primary Healthcare Project

The hospital and the public care clinic overflowed with patients. The Healthcare Project for Saint-Martin was in preparation and the island became a separate district within the Healthcare Services of Guadeloupe. This autonomy enabled Saint-Martin to take care of its specific health problems mainly in connection with foreign immigration. They consisted in a high rate of peri-natal mortality, the reappearance of special cases of tuberculosis observed in children, as well as cases of tetanus and measles in infants. The objective was, therefore, to improve the vaccination coverage and to organize sessions of sanitary education and self-responsibility with regard to primary healthcare. The hospital of Saint-Martin with a capacity of 52 beds, of which 9 in the maternity ward, and a number of births which more than doubled in six years (1984-1990) from 384 to 860, was in dire straits on account of its cash flow difficulties, because the State was lagging by two years in the payment of operating funds. Without financial resources, the objectives of the Healthcare Project seemed compromised. According to figures released by the Marigot hospital, 16,000 Haitians were undocumented and 80% of the births from 1985 to 1990 originated from foreign mothers. The fear of police controls and their personal financial constraints forced most of them to leave the hospital one or two days after delivery. The babies, consequently, lived in sanitary conditions risky for their health.[13]

The problems arising from illegal immigration in the hospital and the public care clinic were in total contrast with the flashy prosperity displayed in the written press of Guadeloupe, and they greatly affected the normal evolution of the entire society. At the meeting organized for the presentation of the Saint-Martin Primary Healthcare Project, the focus was on immigration and the financial burden it represented for the collectivity:

> "Immigration is the core issue crippling the island. (...) On one hand, these immigrants are a financial burden to society in general and to the hospital in particular, as healthcare institutions were obligated to provide public service to everyone, even to undocumented foreigners without money. But on the other hand, these immigrants enrich both the unscrupulous landlords providing them with unsanitary housing and the bosses who underpay them or do not pay them at all. In addition, they have no healthcare coverage and they represent a force of illegal labor, which has reached the highest proportions in Saint-Martin."[14]

The conditions of life in the ghetto-cities were also mentioned:

> "The demographic explosion (...), the massive illegal immigration (...), the existence of real ghettos, no sanitary facilities, no running water, no electricity, no used water drainage, (...) high human concentration zones, over 2,000 people in some compounds, such is the description of this social reality."

In reality, the St. Martin Healthcare Project was mainly developed to cope with the immigrants' situation as they became a priority, although it was normally intended to reach the entire population:

> "The presence and the strong impact of immigrant populations mostly coming from the poorest Caribbean countries, living in deplorable socio-economic

and sanitary conditions, and concentrated in communities living the same lifestyle as in their country of origin, call for an approach based on education and self-responsibility deriving from the Primary Healthcare strategy recommended by the World Health Organization."

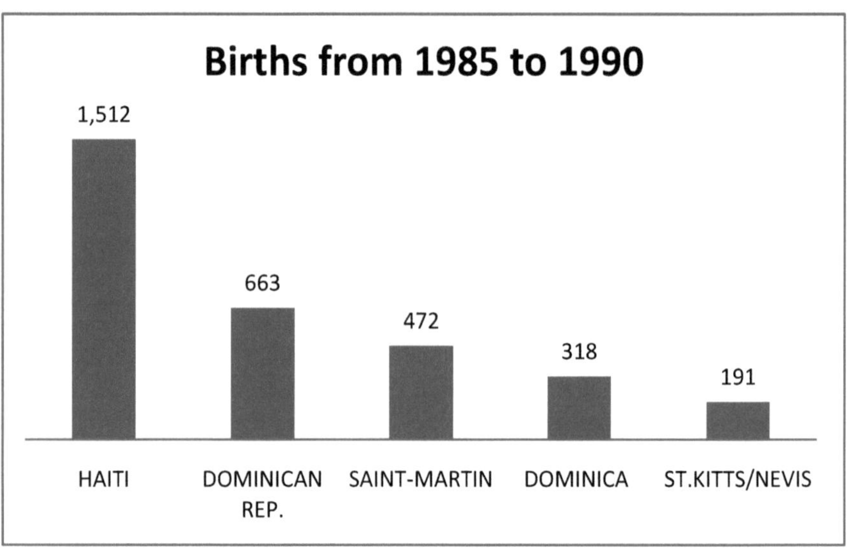

The hospital staff was alarmed at the progression of the AIDS epidemics in Saint-Martin. A report drafted by physicians, Dr. Victor Gibbs, Dr. F. de Caunes and Dr. Alain Rolland, as well as Mr. Jean-Luc Hamlet revealed some disturbing statistics:

> "From 1988 to 1990, 495 persons were identified with H.I.V.+, that is about I adult out of 50. In 1991 out of the 860 women who delivered at the maternity ward of the Saint-Martin Hospital, 254 were H.I.V.-positive. None of these women were drug addicts. 70% of these women were Haitian of traditional culture, often with no knowledge of the disease, and therefore incapable of coping with it in biomedical terms. They were only given some brief information about the disease, with no specific sanitary training before leaving the hospital.
> For children less than fifteen years old examined over an 18-month period, from January 1, 1991 to June 30, 1992, 11 confirmed AIDS-infected children were hospitalized. (…) For 10 of them, the disease broke out within the two first years of their life. 6 are now dead. We have lost sight of 2. Seven of the 11 children had to be transferred urgently to the Hospital in Guadeloupe (C.H.R.U.) in order to pass through that stage in the evolution of the disease.
> For the adults, over the same period, 16 new cases of symptomatic H.I.V. infection were diagnosed at their admission. 6 of these patients had to be

transferred urgently to the Hospital in Guadeloupe shortly after their admission. 4 died and we have lost sight of five."[15]

Gabriel Bez, the chief of the AIDS mission at the Paris Ministry of Health, visited Saint-Martin, and in a meeting organized by Mrs. Karam, he promised to release 400,000 francs to be sent through Guadeloupe in 1992 and an additional 600,000 francs for the organizational and operating expenses of the day hospital. He, however, added:

"An epidemic is never just a biological matter, it is also sociological. (…) What I will emphasize is that an active epidemiology must be carried out, that is to say, a thorough observation of situations. The disease must be counted (…) that is the only way to obtain subsidies or financial resources. In addition, an observation center can be set up in accordance with applicable standards."

Contradictions

Illegal immigration dominated all aspects of the Saint-Martin society. Opinions differed on this issue. For some, it was the best thing that could happen to Saint-Martin. For others, it was the downfall of the Saint-Martin society. Official reports, newspaper reports, interviews multiplied throughout the decade. Points of view varied depending on the lucrative gains derived from the development. This was the source of the chaotic nature of the development, because both contradictory points of view strongly impacted the decision-making process. Contradictions were blatant. There was never any middle-course solution that would benefit the common good. The development was operating on a binary mode. Among the actors of development, there were only those who were for, and those who were against. And the two camps were right. It was the mightiest that tilted the scales on one side or the other. In the mission report drawn up by Claude-Valentin Marie in October 1991 and entitled *Illegal Labor and Irregular Immigration in the Overseas Departments: the Case of Saint-Martin,* it is clearly stated the following:

"For the management of the semi-private development company of Saint-Martin, this development is quite rational and answers to a real demand of the market. (…) The bottom-line today is to properly promote the 'Saint-Martin' product. (…) For others, on the contrary, the real estate development is the result of total anarchy, where speculation largely prevailed over the concern for sound economic management, (…) the system, as it is, is not sustainable, and already the shortage of the demand has resulted into laying-offs and operations of price dumping."

Did these two viewpoints refer to the same demand and the same market? On one hand, reference was made to social homes, and on the other hand, it was made to hotels. On a tiny 54 square kilometer half of an island, could these two strategies of development coexist efficiently? They rather seemed to clash, and the clash yielded an explosive mix which emitted sparks igniting conflagrations at all levels. Paradoxically, the same persons who contributed to the implementation of the tax exemption law system were not the least embarrassed to state that the system was *"too poorly planned."* They referred to the *"big contradiction"* of the French State who was financing a system with *"tax savings"* without providing *"any further assistance to cover the operational and managerial costs involved."* Why did they see all these contradictions only after they had used up tax exemption funds? What was more important: take the money or carry out successfully the development of Saint-Martin? Truly, there was a blatant divergence of views between the statements made by the promoters of *"collective real estate activities"* or *"social investment"* – euphemism for social homes – and those made by *"the investors"* or "*the promoters of private house programs*" –euphemism for hotels and residential hotels. The former considered that the latter knew nothing about the island's economy. The former who lived on subsidies from *collectivities* and the French State for their investment, - that is called *assistance, isn't*? – gave lessons to the latter, for being too dependent on the State and *collectivities*. No doubt that the island has reached the present chaotic situation with these developers, promoters, and investors. For them, it was simply petty personal quarrels with, however, disastrous island-wide consequences. Finally, one could not but agree with them that:

> "Contradiction seems to have become the prerogative of the new Saint-Martin where the very person who has crafted the most destructive collective real estate programs is today advocating a liberal form of economy."[16]

Insecurity and Delinquency

Nevertheless, immigration was a prerogative of the French State, and in Saint-Martin immigration went hand in hand with insecurity and delinquency. The broad daylight murder of Mrs. Anicet, a merchant in Agrement, on Thursday, January 30, 1992, stirred the indignation and the anger of the population. Since the rapid increase of delinquency characterized by rapes, thefts, and aggressions during the previous weeks, Saint-Martiners no longer felt safe in their country. In fact, in September 1990 a delegation of Agrement residents presented a petition of grievances to Sub-Prefect Vaché and Captain of Gendarmerie Laffond concerning the noise, the drug dealers, and the shoot-outs. This quiet district overflowed with clandestine foreigners.

Three hours after the murder, a crowd of 300 persons marched to the Gendarmerie, where a delegation of about five persons, composed of Saint-Martiners and European merchants, was received by Lieutenant Labelle. The protesters blocked the street - *rue de Hollande* - with tree trunks and garbage bins. Then, after Lieutenant Labelle managed to calm down the protesters, the crowd scattered at around ten at night. The following day, Friday, January 31, 1992 in the wee hours of the morning, a reinforcement of 60 gendarmes from Guadeloupe landed at the Grand-Case Airport. The murderer, a Haitian of about forty years old, was arrested at around twelve and taken to the Marigot *Gendarmerie* amidst the insults of some fifty persons, and then he was transported to the airport for transfer to Guadeloupe.[17]

The protesters requested the immediate arrival of the Public Prosecutor, considering that the position of the Sub-Prefect was still vacant, pending the successor's arrival. Meanwhile, elected representatives and associations formed a *Coordination* group, and the population put pressure on public authorities during that week to tackle the disquieting rise of violence and insecurity, with all the risks of confrontation and tension involved. On Thursday, February 6, 1992, Marigot was a ghost town, with the exception of a few restaurants that were open on the Marina and in the center of town. The protest was also motivated by the long waiting for the promised arrival from Guadeloupe of the Prefect, the Gendarmerie Commandant, and the Public Prosecutor, who did not see any urgency for him to be here. About 500 persons quietly marched through Marigot towards the Sub-Prefecture where the general secretary consented to receive a delegation. He indicated to the delegation that he had to arrange a date with the Mayor for the visit of the authorities from Guadeloupe.[18]

The protest march went back outside the Gendarmerie and at around two in the afternoon the road was blocked from there to the Shell gas station in *Hameau-du-Pont*. At the barrage set up near the bridge, words ran high when Lieutenant Labelle approached the bridge followed by 3 trucks of mobile riot officers coming down from Grand-Case. He ordered to lift the barrage. The mob got larger as Lieutenant Colonel Sarrazin, newly arrived from Guadeloupe, read to the protesters the Prefect's injunction to break up the protest and restore traffic. A confrontation broke out between the inflamed protesters and the impassible helmeted riot mobiles armed with teargas on both sides of the barricade. The incident nearly turned into a riot, because many young people were armed with rocks, iron and wooden bars. After the calls for appeasement from members of the *Coordination* group and General Councilor Robert Weinum, the wise decision taken by Lieutenant-Colonel

Sarrazin to send back his men to Happy Bay where they were stationed, contributed to calm down the protesters. Two hours later, they lifted the barrages and allowed the two officers to pass. When calm was restored, the officers received representatives of the *Coordination* group at the *Gendarmerie*. It was decided to organize a round table on insecurity when the authorities arrived from Guadeloupe.[19]

School reflected the state of society and almost every teacher at the Marigot Middle School was on strike on January 30, 1992 to protest not only against the continuous deterioration of the working conditions of both students and teachers, but also against the escalation of delinquency on the school premises. It consisted mainly in verbal and physical aggressions from outside loitering individuals who entered the school and committed thefts of tools used by the service agents, tape-recorders and other items in stock. The growing climate of insecurity was aggravated by *"bottle-flinging brawls at the entrance* [of the school], *overturned garbage bins, rock-throwing, injured students, racketeering, and assaulted students"*. Damaged vehicles in the middle school car park were a daily occurrence.[20]

Fifteen days after the murder, the Prefect, the Public Prosecutor, the Gendarmerie Lieutenant Colonel Sarrazin, the Immigration Police PAF, and other heads of administrative departments coordinated a working visit to saint-Martin to meet the elected officials and the associations. The Prefect unfolded the measures he intended to implement. They included the creation of a council for the prevention of delinquency, itinerant court hearings to be held in Saint-Martin in order to judge certain cases, intensification of the control of foreigners, and expulsion of unemployed foreign workers.[21] However, the dispatching of inspectors from the Labor and Employment Agency to control the work of foreigners in Saint-Martin was put on hold, as it would be a total embarrassment for many employers. The check-points at the airports in Port-au-Prince, Santo Domingo and St. Maarten Juliana, as well as the request to the General Council of Guadeloupe to create a special detoxification center for drug addicts, never materialized. Besides, Lieutenant Labelle indicated that there was one gendarme for 250 inhabitants in Saint-Martin, whereas the quota was one gendarme for 900 in Guadeloupe and one for 1,500 in France.[22] These figures evidenced that the number of law enforcement officers on the island could not solve the problems generated by the unbridled development. Nevertheless, the *Gendarmerie*, which developed from a detachment into a company since 1988, consisted then of 45 gendarmes, of whom 7 for Saint-Barths, with a seasonal reinforcement of 30 mobile gendarmes during the tourism high season. Both the *Gendarmerie* and the public prosecutor's office had their hands full. But it was a well-known fact that expelled foreigners returned at the first opportunity. Intermediaries and false Haitian passports with American visa stamps sold between 1,000 and 1,500 dollars facilitated those returns.[23] Would those measures be effective? Haiti was in crisis on account of the imposition of the commercial embargo by the Organization of American States, the economic downfall, and the political chaos. President Jean-Bertrand Aristide in power since December 16, 1990 was arrested by the army on September 30, 1991 and sent in exile to Venezuela. A consensus government was installed on June 19, 1992 and, according to a Haitian writer, Roosevelt Simplice, *"the population bears alone the costs of the political disarray created by the 'coup d'état' and (...) the OAS embargo."*[24]

The new Sub-Prefect, Bernard Guérin, took up function in Saint-Martin on April 3, 1992 after a four-month vacancy of the position. He was accompanied by Mayor Albert Fleming when he went on his official visit to Paris from November 16 to 21, 1992. He immediately embarked on the execution of the priority plan of action initiated by the French State, namely illegal immigration. Philippe Méjean, Advisor to the Ministry for Urban Affairs in Paris, came to the island and took part with the Sub-Prefect and his General Secretary in a meeting with the persons responsible for local development on June 26, 1992. He confided the following burning reality to the press:

> "It's the first time that I came to Saint-Martin and it seems to me that something has happened to this island, as if it has experienced a unique adventure. Within a few years, there has been a phenomenal urban explosion. It is both interesting and traumatizing, because the inevitable negative impact on the environment must be taken in account very seriously."

The Sub-Prefect was a man working on the field and he knew how to listen to the concerns of the elected officials and the various stakeholders in the economic and social world. In the very first months, he was aware of the burning issues which he tackled frontally in order to restore the trust of the population. He even intended to set up a local committee of integration to facilitate the integration of foreigners within the society.

Situation of Saint-Martin Enterprises

At the general meeting of the Association of European Merchants, ACASM, Paul White, the president of the Association of Saint-Martin Merchants, ADICASM, expressed the point of view of his association on the idea to make Saint-Martin an offshore center. He stressed that *"Whenever something was created in Saint-Martin these last years, Saint-Martiners were not part of it."* It was indeed observed that ACASM only called upon ADICASM when the association presented grievances to the national authorities, with the rightful idea that a united front had more weight than just one organization. The president of ADICASM, therefore, firmly stated to the members of ACASM that the participation of Saint-Martiners was a preliminary condition to the launching of any project of this kind, and that his association would only give its support if this condition was met. This never happened because the Paris government did not agree to an offshore system in Saint-Martin.[25] At a meeting at the Sub-Prefecture with the General Director of the French Central Bank based in Guadeloupe, IEDOM, and the bank directors in Saint-Martin, the association pleaded in favor of bank loans with lower interests to be granted to local merchants. ADICASM was of the opinion that there could be no real tourism development without the participation of the island's inhabitants. Their non-participation reflected in the 30% drop in daily sales experienced by local merchants.

The group of construction and public works enterprises rang the alarm bell. Local enterprises were worried for their future on account of the economic recession and the competition of larger outside companies. In a conversation with the new Sub-Prefect, the treasurer Harvé Viotty explained the situation of the construction companies:

> "The island experienced an incredible growth on account of the tax exemption law. Before, the Saint-Martin enterprises that shared the work among them, but since the 1980s large construction companies have come from Guadeloupe, Martinique, and France with much more resources than ours. Some do not even have a fixed address; they just have a mail-box. So work has become rare for locals, which created a serious imbalance."

He went on to say:

> "Saint-Martin enterprises must be consulted first if they should avoid getting crumbs. Besides, there is a total lack of communication between the promoters and us, because often we are not informed of the works available. (...) or we are informed when it is too late. We would have liked to be informed in advance in order to get a share of the works, of course, but also to

give our views on the type of constructions and housings to be erected on our island. We have seen too many horrible buildings which disfigure the landscapes and do not at all fit in with our traditional houses. For example, the collective housing structures with several floors must be stopped; small human-sized units must be built instead, as it was before. This type of construction would also generate a better distribution of the work. Then, the buildings need to have social and recreational facilities for its occupants; too many of these structures are devoid of such facilities. With this in mind, we request a development plan for Saint-Martin to be jointly put together by the elected officials, the local collectivities, the enterprises, and the associations. (...) It should not be allowed to do anything anywhere!" [26]

The President of the Regional Council of Guadeloupe commissioned two technicians, Messrs Samuel and Lambion, to gather the grievances expressed by socio-professionals in Saint-Martin. Among them, the Saint-Martin merchants brought out their specific situation as natives. Raymond Vialenc raised the following point:

> "Money is getting scarcer and scarcer in Saint-Martin. Before, there were not more tourists, but there were less businesses and hotels. Today, there are more people to share the cake. (…) On the other hand, Saint-Martiners are faced with an important problem, namely, the properties which they own on the Domain beach zone. We own land and buildings in this zone. We have purchase deeds in our possession for long years. But we cannot benefit from the tax exemption program, nor mortgage the land, because that land belongs to the French State." [27]

Yet, European investors could acquire land on the same zone from the State at a symbolic price and benefit from the tax exemption law. Roger Petit, a Saint-Martin businessman, stated the following:

> "The 1986 tax exemption law killed Saint-Martin and while the boat is sinking, some Europeans are jumping off. But we, Saint-Martiners, we have to stay here and make it do. The economic situation is disastrous and I know businesses which stay open for days without making one sale. Nevertheless, rent, salaries, charges, and more, must be paid. If things continue this way, violence will burst out by waves, as it occurred in other Caribbean islands."[27]

Situation of Resident Enterprises

In this month of January 1992, the economy went through a period of crisis. The Gulf War forced American tourists to desert the island. Competition was fierce, not only between the same type of businesses on the French side, over 636 restaurants, snacks, and cafés and more than 200 clothing stores, but also with the Dutch side where wages and social charges were by far less than the French side. Mass tourism, preferred by tourism professionals, proved to be fruitless. Natural landscapes were transformed into a multiplicity of building sites that chased away the upscale tourists. Delinquency and criminality irremediably changed the quality of life on the *Friendly Island*, so much treasured by the tourists who came in the fifties and seventies.

Calling itself non-political, ACASM considered its organization as the economic force of the island, and as such, viewed itself as a political force. At the general meeting of ACASM for the renewal of the board, the main objectives included the clear desire for its members *"to be present in the management of the Commune"* and they were *invited "to register on the voters' list and vote*."[28] Moreover, it was better to form one big group in order to face the present economic circumstances. So the various associations of socio-professionals, craftspeople and professional classes joined into a *Coordination of Associations* including ACASM, ADICASM, ARCHA, AHSM, ACRAM, and APLSM. A joint dynamic series of activities took place on the Marina and in the center of Marigot. In an interview with the *St. Martin's Week*, the president of ACASM, André Zahra, summed up the situation as follows:

> "The situation has been deteriorating for the last three years and we are nearing the worst of the decline for a combination of reasons. Since the closure of the Pan Am airline, we are being told that charter flights have increased as a replacement, but we have not seen many tourists. Besides, it was announced in theory that there would be more seats on Air France. In reality, I have seen flights landed with hardly 30 passengers for Saint-Martin, and I know 17 persons who wanted to come and could not get reservations. … Americans are in recession and we cannot get Europeans, what is left besides the extraterrestrials?
> Here our only livelihood is in a catastrophic situation, and public authorities ignore us completely. … After two years of economic decline we asked our suppliers and our bankers to give us a little break with the beginning of the 1992 high season to balance our accounts, as many of us are still in the red. … If we take the example of Grand-Case, the restaurant-owners … realized that that they need to work together instead of individually; their joint promotional operations have yielded positive results for the last 3 to 4 years. By contrast, on the Marina, everyone sees no further than his door-step. … On the Marina, as soon as a tourist stops by, he is harassed at best for drugs, at worst

> aggressed and racketeered. … by about thirty *rastas,* well known to the police authorities. However, they are always there, and is exasperating.
> … At the end of two years of decline, more and more people are in peril, and if this season is bad again, the bankers who have accepted to be patient will turn off the tap.
> … To safeguard a glimmer of hope for the future, Saint-Martin needs to be officially declared a disaster zone by the state authorities. We are not asking for subsidies but simply a freeze of social inspections with settlement of the late fees."[29]

It is important to note that the *Tuesday nights of Grand-Case* is a success only because the villagers fully participate in the festivities. In January 1992, the editor of *The News* newspaper reported the rather critical opinion of the president of ACASM about an economic study of Saint-Martin carried out by the Chamber of Commerce and Industry C.C.I. of Pointe-à-Pitre from 1986 to 1991. According to the ACASM president, *"the technician, Mr. Bini, does not know Saint-Martin very well."* He added the following information on the mortality rate of businesses, on the absence of a market study, and on the purchase and rental prices for business premises:

> "In addition, the main tourist zone of the Commune, that is the Marina and the center-of-town, has not experienced that problem. Actually, the change of management or of owners happens like everywhere else, but the business sign or name does not change. This is a proof of vitality. It is true that the merchants in the center-of-town are undergoing more economic difficulties than businesses qualified as indigenous, according to Mr. Bini. Often, they offer food products or cheap items to satisfy the local demand, whereas we cater for a more fluctuating group of tourist customers. If tourists do not come, we suffer the consequences much more.
> Another point which I do not agree with concerns the market study. … Of course, adventurers with big dreams are always there, but most merchants are professionals. So before they open their businesses, they inquire and study the market. I must say that market studies are, indeed, rare, but a walk through the streets of Marigot avoids you a costly study.
> The purchase and rental costs of businesses are higher than what the study reveals. For me, the costs of businesses range between 300 and 500,000 francs, and even sometimes 1,000,000 francs. In addition, rents are exaggerated on account of the tax exemption program. Because of this law, rents climbed high and the promoters enrich themselves by imposing an artificial offer." [30]

The *Coordination of Socio-professional Associations* met with the representatives of Inchauspe Bank and BDAF in Marigot respectively, Mr. Inchauspe who hailed from Bayonne, France, and Mr. Serge Revolte from Guadeloupe. In a climate of economic crisis, the Coordination sought the cooperation and solidarity of banks to solve the problem of the debt of their enterprises, to which Serge Revolte retorted that the bank was to be cautious *"and not cover the losses of certain businesses"* because it was its clients' moneys that would be used. This comment opened the opportunity for the president of the Coordination to disclose his point of view of the situation:

> "For the representatives of the *Coordination*, Saint-Martin is not more at risk than anywhere else. This was probably true formerly, but the situation improved, and the business people who invested on the island do intend to settle here, build a future for their children, and take part in the development of the island.
> The problems are rather those of a young society still in search of a direction. Let us not forget that the local market made strides in only a few years, so the facilities must be put in place. We need the help of the banks, because a few years ago they benefited from us coming here and from the tax exemption law. Now that recession is plaguing our economy, banks must show some kind of solidarity with us."[31]

During a meeting of ACASM with the Mayor in May 1992, controversial points were discussed, especially, the take-over of political power by Europeans, an issue which became a real problem for Saint-Martiners a decade later. Europeans had so far only defended their interests as residents, in a situation where Saint-Martiners became more and more a minority on their island, as a result of the official policy to substitute them ethnically. Already, at this meeting, the Mayor tackled the matter on a purely electoral level, and not necessarily in the interest of the population. His position was contradictory. To say that out of 3,700 Europeans, only 800 were registered on the voters' list, and that they were only here to make money and not take part in the life of the community, while blaming them for the candidacy of one of their board members at the cantonal elections under the banner of the National Front, this was merely a source of confusion. The Mayor wanted as much to encourage them to vote as to criticize their right to be candidates in an election. A confused uneasiness permeated the discussion. The president of ACASM did take a stance in connection with the March 1992 cantonal and regional elections:

> "We are active players in the socio-economic life of the island. However, no one requested our opinion, nor involved us in the political life of French Saint-Martin. We wonder why. This is merely "exclusion". Why wasn't there any Saint-Martiner of European origin on the Saint-Martin list at the Regional elections? The only answer given to us was that it was not intentional. Well, we think that these omissions occur too often. All the components of our society have the right to express themselves and be represented. Our votes are sought for, whereas we are not taken into consideration for our representation. I don't think that is logical."[32]

The problem was posed, but not solved, and it would re-appear at the elections for the new Overseas Collectivity in 2007. A list of European residents triggered the indignation of Saint-Martiners. In addition, when the choice by the associations of residents and the authorities at the Sub-Prefecture fell very discreetly, unknown to the public, on a European in 2008 for the representation of Saint-Martin at the National Economic and Social Council, this choice was not perceived as an issue of majority/minority, but really as a show of the incapacity of Saint-Martiners to represent Saint-Martin. The indignation, this time, took on an ethnic, social and regional overtone. One could not overlook the fact that for the last years Saint-Martin has not developed into a society of ethnic and cultural integration – which we will necessarily define further on – but really into a society of economic domination and community-oriented ideology. The statements made by the Mayor testified to the great concern felt by the population:

> "The development took place with much disharmony among the various segments of the population. It created a very unstable situation, because the native population that is running the island has become a minority in their own country. This population is exhausted. The situation is critical. In addition, we must not forget that Edouard Roussat from the French National Front party was a candidate in the last cantonal elections and that the votes he got were metropolitans' votes.
> It is a fact that he is a metropolitan. Saint-Martiners are very concerned about the future of their island."

The loans with 7% reduced interest rates, proposed by the Central Bank and the Regional Council, intended for handicraft and tourist businesses in sound financial standing, were not adapted to the debt situation of the merchants in Saint-Martin. They were of the opinion that to get out of the crisis and give an identity to Saint-Martin, a fiscal and social status was needed. They were planning a status in which, among other things, *"an offshore zone would be created, where there would be no tax levied on companies, and where a separate chamber of commerce would be created in Saint-Martin."*[33] Immediately afterwards, the Coordination of Socio-professional Associations wrote to the Minister of Overseas Departments and Territories requesting this fiscal and social status, and traveled also to Brussels on the same mission. The involvement of all was necessary to achieve this goal. So the Coordination acknowledged the existence of a document on the new status proposed by the Saint-Martin People's Consensus, alongside the document of ACASM. However, it was their project of social and fiscal status that was incorporated in the new fiscal status for Overseas Departments and

Territories proposed by the President of the Region of Guadeloupe.[34] Ten copies of the *Consensus* document were deposited at the Sub-Prefecture on October 15, 1992, date of the second anniversary of the creation of the association by the Mayor, and the document was officially presented to the elected officials and the public on October 23, 1992. Besides, in this period of crisis, the president of ACASM in a conversation with the new Sub-Prefect, expressed, among other issues, his opposition to the new businesses about to open, to the administrative controls of businesses carried out in Saint-Martin with regard to the difference of treatment in Saint-Barths, and especially to the *illegal* opening of Indian and Chinese businesses that, according to him, were tarnishing the business image of the Commune. He indicated that:

> "Saint-Martin is the showcase of France in the American-Caribbean continent. Public authorities and local authorities have a duty to preserve it at all cost: that is our future. (…) All concerned associations are ready to express their opposition to the destruction of this Commune. The only resource we have is the image of France and what it can bring to the island."[35]

Attacks on the environment

However, the development continued its course, despite the fears for the future felt by the business associations, and disregarding the natives' efforts to keep afloat. The sea-filling of the Waterfront, assigned to a group of local companies, went along despite the budgetary restrictions of the Commune. The deep-water pier was taking shape with its 5.50 meter depth even though it could not accommodate cruise ships which required 8 meters. It would, therefore, be just a port of shipment. Several century-old *tamon* [tamarind] trees were destroyed in the new Friars' Bay housing development. The Grand-Case Committee of Defense was formed in order to invite the Mayor to listen to their grievances on a certain number of issues, in particular, a hotel project opposite the Cultural Center on a parcel of land known as Company Yard. a signboard notice of a building permit has just been erected there in the name of SEMSAMAR, without any consultation with the neighbors and a petition was circulating against this project. The committee also demanded that the municipal decrees forbidding jet-skis in the Grand-Case Bay and horses on the sand, as well as the presence of topless females on public beaches be complied with. The Mayor promised to appoint two municipal policemen to this task. Moreover, the archeological association *Hope Estate* contacted the Department of Antiquities in Guadeloupe in order to have them undertake excavations on the site of Orient Bay to rapidly salvage part of the ceramics still existing there, before works resumed at the building site.[36] The association further complained about the presence of equipment belonging to a sand quarry, and the constant theft of sand from the beaches. Afterwards, the R.S.M.A./Guadeloupe undertook restoration works on the surrounding walls of the Marigot Fort which was to become a protected site.[37]

Under the authority of the Environment Observatory created at the initiative of the new Sub-Prefect, the protection of what remained after the destruction by development was a priority. The creation of a coastline and sub-marine natural reserve, a project of *Action Nature* Association, was worked on. However, it took a few years to implement it. Actually much needed to be done in terms of deforestation of the hills, which constituted an unbearable threat, and removal of car wrecks. The latter had to be solved urgently and efficiently if this side had to remain a tourism-oriented island. However, a controversy broke out about the privately-owned rock quarry at Hope Estate in Grand-Case, but also about the commercial activities on Pinel Key. The question was who was responsible for managing the key: the Commune or the State? In the present situation, the Commune issued the building permits. Yet, neither the technician of the National Forest Agency, nor the Public Works Department had granted any concession to the Commune. Was Pinel Key a protected zone or a tourist zone?[38]

The Association of Economic Development, A.D.E., a satellite organ of the Commune, was lending its logistic support to the traditional activities - agriculture, cattle-raising, and fishing - and to possibilities of aquaculture. The Sub-Prefecture hosted a meeting with administrative heads from Guadeloupe, the elected officials, cattle raisers and agriculturists from Saint-Martin in order to devise a plan of agricultural and rural development which provided for the construction of a slaughter-house and presented ways and means to solve the water problem.[39] Despite the high quality of Saint-Martin beef, many cattle-raisers had to fight against the propagation of the Senegalese tick. The seven registered fishermen had to fight against certain fishermen from Guadeloupe who were using the limited territorial waters of Saint-Martin, and against the growing number of illegal foreign fishermen The Mayor met the Sub-Prefect and the head of Maritime Affairs locally to find solutions to these problems. The chicken breeders and egg producers could not compete with the imported products, but they could offer fresh products of a higher quality. A.D.E. through its contacts with the neighboring Caribbean islands, including Guadeloupe and Martinique, organized an Annual Fair enabling local producers to open up to their region to help reduce their difficulties. So A.D.E. staged its third exhibit in 1992. The Association was also interested in employing young beneficiaries of the minimum revenue of insertion to do environmental work, such as pruning, track maintenance, beach cleaning, and care of plants.

Legalization of foreigners

The implementation of the legalization policy for economic reasons in order to restore the balance of an island threatened in its foundations was not only the absolute priority of the French State and the prime mission of the new Sub-Prefect, but also the main achievements of the Commune and its satellite SEMSAMAR, as well as the General Council of Guadeloupe. Although immigrants left Saint-Martin for the United States either directly or illegally via the US Virgin Islands, many returned after their expulsion. The unprecedented legalization operation, which started on March 1, 1993, involved about 3,000 employed foreigners, and extended over 12 weeks. Weeks 11 and 12 were reserved for family assistance, such as elderly persons who could prove that their integration was legalized with a written favorable advice from the Mayor. All immigrants had to prove that they arrived on the territory of the Commune before December 31, 1990. However, the Sub-Prefect could not guarantee the success of this very risky venture and feared the worst if it happened to fail. He, therefore, devoted much vigilance to the application of the legalization process. The island's economy could not cater for the 16,000 immigrants and more that were already there; and the figures were only estimates. To fully understand the extent of the human disaster brought about by the development during the last ten years, the newspaper *The News* reported:

> "All these consequences irremediably lead us to a state of anarchy and bear the seeds of absolute social disintegration generated by marginalization, pauperization, and the exclusion of entire communities. The living space in Saint-Martin is too small to allow the absurd and irresponsible inaction that is witnessed today."[40]

Why so much irresponsibility and greed in the conceivers, developers, promoters of the exogenous development, carried out with the complicity of the elected officials, despite the constant cries of distress of the endogenous population faced with the obstruction of their basic initiatives? How could they pretend to have the interest of the island at heart, when their presence here did not bring about sustainable economic success for themselves? It was obvious that faced with the reality of their own economic failure, the conceivers, developers, promoters and investors who had not yet left the island, were still counting on the engagement of the State of France for them to succeed. In fact, after injecting moneys from the implementation of the tax exemption law into the realizations of the first phase of development, the

State was injecting another type of capital: the distribution of all kinds of welfare subsidies to solve the subsequent social problems. The Commune agreed to make financial efforts by purchasing Parapel Hotel in Concordia to house a squad of gendarmes and by building additional classrooms to cope with the increase of the school population. Yet, the situation did not improve and the measures implemented did not lead to a harmonious and satisfactory societal evolution. By March 1993, at the official opening ceremony of the County Court of Basse-Terre which is the jurisdiction where the accused of Saint-Martin are judged, the public prosecutor made the following revelations:

> "… delinquency was in decrease in Saint-Martin … but it remained higher than the Guadeloupe average. 2,568 offences were recorded in 1992 compared to 2,600 offences in 1991. However, if the offences are in decrease, crimes, expulsion of illegal foreigners, violations of labor legislation, and aggressions to properties are on the rise. For the latter, the figures jumped from 62 in 1991 to 326 in 1992."[41]

It was the least that could be said. Actually, the offences were becoming more criminal and did multiply by five in one year. However, the social renewal that was programmed gave hope to the persons in charge. The State invested one million francs to finance the recruitment of a social development agent who had a double mission: take care of the urban planning but also coordinate social measures such as education, healthcare, or the prevention of delinquency. Social collective housing became the main focus of this policy of integration.

> "For economic reasons, social collective housing is the best vehicle whereby children of the second generation can be taken care of in order to avoid conflicts, such as those occurring in France, or interethnic conflicts."[42]

In other words, social collective housing where ethnic mixing was practiced became the ideal solution to avoid the clandestine status, exclusion, and delinquency. The construction of 40 social apartments started in March 1993. However, works were delayed because the residents of La Colombe in Concordia objected to the large size of the social housing project to be implanted in their residential area. The municipality reduced the project from 16 to 10 apartments and transferred the remaining six apartments to the neighboring area. In fact, the residents did not approve the idea that this project will be used to relocate the foreign people squatting the seaside around the Galisbay Lagoon. By July 1994 this project was available and the six other apartments situated at La Ravine de La Colombe were delivered in September, together with the French Quarter housing project. An anonymous reader published in the newspaper *The News* a letter entitled *Why not an aid to a pragmatic return?* He was not of the opinion that integration was the good solution, and he was not alone. He stated the following:

> "There is also all this population, those who were sitting in the back of the trucks, that illegal workforce, docile and cheap, who was used to build all those tax-free temples of modern tourism.
> Now that *illegal* workers are not needed on the building sites, the men in uniform in increased numbers are getting ready to expel them. Soon the scenes of Haitian chase in the ravines will start!
> To avoid that, they must be helped to go back in their country of origin. Our proposal is simple. On the one hand, we are now quite aware of the traps and advantages of the tax exemption law. On the other hand, there is a potential of investment in various sectors in the surrounding islands. Resorts, marinas, airports, cattle rearing, aquaculture, handicraft, etc ... Programs for the period following the tax holiday must be created, such as a series of fiscal advantages (comparable to tax-free measures) applicable to individuals and legal entities in Saint-Martin who will invest on other islands and employ those foreigners willing to reintegrate their country. ...
> This type of operation has the enormous advantage instead of simply expelling foreigners to tie in the movement of population with the revitalization of their country's economy."[43]

Here is a proposal which the Paris government should consider in the wake of the terrible earthquake that devastated the Haitian capital and its surroundings on January 12, 2010. But this solution seemed absurd at the dawn of the second phase of the development when the goal to make the new society a success, a society created on the rubble of the tax-free development. It is surely not absurd today in view of the societal disaster devastating Saint-Martin presently.

The exponential increase of the population in order to serve an irresponsible and disproportionate development saturated all the infrastructures of the island. The hospital, in addition to its financial deficit in meeting the requirements of public service, suffered from a shortage of medicines, equipment, and staff, from insufficient facilities which were obsolete and inadequate, resulting in costly and traumatizing sanitary evacuations by air. The situation has gradually deteriorated throughout the last ten years. The two-day strike at the Post Office in June 1994 brought to light the employees' claims for the renovation and enlargement of the facility, and for staff increases in the postal banking service. With regard to immigration control and the fight against drugs, the governments of Paris and The Hague planned a new treaty for Saint-Martin as early as 1991 without the collaboration of the island's councils. Rumors of possible customs check-points at the borders between the two sides raised hell within the island's population and elected officials. It was out of the question for the population to allow two European nations to set up a physical border on the island, whereas the European Union was abolishing all borders between the member-states of the Union by January 1, 1993.

The Franco-Dutch Treaty was signed on May 17, 1994 by the Vice Premier of the Netherlands Antilles and the French Minister of Overseas Departments and Territories, and was adversely received by the elected officials and the population of Saint-Martin/Sint-Maarten, as well as by the Parliament of the Netherlands Antilles, on account of its discriminatory nature. In fact, the access without visa to both parts of the island was only granted to citizens of the European Union. Although ratified by the Parliament in Paris, the treaty was awaiting its ratification by the Parliament of The Hague. Nevertheless, the treaty was implemented in Saint-Martin, because in August 1994 two incidents concerning the deportation of residents from the Dutch side in possession of a Dutch passport by PAF officers gave rise to the anger of the inhabitants. At a meeting between local and national authorities of both sides of the island, it was agreed that PAF officers would be informed of the specific relationship between both sides of the island in matter of immigration. A better cooperation between both parties had to lead to a difference of treatment between residents and illegal immigrants. From the perspective of the inhabitants of Sint Maarten, the concern was brooding about a serious threat on the 1648 Treaty of Concordia that regulated life on the island.

Education and Training

The school population followed the same growth as the general population. As for all the elementary schools, the facilities were insufficient and in terrible condition, especially where the kindergarten school of French Quarter built in 1924 was concerned. The parents' association of this school expressed their discontent by occupying the premises and blocking traffic during an entire day, because since 1990 the municipality had promised to make the necessary repair works. After the Mayor's intervention, the repairs were immediately carried out. So the 120 students and 5 teachers started school with a delay of fifteen days. At the beginning of the 1992 school year, elementary classes counted 1,971 students and kindergarten 940.

The happy event at the beginning of this 1992 school year was the opening of a 10th grade under the impulse and determination of the parents' association of the Middle School for several months, presided by Mrs. Helene Hunt, and with the Sub-Prefect's and the Mayor's backing. By July 1992, the Ministry of Education and Culture had given its approval for the opening of the 10th grade in Saint-Martin, transforming the Vocational School into a Polyvalent High School effective in 1995. Managed by the Vocational School, this 10th grade of 27 students was pedagogically part of the Providence Polyvalent High School in Abymes, Guadeloupe. The controversy about the opening of this grade did not prevail this time, as it did a decade earlier. With the 1978/1981 high school classes, it was not fair to remove them since the number of students in those classes had doubled during the two years subsequent to the creation of that 10th grade. This suppression took place at the great despair of students and parents. [44] Yet, the reasons for preserving these classes in 1980 were the same as in 1992, reasons of *"social equity within the public service"* such as was stated by the principal of the Vocational School in an article published in the local press:

> "(...) the existence of this grade is a possibility offered to those who wished to continue their studies in Saint-Martin, on the one hand, and to those who could not afford to continue their studies elsewhere, on the other hand."[45]

At the beginning of the 1992 school year, the Vocational School counted 368 students with 40 teachers and provided training courses in woodwork, auto mechanic, cooking/restaurant service, accounting administration, and sales and business leading after two years' study to a vocational diploma. The Marigot Middle School counted 900 students, 60 teachers, and 37 classes: 13 sixth grades, 9 seventh grades, 6 eighth grades, and 4 ninth grades, plus 6 special education classes. Yet, in spite of insufficient classrooms, shortage of resources and teachers, it was difficult to understand why at the start of the school year the Rector of Guadeloupe transferred to France three Saint-Martin teachers from the Vocational School on duty in Saint-Martin for 7 years. His administration had promised them to appoint them in the Antilles-French Guiana Educational District at the end of the training period for their integration into the body of High School titular teachers. After a strike of some ten days staged by the Teachers' Unions, and a petition circulating in Marigot on November 20, the discussions of the Teachers' Unions with Rector Héon proved to be fruitless. Parliament Deputies Larifla and Michaux-Chevry called upon the French Minister of Overseas Departments and Territories who refused to settle the matter. The referred to administrative measure concerned the nature of the posts. Actually these teachers were occupying posts as assistant teachers and at their becoming titular teachers in 1992, they could not be appointed on the same posts, which were already attributed to assistant teachers for the new school year. An extract from the flyer distributed during the demonstrations is included below:

> "… this decision is a scandal, when we know that there is a shortage of teachers locally. For a week now, we are engaged in an action where schools are closed down. Why did we reach such an extreme?
> Rector Heon accepted to negotiate and made proposals, enabling these transferred colleagues to stay here in their country, which we were ready to accept. Yet to this day, he has not signed and confirmed his own proposals.
> It is revolting, because most *deported* teachers are married, mothers of infants, their spouses work locally, and they have settled her for several years now. What does this policy really hide?
> Mr. Heon, indeed, has come to the Antilles-French Guiana Educational District in order to implement a very precise policy, which cannot be named. In any case, behind this *deportation* there is a firm desire to rid the Antilles of its active intellectual elements in order to make room for United Europe of 1993.
> Population of Saint-Martin, … Think about it: what will all the young people of the country become after their studies when they return home to work in their country?"[46]

Eventually, the protest paid off and the teachers were not transferred. At the beginning of the 1993-1994 school year, 2017 students were inscribed in the elementary classes and 982 in the kindergarten classes. Those figures required the creation of a sixth elementary school of 18 classrooms on the premises of the former Vocational School, behind the Nina Duverly Elementary School.

The Association for Vocational Training of Guadeloupe, AFPAG, arrived in Saint-Martin in 1978 and started training young people for the hospitality industry in the field of cooking and restaurant service during 6 months' sessions. In 1991, all the 12 youths registered for the cooking classes received their CAP diplomas at the first level. The candidates, of French nationality or documented foreigners, had to be registered at the National Agency of Employment, ANPE, and be over 17 years old, to attend the paid classes. Besides, the municipality sent 16 young people on a six months' training to the Adult Training Institute for Hospitality and Tourism in Gradignan, in Gironde, France, but on their return in December 1992, the question of their employment became an issue. In July 1992 INFORM, a private vocational training center, organized its 2nd Trade Forum, but just like for the first one, socio-professionals did not involve themselves in this type of action. At the same time, SEMSAMAR provided training intended for adults under the foreigners' integration plan put in place in Saint-Martin.

APAIS was an association of school remediation, based in French Quarter and subsidized by funds from the *State Urban Policy*. To conduct the sessions, the association received in 1993 four college students on a military service program for one year in replacement of the four militaries who had arrived for the first time in 1992. This initiative, a two-year program of vocational training, was geared to the needs of 150 to 250 young adult immigrants. Finally, Saint-Martin students were taken care of by a group of Saint-Martiners under the banner of ASMIS, the saint-Martin Association for Initiative and Solidarity. In 1993 there were 30 adherents in Paris, 50 in Guadeloupe, and a new branch of 40. The president René Arnell disclosed that the unemployment rate among young Saint-Martiners was much higher than the official figures published by the National Unemployment Agency. The association worked on a summer project encouraging local enterprises to recruit young Saint-Martin graduates.

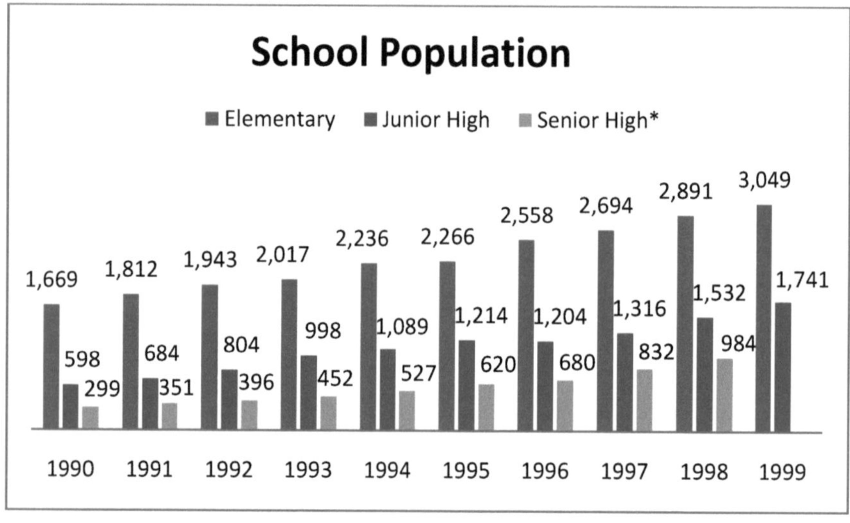

*This figure also includes those following alternate training: school/enterprise[47]

The Saint-Martin International Ecumenical Institution also called PROJECT 2001 proposed a new contract with the island, the Municipal Council, and the French Ministry of Education. After analyzing the school system in Saint-Martin, by January 1991 the conceivers of PROJECT 2001 started working on an alternative bilingual school based on the principle that there should be equal access to education for all. The limitations experienced in the current school system and the degree of frustration in the students prompted those concerned citizens to seek concrete and urgent solutions. The basic principle of the project derived from the notion that any child can learn.

He must be perceived in his totality. So his intellectual, emotional, social, and physical, as well as cultural and spiritual development must be entirely taken into account. PROJECT 2001 aimed at raising the performance level of students by means of a bilingual education as early as kindergarten and elementary levels, while preparing them to continue their studies in a middle and high school.

Statistics proved that of the Saint-Martin students who had reached middle school between 1980 and 1990, less than 10% had graduated with a baccalaureate, the final high school examination. In 1990, about 500 students of the French side attended the schools of the Dutch side at elementary and secondary levels. It was, therefore, urgent for all school-going children of the French side to be able to be educated in a system within their borders that would meet their needs. This dilemma was in direct correlation with the widespread trends and orientations of our society, namely, the change of values and morality, the deterioration of family life, the technological revolution, the evolution of the labor market, the clash of mentalities and cultures, the rise of violence and criminality, the anxiety created by unemployment, and the high percentage of outside teachers. All these changes had deep implications on the school population and affected the children's learning abilities. The conceivers of PROJECT 2001 believed with conviction that students would develop fully if they grow in an environment where democratic values, cultural pluralism, self-esteem, solidarity, the spirit of initiative, the sense of equity and good citizenship would prevail.

PROJECT 2001 intended to prepare students for the international baccalaureate and initiate parental education in the form of seminars and parent/child/teacher workshops, as well as continuous staff training. Everything was in place for the International Ecumenical Institution to open its doors at the beginning of the school year in September 1995. Inscriptions for the first kindergarten class took place from June 14 to June 16, 1995. The renovated French Quarter Elementary School was allocated by the Mayor to the organizing association in order to start the first bilingual kindergarten class. For reasons never elucidated by the president and board of the organizing association, the International Ecumenical Institution was mysteriously blown away by Hurricane Luis on September 5, 1995, after four hard years of preparation. The passing of Hurricane Luis was the pretext used by those in high places who did not want to see this project materialize. It would have allowed children, whatever their origin, to be educated in a bilingual school system and to benefit from an adequate and balanced school environment. It was, once more, a great loss for Saint-Martin, and a gap difficult to fill. Everything that did not match the development imposed on the population had to disappear at all costs. That was the price the people of Saint-Martin had to pay.

In 1997, the Association for Prevention and Assistance toward Insertion, APAIS, carried out educational actions and training programs intended for young underprivileged foreigners in French Quarter. The gendarmes were directly involved in these activities by organizing sporting events for these youths as early as 1995. Under this umbrella, the Prevention Club created a structure in Agrement managed by a Haitian female school educator in order to take care, in the morning only, of the four to six-year old children not attending school, facilitating in this manner their integration in public elementary schools.

The Aftermath of Hurricane Luis

The terrible Hurricane Luis of September 5, 1995, which plunged the island into a roaring darkness of terror for more than 48 hours, proved to be the most devastating of hurricanes within living memory of Saint-Martiners. The winds, at their highest intensity, howled like a voice beyond the grave. Some searched the meaning of so much destruction of material possessions, of natural beauty, and human life, because many suffered less from the bewildering rage of natural forces, and wondered why. The Great Simpsonbay Lagoon, a shelter for boats in time of violent storms, had engulfed lives who thought that they were secure there. The distress was so unbearable that the official figures misrepresented the extent of the disaster, by announcing two casualties for the French side and five for the Dutch side. On the other hand, testimonies and rumors accounted for nearly a hundred casualties, and it circulated that most of the 200 or so boats in the lagoon had sunk. People were talking of dead bodies in cold storages. Army helicopters were streaking the sky back and forth for days carrying huge bags hanging from outside. Luis was followed closely by his companion Marilyn who poured torrents of rain on the island on September 15.[47] Words could not be found to describe the horror of this experience. Yet, it was nothing compared to the January 12, 2010 apocalyptic earthquake in Haiti.

Fearing to see the island drop in a deeper recession, as it was already ravaged by the effects of the economic crisis and the overall situation, many left the devastated island. The most disturbing of all was that the destruction of Luis was increased by the destruction caused by the hands of man. Two groups suffered greatly: the children who had to attend the Saint-Martin International Ecumenical Institution, and Haitian immigrants who were ordered to return *voluntarily* to their country, some twelve days later. The ominous voice of loud-speakers from helicopters streaking the sky informed them that they were no longer allowed to rebuild their shacks on the hills overlooking Marigot and the districts of Concordia and Spring, and that they had to get ready to leave the island. For them, the name of the real hurricane was not Luis, that other hurricane came on September 22 when bulldozers, dozens of gendarmes and handymen sent by the municipality or by the semi-private company of Saint-Martin SEMSAMAR rushed through their living quarters. *Cité Popo* in Concordia, a shantytown of 400 shacks occupied by 1,100 inhabitants, was razed to the ground in a few hours. A week earlier, on September 15, 1995, 37 single tents and 2 double tents were installed over two days in the valley of Concordia. Some one hundred refugees, nearly all Haitians, were accommodated in these tents, not far from their former living quarters.

According to certain testimonies, the first operations of identity controls carried out by armed militaries took place on September 18, 1995 in huts located in the district of Saint-James. Those who escaped to the wooded hilltops were chased after and often tracked down. A naturalized French Haitian family saw the house they were living in destroyed by a bulldozer. Their French nationality did not spare them. They were victims of a blind power. Helpless and disgusted, they left the island once and for all to settle in the United States at their own expense. All the Haitians subjected to these controls were taken to the tent village. On September 23, 1995, at the Grand-Case airport, some one hundred Haitians, men on one side, women and children on the other side, surrounded by gendarmes, waited to be embarked on planes for Haiti. Certain children, suffering from sickle cell anemia and treated at the Marigot hospital, were in possession of medical certificates advising against their repatriation. They all had a single ticket and could ship 2 cubic meters per adult and 0.5 cubic meter per child, plus a vehicle by freight. They were 509 to accept to return voluntarily, among whom certain documented individuals. 190 expulsions were recorded for the period from September 6 to December 31, 1995. It was a generous assistance granted by the French State. But in this setting of great trauma suffered during the passing of the hurricane, and great distress following the destruction of their possessions, certain people on the island were absolutely indignant at their predicament.

At a press conference held on October 2, 1995, Father Celeste, the catholic chaplain of foreigners in Guadeloupe and president of the Support Committee of Caribbean Immigrants in Guadeloupe, who visited the church in Saint-Martin the day before, denounced the policy of the Saint-Martin authorities towards the foreigners, as he underscored the following:

> "To better exploit them, they were not declared. So, they were maintained undocumented, without any protest from the Sub-Prefecture. And today, the

> Prefect of France is expelling them because they are *illegal*. The passing of the hurricane Luis which destroyed everything they possess is used as a pretext to turn them back. And the authorities dare speak about assistance to their return."[48]

The Guadeloupe daily newspaper *France-Antilles* of October 3, 1995 reported that the president of the Association of Haitian Immigrants of Saint-Martin dubbed *"the assistance plan for their return a deportation."* In the same edition Lord Ernest Cabo, Bishop of Guadeloupe, invited France *"to respect the principles of any civilization: the respect of the human being and the right to live in dignity, the right to work and to labor legislation, the right to asylum, and the right of children to education."*

Backed by the French Human Rights League, by a certain number of religious associations, and by national and European unions of lawyers and magistrates, certain Haitians instituted an action at law on account of the treatment suffered and were defended by a group of jurists called GISTI, the Defense and Support Group for Immigrant Workers. The lawyer in charge immediately *"brought the case before the judge against the Prefecture ... and instituted three proceedings before the administrative court, namely, the temporary suspension of the decree, the suspension of its execution ... and the unconditional annulment"* of these decrees, enacted both by the municipality and the Prefecture. The administrative court pronounced judgment on March 25, 1997 in favor of the annulment of the municipal decree dated September 9, 1995, which opened the way for the payment of important indemnities by the municipality, depending on whether the administrative court considered it *"abuse of power or diversion of power"* in the other pending cases.[49]

The Coordination of socio-professionals wrote to the French Prime Minister to request the modification of the inter-ministerial decree on *Natural Disaster* which excluded the wind, since it was *"the most devastating element in the case of the Northern Islands."* The inclusion of the wind would enable the victims to be indemnified by their insurance companies. More than three weeks after the passing of Hurricane Luis, they were still waiting for an answer from the Prefect concerning their claims bearing on *"a moratorium for the payment of outstanding social insurance charges, and for salaried workers involuntarily unemployed to receive unemployment benefits."*[50] In addition, the Mayor of the French side and the Governor of the Dutch side agreed to perform an act of friendship and solidarity in favor of the Dutch side, more seriously affected by Hurricane Luis. The cleaning up of this part of the island was carried out in the true Saint-Martin tradition of *Jollification*.

Many enterprises, associations, service clubs, firemen, physicians, the Association for Economic Development, SEMSAMAR, the municipality, as well as the public and voluntary services of the Dutch side took part in this beautiful initiative.

Moreover, Hurricane Luis disclosed the usefulness and efficiency of the Galisbay Port. The commercial manager, Alberic Ellis, a young Saint-Martiner trained in Havre, France, was instrumental in dispatching food supplies, galvanized roofing sheets, building materials to the population, and in the disembarking of militaries under the program of emergency public service to disaster victims. The completion of the first phase of the commercial port project enabled its opening to traffic by the end of 1994. This advance guaranteed a promising future for this facility in the economic development of Saint-Martin.

Social and Economic Stimulus

Normal life resumed after a full year of emotion and tension to rebuild, and to repair, and to make the insurers indemnify the losses. Although the Victor Schœlcher Private School was opened at the beginning of the 1995 school year, it was officially inaugurated at the beginning of the 1996 school year in its newly built facilities in Concordia. It was a middle school, the continuation of the Saint-John Perse Private Elementary School now occupying the former building in Sandy Ground. Those who attended those two private schools were the children of residents or others who had means to pay school fees for their children. The inauguration was religiously conducted by Father Charles, the president of the association in charge of the creation of the PROJECT 2001 bilingual school, mysteriously blown away with Hurricane Luis. It was a coincidence which made many think!

In the aftermath of Luis, the private kindergarten, elementary, and secondary schools as well as the centers preparing official diplomas, developed rapidly and in perfect adequacy with the ever-increasing school population. The children of Caribbean immigrants normally attended public schools. Already, since the last decade a great amount of immigrant children living on the Dutch side attended the public schools of the French side, with borrowed French side addresses. Those immigrants were now numerous enough on the French side for the principle of solidarity to come into play in matter of education - an undisputable sign of their integration into the French society. The societal partitioning started to be visible as groups with distinct needs and interests functioned in an autonomous mode. The municipality, on the other hand, felt the necessity to improve the level of performance of its staff. They were, therefore, invited to follow classes for the two-year preparation of the Basic Law Certificate, starting in October 1997. This training program was organized by the Department of Permanent Education and Continuous Training of the French Antilles/Guiana University at the request of the Mayor.

The tourism sector was very much shaken by the devastation from Hurricane Luis. Images of the disaster had been seen all over the world and Saint-Martin was practically wiped out of tour operators' and travel agencies' destination lists. The Tourism Office had to regain its credibility in the American market. It had to fight against the negative image that Saint-Martin was a *'closed island'*. The Office devised a recovery plan for its marketing operations in the United States: a telephone number giving out information on the destination, a new slogan, a new series of posters and flyers, the making of a video documentary, and the boosting of the cooperation with airline companies. Starting in December 1997 during the high season, Air France inaugurated its sixth weekly flight with 60% of the seats reserved for the destination.[51] AOM announced its fourth and fifth weekly flight and Corsair added its third flight for the destination.[52] In 1996, the economy kept afloat only because of the injection of insurance indemnifications. Gloom loomed ahead, as the insurance companies experienced financial difficulties from paying out the indemnifications to settle the damages caused by the 1995 and 1997 hurricanes. Premiums were increased by at least 50%. Certain companies even decided to discontinue insurance coverage in the Northern Islands considered at risk. Actually, the French Antilles were going through an intense cyclic hurricane period which lasted at least ten years, should hurricanes Bertha, Georges, José, and Lenny in 1999 be included in that cycle.

In 1998, the multiplication of armed robberies, at the rate of one a day on the French side, aggressions and other offenses against tourists, the dangerous nature of tourist sites like Peak Paradise, Oyster Pond, and the Marigot Fort, were the subject of many letters sent to the island's authorities, in which victims threatened not to return and alert their friends. Other tourists also complained in the press of the unfriendliness, the uncleanliness, *"the odors at the Marina, in the Lowlands, at Orient Bay and in the various streets of the island."*[53] Tourists became scarce in the streets of Marigot. The image of Saint-Martin deteriorated very rapidly on account of the laxity in matter of security - according to the victims - and the fact that no one warned them of what could happen at night. This situation was going on for some ten years already and, despite the measures taken, there was no improvement. On the contrary, insecurity was escalating and affected the arrival of tourists on the French side relentlessly.

Labor and Unemployment

Another gloomy situation which heavily burdened the island's society was the unemployment of the young people of Saint-Martin and labor in general. The young people rang the alarm bell. They were worried about the dark future facing them. Over a hundred students from the public high schools demonstrated in the streets for the first time on March 22, 1997, chanting protest slogans such as, *What future for young Saint-Martiners?* and *We had enough!* They were demanding more police supervision in the surroundings of their schools to chase away the drug dealers, and more sports facilities, especially basketball courts, the favorite game of young Saint-Martiners.[54] The 1997 Trade Forum of the previous month did not alleviate their worries. Jobs existed, but they were not really for them. They challenged the Mayor, who called on resident businesses to hire young Saint-Martiners. Nevertheless training in the hospitality, restaurant, and business sector has been provided locally for the last 20 years, but young Saint-Martiners were not seen in the businesses, restaurants, and hotels of French Saint-Martin. Furthermore, the figures disclosed by the National Institute of Statistics confirmed an absence of registered employees in those areas. According to a survey carried out in April 1997, *"151 restaurants have no salaried employee (...). The same in business, car repair and rental: out of 126 known professionals, 79 have no salaried employee. (...) Overall, out of 5,438 enterprises which the island had at the time of the survey, 3,702 had no salaried employee. (...)"*[55] Those figures were mentioned by the Employment Agency director in public meetings organized by the Mayor, but no one clarified the problem. Rumors circulated that job offers in Saint-Martin appeared in newspapers in France. The First Deputy Mayor, Raymond Bryan, at a meeting of the Municipal Council where the future of the island was discussed, declared: *"the biggest problem"* in Saint-Martin is the unemployment issue and that is an *"institutional problem. Enterprises do not hire the locals of St. Martin, which means that more than 50% of the population is unemployed."*[56] Every year certain socio-professional associations received many résumés of young French people who wanted to work in Saint-Martin, especially in the hospitality industry. No one ignored the extent of unemployment in France. Yet, Saint-Martin, a 52-square kilometer island, was confronted with the same problem with its *3,000 unemployed and 5,000 young people arriving on the labor market in search of their first job,* according to the same socio-professionals.

Could this recruitment in mainland France explain the increasing hiring of *seasonal employees*? They were essentially young beneficiaries of minimum revenue allowances (R.M.I.) and unemployment benefits who came every year from France *to do the season* in Saint-Martin. It was not necessary to declare them because they would lose those benefits and allowances. They worked on both sides of the island. It was a real bargain for employers - a win-win situation both for the employer and the employee. This type of hiring was never a topic of discussion in the meetings concerning the labor situation in Saint-Martin. With regard to young Saint-Martiners, the same old story always resurfaced: their lack of qualification or their laziness, their lack of assiduity or their lack of interest. Yet, it was on the Dutch side that most of our young people educated at the Vocational School found employment. Some were even chefs in very busy restaurants. Unfortunately or fortunately, this new reality lasted forever, because young Saint-Martiners demanded to be declared. Illegal profit was still the bottom-line. Nothing had changed since 1980 in this field.

Social Conflicts

In the wake of the chronic difficulties, physicians, nurses, hospital employees, and service agents marched in the streets of Marigot in June 1995 for a better healthcare policy and a new hospital. The debt of the French State with regard to the hospital was not paid, and the hospital was on the brink of bankruptcy. The staff was on strike from October 15 to 18, 1996. In addition, the legendary *La Belle Créole* hotel, built 20 years ago, had closed down, then re-opened after restoration works, then had closed down again, then re-opened in January 1997 and renovation works were expected to be completed by 1998. The hotel was managed by an American group based in Canada who rehired a certain amount of former employees, but management still hesitated to hire new employees, remembering the conflicts that had marked the 1994 and 1995 years.

The U.D.T.S.M./U.G.T.G. and C.G.T.G. unions defended the interests of the former employees of *La Belle Créole*, in particular twelve among them, members of the employees' committee and the shop steward. They opened negotiations with the owners of the hotel and officials from the Commune by occupying the center of town and blocking all the access roads to Marigot on January 20, 1997, then by blocking the hotel. Clashes broke out between the protestors and the *gendarmes*. Notwithstanding various meetings with the Mayor, the Sub-Prefect, and the conflict mediator, negotiations were at a standstill on January 29, 1997. Union leaders accepted to leave the hotel, but maintained that the twelve salaried employees should be re-hired. In August 1997, the dialogue did not resume and the hotel closed its doors again. In June 1998, a new plan was proposed, namely, the rehiring of 57 out of 107 employees, the transfer of 26 to subcontracting companies, and the indemnifying of the 34 others. When the checks were paid out, some employees decided that they were not ready to sign. Despite the judgment pronounced by the Conciliation Board in September 1998, the doors of the hotel remained closed and liquidation occurred a few years later.

The social climate was becoming stormier and stormier with multiple conflicts. Among the most disturbing ones, the 18-day strike at the Post Office in April 1998 was followed immediately after, on April 23, by the widely attended strike of the teachers. All the public schools were closed on the second day and the conflict ended on May 4, 1998 with concessions granted by the Rector's office. The socio-professional residents also mobilized because of the pending threat of fiscal controls. On June 23, 1997, they blocked the access to a real estate agency in the center-of-town with cement blocks and heavy equipment in the presence of a crowd of merchants, stopping three Paris inspectors protected by a few gendarmes from doing their work. The banners read*: St. Martin, a Commune apart - Recognize its specificities! Yes to the fiscal status - St. Martin, St. Barth: fiscal and social equality - Local taxes, okay. France taxes, no way*[58]. Previously in December 1994, the SEMSAMAR and the Notary's office were blocked in the same way on account of threats of fiscal controls. Then, in January 1999, it was the turn of a hardware business. The year 1998 was the year when bank accounts were blocked, notices to third party holders were sent, properties and salaries were seized. Those in debt were residents, merchants or Commune employees who did not pay their income taxes and local taxes. For the latter, these practices fell under the austerity measures enforced on account of the financial situation of the Commune, whose budget was in the red.

Formerly, the Commune budget was balanced in 1992 with 147,841,000 francs for operating costs and 87,000,000 francs for investment, and Saint-Martin was one of the rare communes of the department of Guadeloupe not in deficit, capable of carrying on its investment policy. However, since 1996, this was no longer the case. The finances of the Commune were in dire straits. The 1997 deficit already amounted to 71,709,843 francs, and that of 1998 was nearing the 72 million francs. The 1998 budget represented an amount of 231,466,953 francs for operating costs and 327,300,887 francs for investment.

The Coordination which became the *Rassemblement* of Associations of Saint-Martin, in its numerous letters to the national authorities, demanded the end of the prosecutions, the discontinuation of fiscal and social controls, and a plan of economic stimulus. Not receiving any answer from the State, the *Rassemblement* of Associations made Marigot a ghost town on February 10, 1999, blocking the entrances of the town with crowds of more than 1,500 protestors, according to the organizers. At about two in the afternoon, the mobile *gendarmes* attacked the blockade at the Marina Port-la-Royale, injuring people and damaging cars. Then confrontations occurred between the gendarmes and the protestors everywhere in Marigot, as well as fires at the blockades. It was an atmosphere of civil war, with many wounded individuals and damaged vehicles.

In the social and economic turmoil of the year 1999, with protests against the fiscal pressure on the local population, and all the administrative and financial irregularities afflicting the economy of the French side, the representative of State tried to implement European standards on the vehicles of the French side. He announced that only vehicles complying with European norms would be delivered registration numbers on the French side. He imposed this regulation on public transportation with immediate effect. However, this imposition reflected a total ignorance of the special nature of road traffic on the island and instituted mere discrimination against the inhabitants of the North. The threat of this imposition forced the local public transportation associations and ADICASM to approach the representative of State in order to convince him to what extent this measure would cripple the lives of the islanders on the Northern side. Indeed, it was a violation of the free movement stipulated in the 1648 Concordia Treaty and a total disregard of the symbolic border with the Dutch side, where this regulation was not applicable. The representative of State argued that European vehicles were much safer than American or Japanese vehicles. This argument was not at all convincing since the European standard vehicles in Guadeloupe did not help to reduce road accidents. Roads in Guadeloupe were recorded to produce the most casualties in the nation of France.

Delinquency and Society

In 1992, violence had already entered the school. It was characterized by thefts perpetrated inside the Marigot Middle School, physical and verbal aggressions committed by individuals outside the school, who did not hide themselves, and by fights with bottles and rocks thrown at students. There was some talk then of creating a council for the prevention of delinquency. This delinquency was exterior to the school population and it only increased year after year.[59] Our analysis is that in 1992 delinquency was a marginal phenomenon hampering the proper functioning of society in general. It was obvious that those elements were produced outside the mainstream society, and had to be dealt with at the source. This was never done, since the new elements continued to integrate and prosper - as was noticed since the very beginning of the development. Therefore, the Saint-Martin society was marginalized and the exterior elements, whether positive or negative, arriving in growing numbers heavily impacted the course of events.

With the policy of integration applied from 1993 onwards and the measures implemented to fight exclusion, it was totally overlooked that human beings could not be integrated without taking into consideration who they are, and by disregarding their culture, because surely they did not ignore their own identity or culture. If integration meant to benefit from a social system in order to attain a better standard of living, if integration meant to benefit free of charge from a school and healthcare system, if integration meant to acquire the French nationality, all that was achieved in 1999. In addition, the unemployment of immigrants was compensated by the introduction in Saint-Martin of the Family Allowance Agency, CAF, which generated excesses and abuses destroying family values in the beneficiaries. The more children given birth to, without a father in the household under the *single parent* allowance, the more money mothers get without working. Mothers could not live with their husbands, but they could have as many children as they could. Making children had become not only a source of revenue but also a means of solving the unemployment of immigrant women. They no longer need to work and it did not make them better mothers. This way of life was in itself marginal, as it resulted in the partitioning of certain autonomous groups within society with distinct needs and interests. This societal phenomenon was visible in the mid-nineties. It was this functioning of society that generated exclusion and socio-ethnic antagonisms resulting in the individualized and clannish conflicts of the following decade. The culture of integration produced division. It was the antinomy of social cohesion at the dawn of a century intended above all to be the century of technology, communication, and information. The development of Saint-Martin was definitely not in tune with that world.

Under the judicial protection of young people, the delinquent youth was assigned to a judicial educator, independently from his environment. The role of the educator was then to establish a dialogue with the delinquent youth. Those young people were rebellious children who were absent from school on a regular basis, and whose only language was violence. They were true delinquents, stealing scooters or guilty of assault on their teachers. Their deviant upbringing manifested itself first at school. This behavior did not match the societal values of the island. It was not surprising that such young person came out of a single parent household, but more importantly his mother was not allowed to live with his father, if she wanted to benefit from the single parent allowance. That was the price to pay. In such a case, what could be the mother-child relationship, when the mother was already frustrated to have to live alone without her children's father? Her life as a woman was marked by emotional instability and imbalance. How could she raise her children properly? If the delinquent boy or girl was considered as "*an independent human being*", he definitely did not feel he was, that is the reason why he integrated a group or a gang. In reality, a child is not a human being apart from his parents and family. He must feel that he is part of that world, and it was impossible in his environment where the system imposed the separation of his parents for the cost of an allowance. So he had to create his own world, that of his peers. Imposed single parent households are more pernicious than natural single parent households found in many Caribbean societies. The social system implemented in Saint-Martin to solve the immigration issue was the cause of juvenile delinquency and the formation of gangs, because that system imposed an unnatural way of life. In 1998, the French Quarter gangs and the Marigot gangs attacked each other on a regular basis on the premises of the Marigot Middle School or in the vicinity of the school. The 1998 delinquency was no longer caused by exterior elements. It was the imposed social system that perpetuated delinquency and violence, for it failed to eradicate poverty. Actually poverty is a state of mind, a way of life and a thought pattern. The 1998 delinquency was not special to the island. It existed elsewhere, and it was catching.

As part of the fight against drug trafficking in the Northern Islands, the 1997 arrests counted 23 drug dealers, 38 user-middlemen and 29 users. Among the drugs used, marijuana represented 68% of the consumption, crack 21%, and cocaine 19%. The local branch of Judicial Police was established in 1994. It was in charge of financial delinquency and money-laundering. But discretion was a necessity in the cases involved in the survey. At a conference organized in Saint-Martin during the European Week of Prevention of Drug Addiction, the director of the regional agency of judicial police in the French Antilles-Guiana regretted the lack of interest of the elected officials in the prevention and fight against drug-trafficking.[60] After 2007, this agency was no longer on duty on the island. Did it succeed to eradicate this calamity?

Culture and Society

From June 3 to 21, 1994 the first Cultural Festival of Saint-Martin took place on the waterfront, where a village of the thirties/forties was reconstructed to accommodate the program of activities. It was the initiative of artist Roland

Richardson, the president of the Historic and Cultural Foundation of Saint-Martin and the municipality. The event was covered by the R.F.O. Television team from Guadeloupe. The very successful celebration was expected to be an annual event, according to the organizers, and the purpose was *"to offer the public another image of Saint-Martin"* whereby the islanders' culture was showcased: painters and artists, food and drinks, film viewing, excursion to historical sites, conference on the theme *Evolution and Culture in Saint-Martin*, boat race, traditional games, musical entertainment, sketches and traditional costume parade.[61] Why *"another image of Saint-Martin*?" In 1994, Saint-Martin was no longer Saint-Martin. The real Saint-Martin was already buried and a manifestation was needed to remind everyone of what Saint-Martin was. However Saint-Martiners were present and it was obvious that their past was still their present. What changed was that it was not visible. Yet, from the organizers' perspective, this first festival was to be *"a vehicle of economic development of our country for Travel Agent Month"*. *Travel Agent Month* brought together 350 travel agents and tour operators from North America, Central America, and Canada on the island during this month of June. Unfortunately, the first festival became the one and only festival. The public never knew why. Afterwards, the organizing Foundation also disappeared. It is true that this event did not depict the culture of those who called themselves *the economic force of the island* and tourism professionals did not deem it necessary to support this type of initiative.

In 1998, the steel-band school of Grand-Case, created in 1989, expanded to the great satisfaction of the managing association called Grand-Case Culture and Music. The steel-band orchestra, composed of young people, participated in many events on the island with great admiration from the public. That is the reason why the president of the association, Franklin Richardson, and its members decided to organize the first international steel-band festival which took place from July 31 to August 1, 1998. A total of about 250 musicians came from the Caribbean islands of Anguilla, Antigua, Dominica, Guadeloupe, Martinique, St. Kitts, St. Thomas, St. Lucia, Trinidad, and of course St. Martin/St. Maarten, as well as a prominent guest from the United States, Andy Narell.[62] After giving a free show on the waterfront on Friday, the main show took place on Saturday at the Alberic Richards Stadium. It was a brilliant and impressive performance to see 150 young people playing together from calypso, soca, and reggae to Beethoven's classical music. The first Saint-Martin international steel-band festival, described by the *St. Martin's Week* headline "Half success for a beautiful first steel-band festival," became also the one and only festival of this type. On the other hand, the public learnt that this festival was not supported by the municipal authorities. This initiative would have contributed to promote tourism on the island:

> "To help with the financing of the project several barbecues and tee-shirt sales were organized on the Marigot market. But it was always difficult to convince the authorities and to set up a financing plan when launching a big first like the organization of an international festival. So, the estimated budget could not be completed as expected and logistically, no venue was granted on the Marigot waterfront, and it was extremely difficult for the association to get a podium!"[63]

Meanwhile, the Haitian cultural week, officially inaugurated by the Sub-Prefect, the Mayor, and Father Charles was a success, according to the press. It took place from June 9 to 14, 1997 and exhibited art and handicraft, dance and religious music shows and ended with a ball entertained by the Haitian bands, Flamm' band and Oxygene. However, artist Robenson Dornevil, the president of the association of Haitian immigrants, was not pleased. Nevertheless, he was neither sad nor bitter. At the extraordinary general meeting of the association on June 28, 1997 *"convened after the financial fiasco of the Haitian cultural week, he followed through on his threats and resigned."*[64] In September 1997, After traveling to France to join his fellow citizens in their protest against the Chevènement circular letter,[65] he became conscious of the real difficulties encountered by his fellow citizens. From there, he sent to the French newspaper this *Letter to the Haitian Community*. The following excerpt is a direct quote:

> "... Dear fellow citizens, the economic, intellectual integration of a people will not be achieved if it is not done through their culture. Consequently, I urge you to think about your future, which is the future of your children. ...
> Liberty is to recognize the liberty of others. Equality is to admit our rights but also our obligations. Fraternity, considering that we are all *foreigners*, must be the glue in our community. ..."

By reminding them the values of their national motto, he was simply telling them not to lose their culture, the essential element of the Haitian people's identity. These words disclosed the true motives of his resignation from the association.

V

SOCIETAL DECEPTION

At the beginning of this twenty-first century, the Saint-Martin society was developing concurrently and almost in contradiction with the new society. The Saint-Martin society should have merged into this new society to form one. All of its members should have integrated this new society. But societal contingencies fall under different laws. Nevertheless, some of us had transferred, for economic reasons, for affective reasons, for reasons of social well-being. Nothing was wrong with that, if that is where they felt comfortable. They too did participate in the societal partitioning, referenced earlier, because their integration was not and will never be total. Deep down within, they knew it. But their reasons to integrate originated from impulses more pressing than those urging them to be themselves. They became the role models of the new society. They served as examples to prompt others to integrate.

Characteristics of the New Society

Those who integrated the new society were in the limelight. They were pushed forward, when it was necessary to make believe that the population was united behind a cause. They were used to make believe that social cohesion was achieved. They were the mouthpiece of the new society, especially when its interests were threatened. That is the reason why, they played this role with so much conviction. They were given much importance in that society. They were recognized by those whom they considered as socially superior. So they felt they were their equals. They were the symbol of success in the new society. They were the very success of that milieu which somewhat cocooned them. They felt protected against any outside force. That is the reason why they had to keep their own group of origin at a distance. But in reality, they played a role and they knew it. They felt comfortable to function in this new society. But as soon as they associated with members of their group of origin, they were less at ease, because their preeminence was contested, and this could destabilize them and confuse them. If they were destabilized in public, the spokespersons of the new society immediately ran to their rescue by decrying those who destabilized them. They needed to be reassured. That is the reason why these confrontations had to be avoided. Their alienation had to be total. Most of them used this form of internal adjustment permanently. The alienation affected their personality, their perception of themselves, and even their identity.

The dominant group also suffered from a form of alienation, because they too played a role in this new society that they created from scratch. The difference was that they created it. They were themselves only when they were outside of this society, in their group of origin. It was possible for them to move from one type of identification to the other, as the society they created was successfully taking shape; its predominance forced everyone to believe that it was the only existing one and that everyone was part of it. The notion of locality was fundamental to this creation. They could change their identification according to the location where they found themselves or according to the society they were associating with. But these transfers did not affect their true nature, their perception of themselves, and their identity, because they knew that their creation was an illusion, and that they remained what they really were. The partitioning phenomenon played out also in their case, because they too had to undergo adjustment, depending on whether they were in the new society or in their society of origin. Nevertheless, this mental gymnastics was superficial, because they knew that this new society was only a mirage, an optical illusion. Generally, it corresponded to the democratic process whereby number is a determining, if not existential, factor. In a democracy, the majority/minority concept is fundamental, and to exclude the other is not immoral. Therefore, it is easy to exclude a minority group. The notion of exclusion is an integral part of a democratic society. This is what is referred to as its perverse effects, the negative consequences inherent to a system created with good intentions. We stated in a previous book that the new society was not genuine:

> "This society created from scratch is (...) a well-structured society based on a hierarchical and stereotypic order where democracy, devoid of substance, is no longer a conscious and thoughtful principle, but merely an empty ritual."[1]

This new society really existed only in its locality. It had fundamental existence only for those who had integrated it in order to feel comfortable. It was a creation flattering the pride of both component groups. They were satisfied to be mutually good to each other and it was a beneficial feeling, with humanitarian overtones for some. The mutual dependence of the component groups, inherent to the new society, was also beneficial. It was reflected in the repetitive use of the words *new* and *our*, reinforcing the feeling of shared ownership and responsibility. It was reflected in their conviction that the new society originated from them for the benefit of all. It was a society in which its members were closely connected by apparent links of indestructible mutuality and solidarity, similar to clannish societies. There lay its strength. However, the interests of the dominant group had to be served by everyone; if not, the dissident member was sanctioned with rejection.

From the perspective of the Saint-Martin society - which did not disappear - this new society was seen as a mystification. It was, therefore, necessary not to integrate it since it was an illusion. Those who created it did not believe in it, because they were able to withdraw from it at any moment, according to their interests, without losing their identity.

The Saint-Martin Society and the New Society

The century started with the full awareness that the new society was not doing as well as it was believed: the Commune of Saint-Martin was under higher supervision. Nevertheless, the average citizen did not know exactly what this meant for the elected representatives, since nothing changed exteriorly. In fact, *to be under supervision of the Regional Audit Court* did not simply mean a change in the internal functioning of the Commune. The average citizen noticed that the Regional Audit Court ordered the closing down of various satellites of the Commune, for example, the Agency for Economic Development A.D.E., the Association for the Promotion of Education A.P.E.S.M., such structures that were in direct contact with the population. The average citizen also learnt that certain close partisans of the Mayor were provided with cellular telephones and that the bills were paid by taxpayers' money. He vaguely heard that some senior civil servants of the Commune were paid much higher salaries than they deserved. In addition, the average citizen understood that the Regional Audit Court also contested the activities of the SEMSAMAR. This semi-private development company had to stop its subsidies to certain associations, namely, the Museum of the Hope Estate Association, which experienced financial difficulties until further injection of funds was made by SEMSAMAR in 2003 to cover its salaries and operating cost, in anticipation of its temporary closing. The museum reopened in 2008 when new subsidies were granted for its operation. The average citizen learned that SEMSAMAR used to prepare the budget of the Commune until 1996, that its director was the treasurer of the Tourism

Office until 1994, and that it paid the bills for the gendarmes' cellular phones.

This was just the visible part of the iceberg, with regard to the reports which were made public in 1999 and can be found on the Internet[2]. So when *Les Infos*, number 223, a news magazine of the Northern Islands, came out on February 22, 2002 in the morning, with the following headlines over two-thirds of its front page, "*Commune Staff – Grandiloquent titles – Doubtful Qualifications* ... and other less pleasant headlines extracted from facts revealed in the Regional Audit Court report, its editor was far from thinking that this was the final edition. Before the end of the morning, the newspaper disappeared from the bookstore and newspaper stalls. It was rumored that the Mayor ordered the immediate withdrawal of the 223rd edition and the closing down of the newspaper. The entire staff was instantly out of a job. However, in 1999, no newspaper dared to publish even one line of that report, supposedly not to be ranked among the Mayor's opponents, as the municipal elections were to be held in March 2001. But one year after the Mayor's fourth reelection, what risk was the newspaper running by expressing its views concerning this report? Well, in Saint-Martin, this newspaper was risking its very existence.

The report, presented to the Overseas Secretary of State by François Seners, former Sub-Prefect of Saint-Martin and Saint-Barthelemy from 1986 to 1989, came out in December 1999. It was entitled *Saint-Martin, Saint-Barthelemy: What future for the Northern Islands of Guadeloupe?* It was a candid and realistic analysis of both islands. Mr. Seners acknowledged facts that were considered taboo locally:

> "The Saint-Martin society is today a fragmented society where the antagonisms between the various communities override social cohesion. The economic difficulties have widened the gap between groups and stirred up tensions, which are expressed more and more overtly. Could it be otherwise on an island where the islanders, for a long time masters of their environment, their culture, and their way of life have been reduced in fifteen years of unbridled development, to a minority as much demographically as economically? (…)
> Two phenomena of social destabilization have resulted from this uncontrolled demographic evolution.
> The first is in connection with the expectations of the foreign population. (…) These young people, who did not really integrate and whose frustrations are becoming visible, are surely casting a gloomy cloud on the social future of the island. (…)
> The second phenomenon of social destabilization is the open antagonism between the Saint-Martin community and the metropolitan community. Many Saint-Martiners have a hard time dealing with this double marginalization -

cultural marginalization and economic marginalization - which gradually overwhelmed their very existence for the last fifteen years."

This excessively fragmented society, facing economic, social, and human hardships to cope with this queer diversity, left all observers baffled at this incomprehensible mixture, especially as the observer did not see Saint-Martiners, the natives of the country, and he did not know who they were. Should he see any, they were never in sufficient numbers to deserve the qualification of *people from Saint-Martin,* from his viewpoint? No semblance of a specific culture or identity was visible, as it was on the other islands. In a cultural show, an accumulation of cultures or the celebration of a well identified foreign culture was generally the focus of the event. Since the integration policy promoted the legalization of foreigners, and enabled their registration, the Sub-Prefecture was able to disclose less approximate figures than prior to 1993, starting from the beginning of this century. Official records counted 114 nationalities in 2003, 117 in 2005, and 115 in 2006.

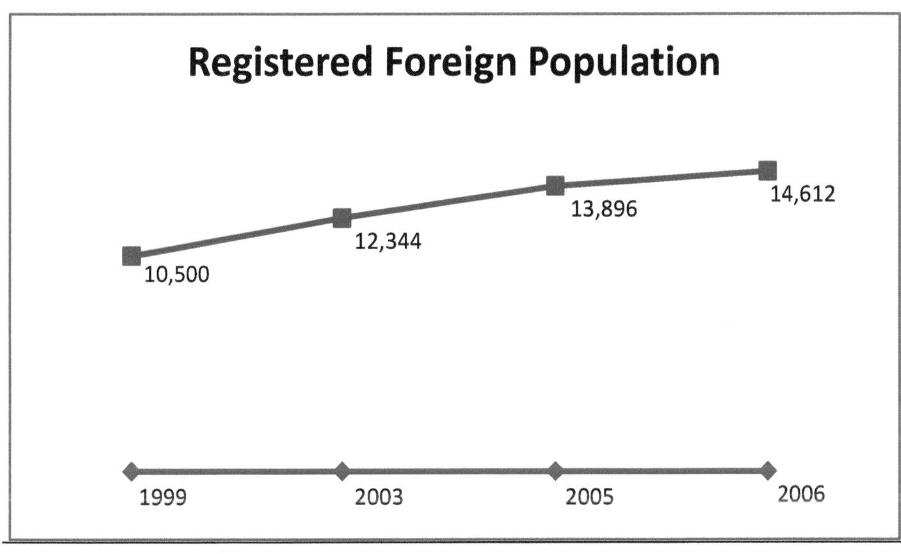

Source : Sub-Prefecture

Societal life seemed to be the accumulation, the juxtaposition, the mixture of individuals giving an impression of harmony or cohesion according to the circumstances, according to the observer, or according to the vantage point. The impression that one had that the Saint-Martin society reflected both what was seen and its opposite determined its degree of complexity. This fueled the propaganda of social cohesion, disseminated by the dominant group in charge of the island's development, under the staunch authority of those responsible for implementing the urban funding policy and the foreigners' integration policy regulating life on the French side. At this stage, the European visitor felt comfortable here, the Caribbean visitor was surprised, and the French Antillean visitor could be either shocked or indifferent. Those who always lived here had to try to maintain their balance on these quick sandy grounds.

The visit of the President of the French Republic in March 2000 offered the elected officials the opportunity to disclose the catastrophic situation of the island: five hurricanes in five years, an 40% unemployment rate, an ailing economy, more than 80 nationalities on the island, the uncontrolled drug trafficking, increasing illegal immigration, and the escalation of insecurity imperiling the tourism economy. President Chirac encouraged everyone to work with mutual respect of everyone's culture. It was difficult to achieve. The various communities had a real existence, especially those who benefited from the foreigners' legalization policy inaugurated in 1993. This policy included all the measures of insertion facilitated by the construction of collective housing in Concordia, Agrement, French Quarter, Cul-de-Sac, and Grand-Case. These new buildings changed the landscape of the island. It promoted the creation of insertion associations, such as APAIS in 1994, ACED in 2002, of recreational associations for young people living in collective social housings, and cultural associations. All these associations were subsidized by the State urban funding policy. ACED, the Association fighting Exclusion and Delinquency had the young immigrants work at cleaning and embellishing the green areas, while allowing them to follow the training necessary for their integration in the job market by the end of the two-year training.

The national organization which had contributed the most concretely to the integration policy of foreigners was the Family Allowance Agency of Guadeloupe, currently called CAF. It provided its services locally only since 1994. It was obvious that the introduction of a branch in Saint-Martin was part of the integration and family regrouping policy implemented by the French State to eradicate illegal immigration on the territory of Saint-Martin. On the Mayor's invitation, the president and director of the CAF held an information meeting at the Town Hall of Saint-Martin on June the first 1994 for a numerous attendance on the occasion of the *Year of the Family*. The director of the CAF disclosed that *"out of the 75,000 beneficiaries in Guadeloupe, Saint-Martin which is now demographically the second Commune* [of Guadeloupe since 1990] *counts only 2,500. This ratio is ridiculously low."* He challengingly announced:

> "Today the CAF must reinforce its presence in Saint-Martin on account of this low rate of beneficiaries. Consequently, before July the first, a full time agent will be appointed locally. His mission will be mainly to provide information, and he should very rapidly familiarize the population with certain types of social actions, such as allowances and aids, housing, loans, canteen benefits or again summer camps and the creation of public day nurseries."[4]

The building expected to house these services was built by SEMSAMAR and became a place which was constantly visited by supposedly documented immigrants. The closeness of this service had enabled young Saint-Martiners to take advantage of it these last years. Nevertheless, CAF beneficiaries and other social beneficiaries were in majority Haitian and Dominicano immigrants and they crowded the Marigot post offices around the 9th of each month, in particular the main office in the center-of-town, for many years to collect their benefits. Long lines of people waited outside the building and a security guard at the door allowed access by groups, as the lines inside permitted it. This has become a common spectacle of the Marigot landscape up to this day, which has always given rise to critical remarks by many passers-by.

In 2004, the coordinator in charge of the DASD branch in the Northern Islands under the patronage of the General Council of Guadeloupe called a press conference to explain the actions and budgets of its services in Saint-Martin. They consisted in public healthcare clinics, the care of infants and pregnant mothers, social assistance to children, assistance to the elderly and the handicapped, and service tickets. The costs for the full time salaries of the 33 employees from Guadeloupe working in these services amounted to 802,873 Euros in 2003, and their travelling expenses back and forth turned around 43,000 Euros. He confessed that 80% of the users of the DASD services were foreigners, sometimes undocumented immigrants. He added:

> "The laws of France, which may appear permissive, have attracted an enormous amount of foreigners to Saint-Martin. Those people came here to work, without being declared, and the questions posed were never answered. (…)
> We sometimes repatriate to his family a foreign child who is living alone in Saint-Martin. We help homeless metropolitans - their numbers are increasing – by sheltering them for a few days and providing them with a few meals. (…)
> As for the foreigners who are already living here, they could integrate the society if they can avoid sticking to their country's habits."[5]

The 1994-1999 Plan Contract amounting to 14 million francs was allocated to the urban funding policy for the construction of social housing and the rehabilitation of insanitary dwellings (R.H.I.) in French Quarter, which was to be carried out by SEMSAMAR. APAIS was responsible for the training and supervision of young immigrants. However in 1996, the director of SEMSAMAR and head of the *urban funding policy* project anticipated *"a social explosion"* should this policy fail. He stated, *"the integration was more difficult for the second generation"* and he added that it was necessary *"to create about 5,000 jobs between 1996 and 2000."*[6] Considering that it was impossible to create those jobs, the economic and social disaster of the following years was therefore foreseeable and foreseen. Why was nothing ever done to put an end to these deadly policies? That is the question.

The second 2000-2007 Plan Contract amounting to 40 million francs, three times more than the preceding one, was designed to salvage injection a particular sector. The funds were spent on the professional insertion and employment of foreigners by training the underprivileged young people, by providing after-school remedial classes, by alphabetization classes, and by the creation of associations providing leisure and recreational activities in the social housing areas. All this was put in execution by the training services of SEMSAMAR, but there was no control to determine exactly the actual use of those funds. However, these funds were chosen to be spent on the training and employment of foreigners at a time when the economy was undergoing a constant downtrend and the goose with the golden eggs was dying.

As soon as Mayor Albert Fleming was elected for the fifth time in March 2001, the Association for the Prevention and Assistance to Local Insertion, APAIS, organized an information meeting for the Haitian community on April 3, 2001 and for the Dominicano community on April 4, 2001 at the Cultural Center of Sandy Ground on the theme, *Immigration, rights and obligations.* The meetings were held under the honorable presidency of the Sub-Prefect, the Mayor being replaced by his First Deputy Mayor, and other intervening speakers representing OMI, CAF, DASD, PAF, and a representative of the Consuls of each country, among others. Such affluence was never seen before. There were more people outdoors than indoors. The crowd was estimated at close to 3,000 Haitian immigrants on April 3. The Sub-Prefect explained them the procedure to obtain the residence card for foreigners. The recognition by the State and the Commune of only these two groups of immigrants gave them a greater importance over all the other foreign immigrants. They were told that they had the same rights as all French residents - and that is what they remembered the most. In fact, in 2005 a PAF lieutenant declared, *"Foreigners know all the administrative tricks to avoid being expelled."*[7]

This was a blatant difference of treatment with the English-speaking islanders, when the state authorities decided in 1980 to turn the island into a

French island and to introduce institutions that had never existed before. These authorities never tried to explain anything to facilitate their integration into the new system. On the contrary, the islanders were penalized by the administration for the use of their mother tongue. English was and still is the official language of communication with all the surrounding islands and essentially with the Dutch side. According to the island's 1648 Treaty, the inhabitants of both sides of the island enjoy free movement, and the opportunity to work and to reside. So in 2008, it was astonishing to hear the reaction of the Public Prosecutor of the County Court of Basse-Terre who lost his temper on a Saint-Martiner at the Marigot Courthouse. This Saint-Martiner was a former taxi driver of the French side residing on the Dutch side and the holder of a Dutch driving license. The Public Prosecutor declared:

> "The people who live in Lille [a city close to the Belgium border] do not drive with a Belgian driving license, the inhabitants of Alpes-Maritimes [a department close to the Italian border] are not holders of an Italian driving license, and the Basques [the inhabitants of Pyrenees-Atlantiques close to the Spain border] do not drive with a Spanish driving license."[8]

Societal Disintegration

At the same time, in April 2001, the AOM airline withdrew its Paris/Saint-Martin direct flight for purposes of restructuring the airline company, and GO GO Tours, the largest provider of American tourists, sent warning messages to all its travel agents concerning the sales of the Saint-Martin destination. Actually, many American tourists complained about the recurrence of robberies, armed aggressions and other unpleasant happenings during their stay. Daily acts of delinquency which were becoming more and more violent, rapes of children and women, attacks at gun-point and broad daylight aggressions, and recently murder, greatly disturbed the life of residents, merchants, and private individuals, in spite of the new actions undertaken by the municipal police and the Gendarme forces in collaboration with the Dutch police. These actions consisted in joint road checks, more frequent night patrols, the opening of the Simpsonbay police station at night, but also increased working hours of private security companies and the use of cameras.

A Collective of associations was created in order to draw the attention of the elected officials and the Sub-Prefecture authorities on the increasing insecurity. In 2002, the general public was mobilized to protest against the impunity which drug dealers benefited from, against the visibility of their activities even in the center-of-town. Public marches against drugs and violence were repeatedly organized in Sandy Ground and Agrement. The leaders of the Rastafarian Movement called the attention of the Dominicano community, accusing them of being the perpetrators of most of the robberies in Saint-Martin. The parents were not spared. They were accused of abandoning their responsibilities towards their teenagers. The slogan used by the inhabitants of Sandy Ground resonated everywhere *"Enough is Enough"*. Letters from tourists and residents alike, giving account of their misfortunes on the French side flooded the newspapers. In an open letter to the Sub-Prefect, a resident declared, *"We are at the point of no return. Normal people are petrified with fear."*[9] Night life was becoming extremely dangerous and tourists complained that no one warned them of such danger. They felt trapped. Burglaries occurred in all the districts and in all social classes, even the residential districts of Mont Vernon I and II. In 2008, the Lowlands road on either side of the border was still infested with attacks at gun point and robberies. The Association of Lowlands landowners took charge of the security of their residents in the best possible way *"by increasing lighting, alarms, dogs and everything that could keep the criminals out."*[10]

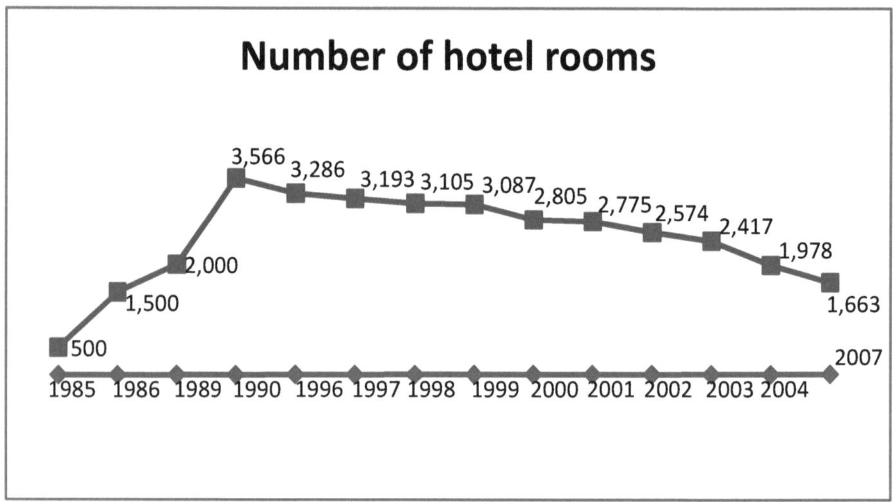

Saint-Martin was in bad shape. ADICASM voiced their concerns because their members declared that they were on the brink of bankruptcy. They considered themselves to be the only force on the island contributing to the economic development, because they created jobs and they hired the local population who stayed on the island. They asked the municipal administration to check those who were not paying any taxes instead of increasing the taxes of those who were paying. The economic downturn, in spite of the creation of numerous businesses in Saint-Martin, proved that drain of money was paramount on the island. The local investors were, however, penalized as they could easily be found. According to them, the administration should identify the businesses that were not declared in a more efficient way. Those businesses paid their employees less than the minimum wage, and those employees were not Saint-Martiners. Those unfair practices were unbearable to them. They indicated that only 25% of the population paid taxes, and 90% of those 25% were Saint-Martiners. They added,

> "When the State fiscal administration puts the pressure on those delinquents to pay their taxes, they go on strike and Saint-Martin turns into a ghost town. And it is so funny that the same politicians who want to increase taxes today come out to defend those people against the State."[11]

On the other hand, a general malaise prevailed in the Haitian community, even though the entire policies of the French State and the Commune were exclusively focused on their integration and their material well-being. In an interview with the Guadeloupean magazine, *Sept Mag*, the president of the Saint-Martin Association of Haitian immigrants, the first immigrant association created in 1989, disclosed that *"the community does not really recognize itself in the various associations that are supposed to represent them."*

> "Since 1993, the number of Haitians has been steadily increasing on the island. … Today, our children are born here; we were able to retrieve a sense of direction and managed to integrate. The reverse of the medal is the disappearance of a true ethnic solidarity. We have become individualists. … Our country is truly full of wealth. If there was really a political will, we would have the resources to develop our island. Furthermore, if one day Haiti manages to achieve this goal, I am sure that most Haitians in exile will prefer to return home." [12]

The other members present with the president at the interview were not of the opinion that everything was going well for them in the labor market. One of them indicated that racism *"is not that blatant, but it did not disappear altogether. ... Several of them have been hit by an employer who did not declare them and thought he had all rights"* and he continued,

> "They came to look for me and I went with them to the Gendarme headquarters. There, we were told plainly that if we were not legal on the island, they could not take our complaint."[12]

For this very reason, illegal labor persisted because the unscrupulous boss could not be prosecuted by an illegal worker. Since the appointment of a assistant public prosecutor at the Saint-Martin Courthouse, complaints made by illegal workers seem to be accepted - unless it is done by denunciation - considering the amount of judgments rendered on account of the employment of undocumented or undeclared workers since 2008.

The First Deputy Mayor, Jean-Luc Hamlet, complained in a newspaper of the Dutch side about the constant increase of the homeless population who came from France and elsewhere with the intention to find work here. But after some time, they became beggars on the streets or they went to the State welfare services for help. Often, he said, those who managed to return to France would use the funds received from the welfare services to come back to the island. It would be interesting to know what attracted them to the island. Poverty was real for those who could not afford to feed themselves, even though they had a dwelling. According to the First Deputy Mayor, this was a real problem for the municipality.[13] In fact, poverty was imported. And all the *wealth* created in Saint-Martin could never compensate for that poverty. It was not an easy task to make so many different types of people cohabit on such a tiny territory. That is the reason why the Center for shelter and social reinsertion was created by *The Cloak of St. Martin*, a charitable association presided by the former parish priest. After the villagers of Saint-Louis/Free Town had staged a protest against the construction of this Center in their village in 2001, the Center opened five years later in a wing of the former hospital. During the day, the center accommodates 25 persons in the restaurant, who can have a shower, rest, and socialize. At night, it can shelter four persons in two bedrooms. The center caters in priority to women victims of violence and to drug addicts.

It was further reported that a middle aged Haitian couple was renting some twelve rooms measuring from 15 to 30 square meters in the basement of their house in Concordia to some twenty persons living in very precarious and insanitary conditions. There was no window opening on the outside, no ventilation, no connection to running water, no bathroom, no kitchen area, only a W.C. Electricity reached them through an unprotected cable directly run from the owners' apartment to one plug. Outside, plastic drums collected rainwater. An outside tap linked to the owners' water line provide the tenants with running water which was sold to them at 5 Euros the bucket. All the tenants, together with infants, were of Haitian nationality and paid a rent of 300 Euros monthly, without a lease agreement, some living there for several years.[14] The integration program dating back to 1993 had not changed the way of life of certain immigrants.

In 2004, a private school in *Hameau-du-Pont* fell under the heat of criticism at the voting of the Commune budget during a council meeting. The First Deputy Mayor explained that this school was managed by the association *Learning Together* since the year 2000. The Local Educational Contract put in place by the municipality provided certain associations with teaching support for the benefit of 6 to 15-year old children. He declared,

> "This is how two agents under the *Initiative Contract for Activity* (CIA) were put at the disposal of the association. Their role was to fill in the vacant remediation posts during the period prior to school vacations. It is falsely rumored that the municipality of Saint-Martin was in charge of the functioning of an *illegal* school. That is not correct."

And the journalist added:

> "The case of those children attending the *Learning Together* School reveals once more that the issue of immigration remains one of the major realities of Saint-Martin and that *clandestinity*, the unique refuge for undocumented persons, is manifesting itself in all its forms. (...) Today, this school is closed for security purposes, and the short-term question is: what to do with these *former* school children? The First Deputy Mayor answered by stating that 'Each case will be dealt with individually'."[15]

In October 2004, an anonymous letter sent to the Sub-Prefecture disclosed that a young political asylum applicant, an info-graphic artist by profession, was regularly *bringing in* Haitian citizens with the complicity of a friend. The investigation was opened, and telephone tapping revealed that trafficking was actually taking place for Haitians to stay in or transit through Saint-Martin to enter the United States via Juliana International Airport. A young Saint-Martiner, then the Sub-Prefect's chauffeur, sold for thousands of dollars dozens of blank official documents, foreigner's residence cards and passports, to which he had easily access. He sold them to two intermediaries, the young info-graphic artist and a young woman, among other. With his advanced technological equipment, the young Haitian filled the blank documents, laminated them, and stamped them for the cost of 100 to 150 dollars per document. The clandestine persons had to pay him 3,500 to 6,000 dollars for the trip from Haiti to Saint-Martin. The trafficker or, in his absence, his concubine's chauffeur picked up the clandestine persons at their arrival at Juliana Airport. The couple put them up at their home, confiscated their passports while waiting for their new papers and until complete payment of their debt. Another trafficker, a pastor by profession, bought false residence cards *"to come to the assistance of his sister and his female cousin"* who could not leave Haiti legally, and also served as middleman. Another trafficker, the pastor's supplier, bought *"more than 40 fraudulent official documents"*. A last trafficker who left Saint-Martin hurriedly was *"the writer of a letter threatening to kill certain prisoners and their families if they continued to implicate him."*[16] Finally, 18 persons were arrested, 15 detained in Guadeloupe, 2 kept for questioning, and one expelled to Haiti.

Searches at the home of the info-graphic artist-forger unveiled very sophisticated important computerized equipment and an assortment of false papers engraved on CD: Schengen visas, Sint-Maarten and Saint-Martin residence cards, driving license, diplomas, among others. At a press conference on December 7, 2005, the PAF Captain and the Lieutenant estimated that this traffic dated back at least to 2002, and had enabled not less than about forty immigrants to leave Haiti clandestinely each month. With the exception of the civil servant from the Sub-Prefecture, all were Haitians and most of them educated and salaried employees: a security guard at the Marigot hospital, the pastor of the Church of Christ in Agrement, two agents who bought tickets from American Airlines with an American Airlines Gold card, and racketeers who sought for clients in Haiti. The final destination of the clandestine persons was the United States via Saint-Martin where they worked to earn the money for the second segment of their trip to the US Virgin Islands. Dozens of clandestine immigrants arriving from Haiti were arrested at *Pole Caraïbe* Airport in Guadeloupe, as officials there were alerted by the multiple uses of the same passports. The verdict pronounced on October 8, 2009 appeared to be a mild judgment, considering the enormous consequences of this disgraceful traffic, as characterized by the exploitation of misery under the cloak of humanitarian and Christian charity.[17] The big victim was Saint-Martin, our native island, which is far from recovering from such degrading circumstances. Who will Saint-Martin sue for civil injury?

Citizenship and Security

The damages of this degradation had to be minimized because everything had been officially tried to eradicate illegal immigration, to avoid exclusion, and to relieve poverty. Millions of francs, then millions of Euros, were spent to that effect. All the energies necessary for this humanitarian task were mustered. And yet, violence escalated to senseless murders. Delinquency had no limits. The successive revitalizations of the tourism economy ended up in the closing down of many hotels and businesses, the exodus of European residents to the Dutch side and elsewhere in the region, the forced exile of our young Saint-Martin graduates and professionals who increased the already large Diaspora in the Netherlands, England, Spain, Canada, and the United States, for most of them. The Saint-Martin society exploded into a multiplicity of societies, different one from the other, the visible ones and the underground ones. And to minimize this disintegration and to avoid acknowledging that all possible measures had been exhausted, the authorities came up with a brilliant idea, a new citizenship was born, the citizen of Saint-Martin. They were inevitably plunging into blatant division, and the Charter of Community was convincingly invented.

The first *Week of Citizenship and Security* under the leadership of the local committee of security and prevention of delinquency, co-presided by the French State and the municipality, and financed by the State Urban Funding agency to the extent of 22,000 Euros was in the making since October 2001. It had to take place every year and was *"important for the future of Saint-Martin"* according to the organizers. The steering committee made up of the members of the association, Saint-Martin Future and Development, the brainchild of SEMSAMAR, was in charge of the organization of the activities which ran from Sunday, March 16 to Sunday, March 23, 2003, a highly symbolical date for Saint-Martiners, as it represented the 355th anniversary of the 1648 Treaty dividing the island. This treaty has governed the lives of Saint-Martiners up to this day, in spite of the ruthless threats directed at the Saint-Martin society for the last twenty years. Involved in this organization were the following administrations – Middle and High Schools, Judicial Protection of the Youth, State Public Works, Local Mission*; the following associations – Agire, Get Together Committee; and the Gendarmerie, the Sandy Ground and French Quarter Cultural Centers, as well as religious leaders. Security associated with citizenship was the twin theme of this *first* Week, and the purpose was to motivate the population *"to respect the laws and rules enforced on the territory where they live"*. The main action was *"to bring all the communities together around a charter of understanding"*. This charter called Charter of Community, comprising nine articles after the manner of the 1648 Treaty of Concordia, was drafted by the organizing association, Saint-Martin Future and Development. It was said to formulate the rights, liberties, and duties of the inhabitants of Saint-Martin, was read by the Youth Municipal Council, and ratified by the Sub-Prefect and the Mayor at the opening ceremony featuring an ecumenical religious service.[18] It was a true parody.

---

* The Local Mission is a State Agency for employment and training created to help young people from ages 16 to 25 to integrate socially and professionally in the job market. It was introduced in Saint-Martin as part of the State integration policy for immigrants.

The municipality's newspaper, *Our News*, published a letter from the Archbishop of Guadeloupe intended for the parishioners of the Catholic Church recommending the boycott of the activities of Citizenship Week and emphasizing that the only legitimate priest of the parish of Saint-Martin was the currently appointed parish priest. Then by mid-week, the *St. Martin's Week* took stock of the first activities:

> "… Unfortunately, it must be acknowledged that the participation in the various events proposed did not rise to the organizers' expectation. At first glance, here is what can be said: the conferences/debates intended for adults were very poorly attended. However, it seems that the young people and students were more consistent, probably because their teachers and schools motivated them and urged them to attend. …The conference/debate on citizenship only attracted about twenty persons for exchanges of ideas that were often far from the topic proposed.
> Other disappointments were experienced. The following day on Tuesday, the Forum for prevention- and security-related trades went on with scanty attendees. Still worse, by early afternoon, the show on the waterfront displaying security-related trades was cancelled for lack of public attendance. The play staged by the students at the Courthouse gave a great boost to this week of festivities, and on Wednesday, March 19, a conference/debate hosted by the Gendarmerie Squad for the Prevention of Juvenile Delinquency brought together a wide panel of 10th and 11th grade students. Another satisfactory event attended by the young people once more was the citizenship rally involving nearly 70 participants of the Local Mission."[20]

Like all the *first* of these last years, this Citizenship Week was the only one and it ended without commemorating the signing of the Treaty of Concordia, as initially planned. *FaxInfo*, a daily newssheet, remarked the absence of political leaders at these events. Three elected representatives questioned had good reasons not to be there, whereas another did not wish to express himself publicly on the topic.[21] On July 21, 2008, Saint-Martin Future and Development celebrated its 10th anniversary by again publishing the Charter of Community in French and in English.[22]

The formulation of citizenship in this Charter of Community seemed to be restricted to Saint-Martin and started with the sentence, *"The inhabitants of Saint-Martin, by establishing an increasingly closer and more binding union of communities between them, have decided to share a peaceful future based on values (...), which constitute the foundation of the Republic"*, then it insisted that, *"This union of communities wishes to remind everyone that the enjoyment of the Citizen of Saint-Martin's rights brings about responsibilities and duties towards others as much as towards society and future generations."* To associate *union of communities* and *Citizen of Saint-Martin* was disturbing for a native of Saint-Martin and it incited an analysis of both concepts. Was there a Citizen of Brittany or a Citizen of Alsace? This question by itself brought out the whole ambiguity of this new concept. Citizenship within the Republic is that of France. Did they want to make believe that there exists a citizenship of Saint-Martin? On the other hand, the *union of communities* in a Republic that is one and indivisible was raising confusing notions. Were they saying what they did not want anyone to believe? Was Saint-Martin really a *"close and binding"* union of communities? Yet, many officials throughout the development warned against the threat of developing a community-based society. Had they fallen into the community-oriented ideology with this Charter of Community? Considering the experience of Saint-Martin during the last thirty years, it is obvious that the fragmentation of the Saint-Martin society led to the formation of distinct communities on the basis of ethnicity, enclosed and antagonistic. The *union of communities* was a hoax.

True citizenship is, indeed, that of all the holders of the standard French identity and nationality card. In Saint-Martin especially, like in all colonized countries, nationality and identity, as it is lived by the islanders, are two absolutely distinct notions. There is no nationality or citizenship of Saint-Martin. There is, at most, an identity of Saint-Martin defined by criteria formulated by Saint-Martiners themselves. Citizenship and nationality are defined by criteria included in laws. An individual normally defines himself by his ancestral and cultural origin and by his nationality. Besides, true citizenship is also the one attributed by naturalization decrees. For a few years now, the State representative has issued these decrees in a highly publicized ceremony. The criteria for acquiring the French nationality are sealed in the laws of the French Republic.

In November 2001, the Sub-Prefect, assisted by the head of the department for foreigners and the head of the service issuing residence permits, gave out naturalization decrees and French passports to four new French citizens. A couple from Dominica and their 20-month old son born in Marigot had arrived in Saint-Martin from Guadeloupe in 1985. Their naturalization application dated back to 1995. The other new French citizen, a 22-year old Haitian, arrived on the island at the age of one year. He was a head cook motivated by his desire to continue his professional training in France and in Europe. He was, therefore, making his mobility easier by obtaining a French passport. The Sub-Prefect recommended them to register on the electoral lists. In all, seven naturalization decrees were issued in Saint-Martin in 2001, and in 2005, at the following naturalization ceremony, 115 decrees were granted.[23]

The interim Sub-Prefect, General Secretary of the Prefecture of Guadeloupe, welcomed about twenty new French citizens in a very official and solemn ceremony. In all, in 2006, 274 decrees were granted. In October 2007, the Commune became an Overseas Collectivity on July 15, 2007 and that year the Delegate Prefect was assisted by the President of the Overseas Collectivity and an opposition Territorial Councilor to welcome the 223 new French citizens, of Haitian origin for most of them, in a ceremony as solemn as the previous ones.[24] It was the first time that the political leaders attended this ceremony. In April 2008, six months after the previous one, the welcoming ceremony into the French nationality was intended for 145 new French citizens originating from 15 countries, 90 among them were born and residing in Saint-Martin. This ceremony took place in the presence of the President of the Overseas Collectivity and the new resident Assistant Public Prosecutor of the Court of Saint-Martin.[25] In July 2009, at the welcoming ceremony, the Delegate Prefect welcomed 263 new French citizens, of whom 191 from ages 13 to 18, foreigners born on the island.[26] This increase in the number of naturalized French citizens in Saint-Martin was certainly the result of the public information meetings for immigrants held in April 2001. The increase defiantly exceeded the number of naturalizations granted in any French Overseas Departments, including French Guiana. Such figures reflected the overall demographic excesses that were encouraged since 1986.

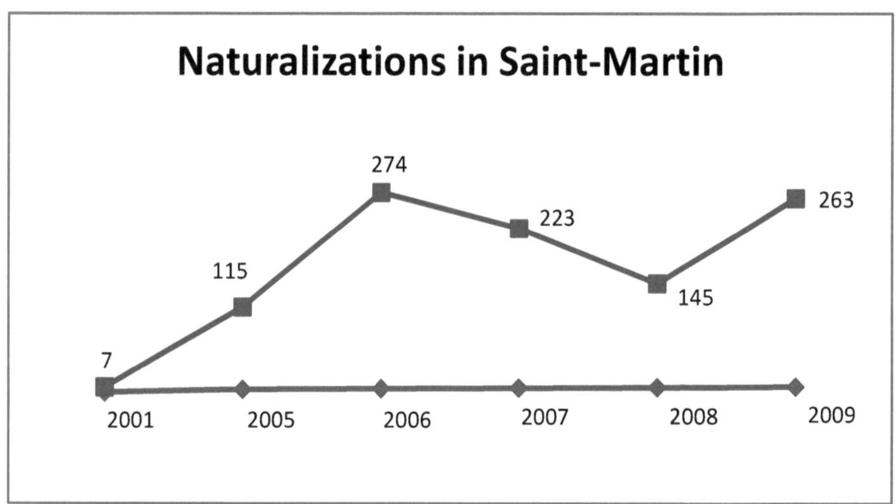

Since the creation of a branch of the National Agency for the Admission of Foreigners and for Migrations, ANAEM, in premises put at its disposal by the Collectivity in September 2008, and a new ministry of immigration in the

Paris government, the migrating influx was better controlled. In fact, ANAEM of Saint-Martin received 90 foreigners in training in their For'IDN center since its creation and 24 trainees afterwards. The State also proposed *"a 2,000 Euro premium to foreigners who wanted to return to their country and granted aid to set up businesses in their country of origin."*[27] Surely, the numerous legalizations and the family regrouping carried out by the French State since 1993 would still encumber the evolution of Saint-Martin for quite a long time, despite this new policy recently implemented.

Widespread Exasperation

The year 2008 started with the wishes of the New Inter-professional Federation of the Overseas Collectivity, FIPCOM, which was called FISM prior to 2007, that is Inter-professional Federation of Saint-Martin. Those wishes exasperated more than one Saint-Martiner, because the tone and the wording recalled the language used in the nineties by some newcomers, when the new Saint-Martin and the new Saint-Martiners were created. In 1997, a press release entitled, *The old Saint-Martin has lived, The New Saint-Martin is in progress,* outlined the *"five main ethnic groups"* forming the population of the nineties, in which *"Everyone is claiming his place"*. The author asked three questions:

> "From this juxtaposition of sometimes antagonistic cultures, can we expect the emergence of a *modus vivendi* defining a new Saint-Martin identity?
> Will the indigenous people accept without reaction the proposals of those with the economic power or those with the highest demographic percentage or the intellectuals and other thinkers? (…)
> Must one language continually oppose the other; must one language impose itself upon the other?"[28]

What had this new society become in 2008? Had it collapsed? A new citizenship had already been inaugurated. And what had *"the indigenous people"* become? Had they been exterminated as in the time of Christopher Columbus? FIPCOM, the new Federation of Socio-Professionals, solemnly stated the following in a press release:

> "2008 will be the birth of a new multiethnic community who, like the flamboyant tree, takes care of all its roots in order to spread out its branches. (…)
> All those who can prove that their main residence is on the French part of the island by January the first, 2008 are CITIZENS OF SAINT-MARTIN. (…)

> "Before", we lived in tribes, in bubbles, by arrival date, by profession, affinities or interests, by origins."[29]

When was *"before"?* Was FIPCOM referring to the new society prior to 2008 or the society of indigenous people prior to 1980? WAOUH!!![30] Was the Federation claiming to talk on behalf of the entire population? Didn't they know that the island society has been multi-ethnic from its inception and that it had managed throughout the centuries to harmoniously integrate the main cultural features of the various ethnic groups present here? These features imparted qualities of openness and tolerance which characterized the Saint-Martin society until the 1980s. Were they giving lessons of multi-ethnicity to the Saint-Martin people? The Federation continued,

> "Today, many companies, businesses can function thanks to the development of the Dutch side. Attracted by the economic growth of our neighbors, we have spread out our professionalism there.
> "Tomorrow", our market is "our country".

How far will they go with their mystification?

"Enough is enough" was the theme of a meeting organized in May 2008 by the family and friends of Eugene Brouta in French Quarter in the presence of his lawyer. The incident nearly ended in a riot, which caused the elected officials of the Collectivity to rush to the scene. *"The case of Eugene Brouta is not an isolated one and we have many testimonies of disrespectful treatments towards the population".* During a routine road control, an altercation broke out between three gendarmes and the victim. According to a letter from the family, *"he was kicked in his stomach and genitals and had to be hospitalized. The following day, the gendarmes continued their aggressive attitude towards the young people of French Quarter by threatening them that next time it will be worse."* The protestors were enraged at the treatment inflicted to this young father of four by the gendarmes. They blocked the road with heavy equipment, put fire to a vehicle belonging to the gendarmes, and after piling garbage bins in the middle of the road set them afire. The presence of a Territorial Councilor claiming that he was representing the President of the Collectivity, who he said was off island, only aggravated the atmosphere. The French Quarter residents complained that when they call the gendarmes for the many robberies they suffer, nobody come to them. Finally, the President of the Collectivity arrived with his entourage. It was not easy to calm down the crowd. The Delegate Prefect arrived on the scene to speak to the protestors by assuring them that an investigation will be carried out, and

that the witnesses will be heard to determine exactly what took place. The Assistant Public Prosecutor also arrived on the scene in the afternoon and the protestors accepted to lift the blockades after having obtained confirmation that justice would be done.[31]

An issue of political representation, having become the Fuentes Affair, gave rise to the protest of several groups of Saint-Martin socio-professionals concerning the appointment of a European - a UMP Territorial Councilor - to the national Economic and Social Council, whereas several Saint-Martiners were candidates for this position. They were Joseph Romney, a Customs Inspector and the Director of Fiscal Policies within the Cabinet of the President of the Region of Guadeloupe; Jean Arnell, a young Information Technology Expert and a board member of the local Chamber of Commerce; and René Arnell, a young company manager and director of SODEGA Saint-Martin, a State funding agency. The appointment of Mr. Fuentes, a former Director of the French Commercial Bank (B.F.C.) and a company manager, remained a secret for long months. Three organizations, ADICASM, the Economic and Social Collective, and the Citizen Movement Collective, gave vent to their denunciation of this appointment. Open letters were sent to the Delegate Prefect with copy to the President of the Collectivity, and to the local press. A press conference took place on July 4, 2008.[32] All three organizations requested the annulment of this appointment. Their position was the following:

> "... Mr. Fuentes arrived on our island less than ten years ago. He is not aware of the affairs of Saint-Martin. He cannot justify his integration in the Saint-Martin culture. He is not a Saint-Martiner, and it is for these reasons that he cannot claim to represent Saint-Martin in any way whatsoever. ..."[33]

The President of the Collectivity expressed his views justifying the appointment on local radios by stating that Europeans formed 35% of the population. He meant that they were more numerous than Saint-Martiners. This was the first time that he dared to make this revelation publicly. Likewise, the Delegate Prefect explained the appointment procedure. Finally, the problem was not addressed in its entirety. If Saint-Martiners were living in a state of denial of what was really happening on their island for the last twenty years or so, they definitely had a rough wake-up call. In an open letter entitled, *The June 27, 2008 Appeal of the People of Saint-Martin to the Elected Officials of the Collectivity*, Saint-Martiners were demanding, among other things, that *"all representation of Saint-Martin at the local, national, or international levels be done by Saint-Martiners"*, and reminded that *"Saint-Martiners have a HISTORY, Saint-Martiners have an IDENTITY, Saint-*

Martiners have a MEMORY". They asked their elected officials: *"When will you react to the discrimination directed against us?"* and ended with this outcry:

> NO, WE ARE NOT RACIST! WE WANT TO EXIST!
> NO, WE ARE NOT XENOPHOBES! WE WANT TO EXIST!
> We are only asking to be recognized in our country and to be respected as Saint-Martiners
> WE WANT TO LIVE NOT SURVIVE.

The appointment of Mister Fuentes was maintained at the national level, and his term of office was extended, in spite of all these interventions.

The aggressions and armed robberies, or violent robberies against tourists, merchants, and individuals became more and more frequent and more and more ferocious, as they occurred in broad daylight. For the year 2008, letters from tourists and residents sent to the press did not stop. They were entitled, *I will never come back*. They observed, *St. Maarten/St. Martin is a den of thieves; it is no longer the Friendly Island*. The locations were: *Grand-Case, Peak Paradise, Orient Bay, Oyster Pond, and the Waterfront!* The headlines were *Marigot Velo Caraïbes: 2nd burglary in 3 months - Another armed attack in a store - American tourists aggressed on the Waterfront - Another aggression at Orient Bay - Armed attacks: the series continue - Everything is done to rob the residents of Oyster Pond - The director of Mercure Hotel is fed up - Between laws and realities, night life is doomed.* Then, as an introduction to this letter:

> "Marigot is dying after six in the afternoon, Grand-Case scares after nine at night, walking at Bay Nettle is impossible, Oyster Pond is forgotten, and music is forbidden at Orient Bay after one in the morning. Meanwhile, they attack at gun-point, they plunder, and criminality is making its nest, discouraging the most fearless tourists from coming to spend an evening on the French side."[34]

And all this was happening in spite of the joint road controls with the Dutch side police: 480 vehicles checked in Oyster Pond in one night! It was endless, everyday in the newspapers. In 2009, the headlines went on, *They aggress, brutalize, and plunder in our home* - two identical headlines one after the other in the same issue, *Wounded by bullet in French Quarter - Grand Saint-Martin: a family savagely aggressed in their home*. Drug trafficking also made its victims among the *mules*. In March 2008, a 15 year-old girl of Dominicano descent died in an apartment in France after swallowing about one hundred cocaine *bolitas* on a mission from Saint-Martin to Orly Airport in Paris. Saint-Martiners were exasperated that all those young people were called Saint-Martiners by the French side press, whereas in France they would be referred to as *of immigrant descent.* Saint-Martiners were fed up with their image being constantly dragged in the mud.

In July 2009, the Central Caribbean Football Tournament brought together young people under 15 and under 17 from Saint-Martin, Sint Maarten, Guadeloupe, and St. Kitts. 32 of the 44 players of the neighboring team of St. Kitts came under attack after the end of the last match by players from the French side, whereas the tournament was a success up to then. Eight players from St. Kitts sustained injuries and were hospitalized, one of them with a fractured nose. The officials from Saint-Martin were dismayed at this inopportune violence.[35] The St. Kitts group feared for their security and the news broke out in the press of the neighboring island. The Director of Sports of the Collectivity finally made the following revelation to the local press:

> "In 25 years of playing with the Kittitians in a spirit of mutual understanding, it was *hurtful* that this incident occurred, which never happened before. ... These kids who play in our teams, in schools and gang fights need to be checked to find out who they are. You see, Haitians, Jamaicans, Guyanese, etc. leave their country of origin. Those with good manners bring their good manners, and those with bad manners bring their bad manners. We feed them, clothe them, and give them a new home and a new nationality. Now, when things like this happen they say it's the French Quarter boys, or it's the Dutch boys. Our kids do these things. I am not saying no, but the majority of the time we cannot say that it is local kids."[36]

This incident destabilized the friendly exchanges that Saint-Martin has always had with St. Kitts. Saint-Martin and St. Kitts enjoy family and friendship ties dating back to many centuries. Saint-Martin had never a reputation of aggressiveness. This embarrassing situation obliged not only the President of the Collectivity to go to their hotel to apologize to the St. Kitts victims and parents, but later on, the Territorial Councilor in charge of Culture, Sports and Youth travelled to St. Kitts with a delegation of three sports leaders to apologize for this unfortunate incident to the Prime Minister, the Minister of Youth, the Minister of Sports, as well as sports leaders. They confirmed that all the expenses incurred would be the responsibility of the Collectivity. Such circumstances had never been experienced in Saint-Martin before.

Saint-Martin counted 16,000 young people under 25. We were in 2009 and, according to the French law enforcement officers, adult presence was inexistent at home. In fact, those young people, most of them born in Saint-Martin, who since 2005 had contributed to the growing increase of naturalized French citizens, were the children of mothers who had lined up every month at the Post Office to collect the social benefits necessary for their survival.[37] But they were no longer entitled to that money when their children reached the age of 16, and jobs have been scarce for the last 15 years. These mothers were often obliged to leave the island to survive, and they would leave the children behind for their schooling in care of the older brothers. The girls would follow the same path as their mothers and become, in their turn, beneficiaries of the CAF and other benefits. It is to be noted that continuous attendance in the French schools was the main requirement for these children to obtain the French nationality. Being born in Saint-Martin was not sufficient. That is the reason why these children attended the French schools in great numbers. In addition, they did not have any identification papers yet. The mothers could not take them when they left, as they did twenty years ago. Furthermore, these children could not go to visit their families in their mothers' country of origin without a passport, even though some mothers were from islands as close as St. Kitts/Nevis, for example.

For having collected *CAF money*, these offspring had to suffer the consequences. This was the price that mothers and children had to pay. Whose fault was it? In the eyes of the mothers, these children were *the State's children*. And the children were frustrated to have to be abandoned by their parents, so they let off steam in a violence which, as they grew older, drove them not only to antagonize each other, but virulently confront those whose parents were natives of Saint-Martin. It was obvious to them that their mothers were foreigners and were subject to harsher conditions of life. They had a grudge with the world. They have been repeatedly told that they were Saint-Martiners and some believed it. As they became older, they realized the difference. They bubbled with an inner frustration. Often, they were abandoned or completely ignored by their fathers, a Saint-Martiner or a foreigner. Moreover, it was dramatic for the mothers, when at random they were controlled and it was discovered that they were living with a man. They were ordered to reimburse the money. CAF money was misery. And what misery! An unnatural perverted life! This is one aspect of the psychological explanation of this violence in those young people, as it can take on various forms and degrees of intensity.

The Gendarmerie was directly involved. The Squad for the Prevention of Juvenile Delinquency (B.P.D.J.) kept up its interaction with these young people by organizing football matches, by having them take part in boat outings or even a trip to Paris. The goal was not to win the match, but the rules consisted in playing without violence and without insult, under penalty of sanctions, and to make these young people conscious of the fact that violence did no pay. Seventy young people from various clubs and communities as well as gendarmes participated in these matches. B.P.D.J. received the cooperation of the Baie-Mahault branch in Guadeloupe, and the project was financed by the National Agency for Equal Opportunity and Social Cohesion.

2009 was a deadly year for the 20 year-olds, as they were victims of car and motorbike accidents, and murders. Car and scooter thefts had increased these last years, and also the fights outside the two Marigot Middle and High Schools, and their continuation in the center-of-town, in the public eyes and to the knowledge of all. Nevertheless, as those unfortunate occurrences intensified and the senseless violence in the months of September and October 2009 stunned the general public, exasperation reached its highest peak. The murder of a young Saint-Martiner by a new Saint-Martiner for a parking spot, followed immediately by the murder of another young Saint-Martiner whose scooter was stolen by an unknown individual, his murderer, gave rise to a spate of angry questioning and accusations sometimes without answer or solution. Pointing fingers was not productive

When the center-of-town merchants became the victims of acts of vandalism committed by these middle school students, it was *the drop that made the bucket overflow*. In fact, on October 15, 2009, when the owners of a center-of-town store opened their ready-made clothing boutique, they noticed dirt stains on the newly painted walls. The pot on the sidewalk in front of their store was broken and the plants had disappeared. The day before a group of middle school students had punched on their glass window, flung eggs, and fought in front of their store. Frightened, the lady did call the territorial police who arrived on the spot half an hour later. This late arrival ended up in an altercation between the policeman and the owners, and the filing of a complaint against the policeman. Rock and egg-throwing at passers-by, pulling up decorative plants, and damaging store signs were unbearable.

> "Apart from that incident, the merchants complained of the violence which they face on a regular basis. At this time, the egg-throwing that sometimes degenerate into more aggressive acts, really disturbs the tranquility of the *rue du Général de Gaulle*."[38]

Already in the month of June 2009, gendarmes had intervened in the center-of-town to stop a fight between middle school students. The public road belonged to them when they left school at twelve and at four in the afternoon, and *rue du Général de Gaulle* was on their way. Those acts of provocation urged the merchants in the morning of October 16, 2009 to form a *Collective of Merchants on Rue du Général de Gaulle*. They collected about fifty spontaneous signatures for a petition to be handed to the President of the Collectivity with a request for an appointment. The President and the Chief of the Territorial Police received the Collective on October 21, 2009. The merchants demanded more frequent presence of Territorial Police officers when the students came out of school and at the closing hours of their stores. As elected officials so often repeated to the young people in the past that they were the future of Saint-Martin - *We need you* they used to say -, this new generation proved that the future of Saint-Martin was seriously compromised. In fact, they did not address the same young people. What came out of these events for the natives was the conviction that those young people were not *their* children. Never before, the middle school students of 1980, the year when they formed the majority of the population, would have indulged in such violent, aggressive, and disrespectful behavior. It was still the days of the *Friendly Island*.

By October 13, 2009 another petition arrived on the desk of the President of the Collectivity from an association using the Galisbay Sports Complex. The Saint-Martin Gym Club protested against the poor management of the Sports Complex and the uncivil behavior of the security guard. A dispute arose between the security guard and the instructor of the club, following the more than twenty-minute *sequestration* in the dark of young athletes, which provoked the revolt and indignation of their parents. On the other hand, the other users complained about the dues that the Collectivity instituted in April 2009, the proceeds of which were to cover the expenses for using the facility, and also about the bad condition of the Collectivity's sports infrastructure.

During that same month, three gendarmes from the Squad for the Prevention of Juvenile Delinquency (B.P.D.J.) organized a street basket tournament for about sixty 8th and 9th grade students from French Quarter, Cul-de-Sac, and Concordia at the Louis Vanterpool Stadium of Marigot, in order to determine the causes of their absenteeism at school. These students accumulated the highest number of non-attendance at school. The association *Liaisons Dangereuses* was also involved. In addition to the sporting activity, personalized interviews were programmed with a psychologist, a speech therapist, and a special educator from the Social Services of the Collectivity. A social worker interviewed the parents. The teams consisted of about fifteen students from the various schools "*to avoid any fights between students of the same district.*"[39] The Collectivity was obliged to give its contribution to solutions for this suffering society, and that is what it agreed to do through training programs at all levels of needs. Those programs were common practice throughout the development. Operation Youth Solidarity of the

FISM, initiated in 1996 and financed by the Regional Council, consisted in placing young people between the ages of 18 and 25 in businesses on a part time basis during the vacation months of July or August.[40] But after the training, after being a trainee for a month in a business, where were the jobs, since the economy was in a constant downturn? Shattered hope! Could it still be called hope in a situation where many felt that the present circumstances had outgrown their expectations?

Actually, everyone in this new society was exasperated, and everyone clashed with each other mercilessly. Foreign parents who had the means to send their children to college abroad were also confronted with the petty annoyances of the state administration which slowed down the progress of their children. A seven-parent delegation, all merchants on the French side for 25 years, whose children were born in Saint-Martin, complained about the fact that they had to wait at least one year to obtain the residence card which their children needed to apply for a visa to go to Canada or the United States. The circulation card which they used to travel expired automatically at the age of 18; afterwards, they had to start the procedure to obtain their residence card which lasted about a year. Meanwhile, they were given an application receipt which allowed them to travel, but not to obtain a visa. This situation caused the parents' frustration, because at the end of their secondary studies, their children were losing a whole year before they could continue to college.

The violent behavior of young teenagers originated from the precariousness of the living conditions imposed on them. The generosity of the social services did not improve their standard of living and they plunged into a mental state that was detrimental to them. It was the first time that the French local press reported so openly the state of poverty in Saint-Martin. It must be noted that such poverty did not exist before the 1980s. Unemployment did not exist then, delinquency and violence either, it was the *Friendly Island*. It was paradise - not wealth - for the islanders and for those who came to live in harmony with the native population. Dollars did not run the streets. In October 2009, an article in the *St. Martin's Week*, in an attempt to provide a sociological explanation of that violence, gave an overview of this reality. It is shocking for those who do not know the world of *ghettos*.

> "As poverty gradually increases, the number of homeless youths living in precarious conditions also increases. The number of children wandering in the streets has been growing steadily, especially in the *forsaken* districts. Most youths do not go to school, because they cannot afford it. They are born in families whose revenues are extremely low, and they are confronted with all sorts of violence at a very early age. Few among them can, therefore, hope to find a job in the economic sector. So, most of them very early turn to drug

> trafficking which is a very profitable activity, with the hope to live a better life by helping their families financially.
> Moreover, the free circulation and proliferation of firearms …; the fact that the use of *hard* drugs, like cocaine and crack, has become common practice; and an environment of sheer destitution that is increasing day by day in certain districts; all this has created a climate conducive to the explosion of violence among the younger ones. Alcohol abuse, family and social disorganization are also factors to take into consideration in order to better understand the present situation."[41]

In addition to the misery of the younger ones, the Red Cross drew the attention of the reading public on another kind of poverty, that of adults. It has been steadily increasing, and the Red Cross dutifully tried to alleviate it. The organization does not receive any public subsidies; its resources derive from the proceeds of its annual charitable gala and from private donations. The end of the year 2009 was the opportunity for this organization to solicit the generosity of the general public. Its facility in the former hospital was put at its disposal by the Collectivity. The organization explained the poverty in Saint-Martin as follows:

> "Saint-Martin is a two-faced island. One is the beautiful tourist territory with its beaches, beautiful hotels, wealth, and modern society. The other is the life in the districts where families, often single parent families, cannot make ends meet. Since the month of April 2009, the Red Cross has received nearly 300 families with their terrible life histories. … They are numerous, those homeless people who come knocking on our doors. … The Red Cross has listed more than 250 homeless persons whereas the authorities hardly numbered 50. … At present, these homeless persons shelter in *squats* in and around the center-of-town, where the law of the jungle prevails. There, insanitary conditions are unimaginable to the average individual. Aggressions, rapes, fights are common occurrences. What do the social services of the Collectivity do for those destitute vagrants? There is no program, no public structure to deal with this terrible problem which is spreading in Saint-Martin."[42]

With the downfall of the tourism economy, the visibility of economic inactivity, the closed-down shutters of merchants who have given in to discouragement, the depopulation of the center-of-town, the exodus to the Dutch side of many resident enterprises, the bubbling activity of the Dutch side, but also the obvious courage of Saint-Martiners for whom leaving is not an option, the year 2009 is perceived as the prelude of a diffused hope that everything is not lost. The new society is sick, sick of its domination, sick of its arrogance, sick of its strength, and sick of its disrespect of the society prior to 1980.

Saint-Martin must serve as the laboratory for the extreme deviances and excesses observed in post-slavery and colonial societies. For us to move forward, these deviances and excesses must be stripped out of governmental policies. If there is a place where it must start, that place is Saint-Martin. Here, all the ills live side by side with a maximum degree of concentration on a tiny 54 square kilometer half island. It must start in Saint-Martin where hoaxes are short-lived. The same societal pattern, reproduced at a larger scale in many Third World countries and emergent countries, required decades to detect its contradictions and failures. In Saint-Martin, everything happened simultaneously, the failures of the new society and the exclusion of the society to eliminate.

In the new society that was growing and gaining importance as the Saint-Martin society was fading into inexistence, everyone behaved as if all the members of the Saint-Martin society had slid over to the new society, so when members of the Saint-Martin society tried to keep their heads above water to breathe for their survival, they were deemed insignificant by the absolute force. The year 2009 revealed itself as the catalyst of the conviction that the Saint-Martin society had not completely disappeared, even though the local and national authorities have disregarded it since 1993. This society had never merged with the new society, as it was made to believe. The new society was but a deception. The imposed systematic poverty was imported. The victims had no means of pulling themselves out of it. The societal requirements made on them were unnatural and perverted: they were in opposition to their natural instinct of survival. This study intends to send a message to public authorities warning them against imposing new societal patterns conceived with the sole intention to provide nourishment to greedy individuals.

CONCLUSION

THE AWAKENING OF 2009

The Saint-Martin society of 1980, which the newcomers did their very best to eradicate throughout the last thirty long years of unbridled development, had dwindled to nothingness. They replaced it by a new society with new Saint-Martiners, and invented a new citizen, the Saint-Martin citizen. At the passing of the bulldozer of development, some preferred to jump aboard the train for which the bulldozer cleared the way. Others continued to live their culture, their traditions quietly in their own way.

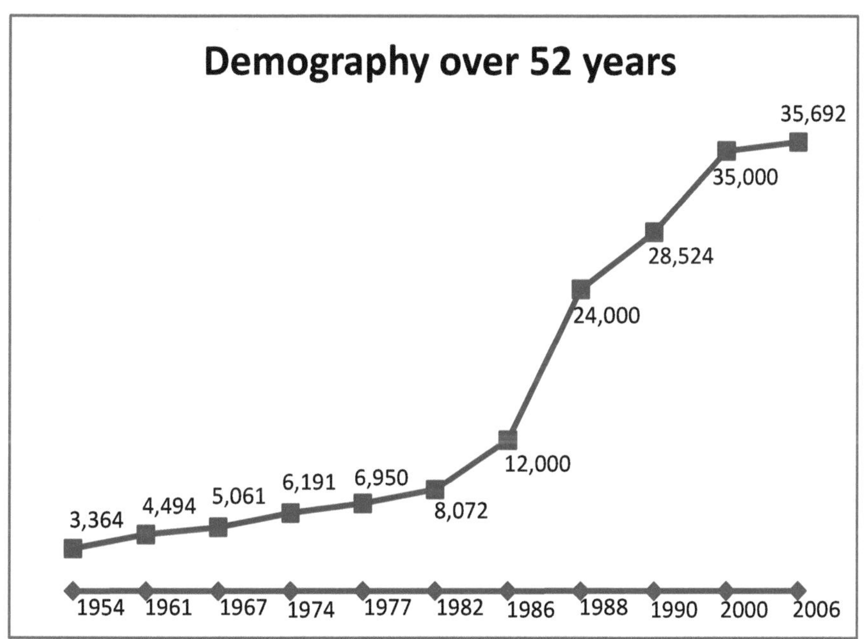

Little things strengthened the natives' conviction that their society cannot be that new society that is dying a natural death with raging violence. The Saint-Martin society is actually the fêtes of the Triple Village, Saint-

Louis/Free Town/Rambaud, the arrow-root *jollifications* of Colombier, and our so-called overeducated youth that the new society forced into exile and is prospering elsewhere with their native island in mind. The Saint-Martin society is actually the Gunslingers and the Jolly Boys in Grand-Case, Tanny and The Boys, the Rolling Tones, the Soualiga Brass and Drum Band, the Ponum dancers, and Chester York and Sons and Grandsons Steel Band in Great Bay. It is actually our artists and painters immortalizing our landscapes and faces, some of our little houses already gone with the development. It is also our poets and songwriters echoing our struggles, sufferings and joys. It is our craftswomen dressing up their dollies in the *frocks* of not so distant days. It is also this Municipal Councilor who in 1978 had publicly denounced his political leader. In 2006 at the end of his political career, when in charge of the Commission of Urban Transportation, he reminded us that public transportation - school buses, tour buses and taxis - were still a sector mostly held by natives. He insisted that it is a cultural tradition handed down from father to son. This profession was threatened by the parallel activity of *gypsy* taxis and buses with no solution for some twenty years. He decided to organize locally a training session for Saint-Martin drivers.

The Saint-Martin society is actually all those residents who have never believed in the viability of the new society, which they had difficulty to accept. They knew Saint-Martin prior to 1980 and those Saint-Martiners whose memory they dearly cherish. The Saint-Martin society is actually those guesthouse owners who came together as *The Relays of the Tamon Trees*, an association under the chairmanship of Pastor Eugene Hodge, the owner himself of a 12 room guesthouse. There are 19 of those typically Saint-Martin guesthouses totaling 240 rooms. But the new society does not give any consideration to a 100% Saint-Martin hotel trade, and yet it exists. The owners of those facilities under 20 rooms each often have another profession. Promotion of the facility is done by word of mouth by their guests, who are Americans in winter and Europeans in summer. They also cater for Caribbean guests from Puerto Rico, Martinique and Guadeloupe, mainly. They offer a family-like personalized service to their guests, and more than half of these guesthouses are *overbooked*. The association aims at encouraging these small hotel owners to improve their service, because they believe that the future of Saint-Martin tourism lies in these authentic convivial facilities.

The Saint-Martin society is also the villages of Colombier, Friars' Bay, Rambaud, Saint-Louis/Free Town, and Peak Paradise. These villages are the breadbasket of the island, the cradle of culture, and the heart of rural life. Far from the sea, they did not arouse the cupidity of the newcomers. Nonetheless, the villagers of Colombier had refused the building of a huge hotel in their picturesque valley in 1986. The villagers of Saint-Louis/Free Town had refused the building of a Shelter for drug addicts in the middle of their village in 2001. Rumors of the building of social housing at the entrance of the only road into their villages gave rise to feelings of indignation which strengthen their determination not to allow their living environment to be tarnished. The villagers of the Triple Village will continue to preserve their heritage by honoring the memory of their cultural icon, Laurelle Richards, affectionately known as Yaya and considered as the Queen of the villagers, who suddenly left them too soon on Wednesday, May 26, 2010.

The Saint-Martin society is actually this young fisherman, the son and grandson of a fisherman who, after studying in the hospitality field in Martinique and working for a real estate company, gave up everything to engage into deep-sea fishing as his life profession, whereas his father fished in the traditional manner. His customers are the natives, and tourists from Latin America and the United States. He earns a good living and hopes that one of his sons will continue the family tradition.

The Saint-Martin society is, undoubtedly, the *Solidarity Rastafari* gardens created in 1995. They are cultivated by about forty men and women from Martinique, Guadeloupe, Trinidad, St. Kitts, Anguilla, Saint-Martin, Jamaica, among others, working to preserve the cultural and natural heritage of Saint-Martin. They are now in the valley of Bellevue since February 2007 on 37 acres of land put at their disposal by the owners. In season, they produce lettuce, cucumber, beet, pepper, white onion, leek, turnip, celery, parsley, spinach, carrot, and papaya. They use neither pesticide nor fertilizer. However, they lack water and they have to get it at the Marigot public well. They not only welcome school children in order to instill into them the love of gardening, but natives, French and foreign residents also purchase their produce on a regular basis.

The Saint-Martin society is also the hero of this octogenarian couple from California who is telling their beautiful story in the *Daily Herald* of September 24, 2009:

> "Last week, we punctured a tire as we pulled into Juliana Airport to pick up arriving friends. My 80-year-old husband pulled up to the curb and I went to find assistance to change the tire. We were not familiar with the jack in the trunk.
> Two security guards posted at the curb were only concerned about keeping the traffic flowing. "No parking" they cried out. We explained to the fellow in charge that we had a flat tire and asked him if he had a cellular phone or if he could direct us to someone who could help us fix the flat. He looked at me as if I spoke a foreign tongue (perhaps I did?) and just repeated, "Move the car. You can't park here."

> I went to the car rental booths inside the terminal, but no one could help either. In sheer desperation, I approached the tall fellow in charge of the taxi service. “Let me look at it,” he said, and followed me to our car while the security men went on with “Move it” and our guests were looking for a place to place their luggage.
>
> Our hero – and new island friend – changed the tire in about five minutes, and we were ready to go. He didn’t even want to take the few dollars my husband gave him.
>
> The tall man in the yellow shirt at the taxi stand will always symbolize “The Friendly Island” to a little old lady from California. Perhaps those other folks were immigrants?”[43]

We are faced with a challenge today: the Saint-Martin society or the communitarian-based society?

APPENDIX 1
THE 1648 TREATY OF CONCORDIA

Today, March 23, 1648, have assembled Robert de Lonvilliers, Knight and Lord of this place, Governor of the island of Saint-Martin on behalf of His Most Christian Majesty (i.e. the King of France) and Martin Thomas, likewise Governor of the said island, on behalf of the Prince of Orange and the States General of Holland, and Henry de Lonvilliers, Knight, Lord of Bennevent, and Savinien de Courpon, Knight, Lord of La Tour, Lieutenant-Colonel of the island, and David Coppin, Lieutenant of a Dutch company, and Pitre van Zeun Hus, also lieutenant of a company, both parties have hereby agreed to the following:

I

That the French shall remain in the quarter where they are established presently, and that they shall inhabit the entire side facing Anguilla.

II

That the Dutch shall have the quarter of the fort and the land surrounding it on the south side.

III

That the French and Dutch established on the said island shall live as friends and allies, and that in case of either party molesting the other, this shall constitute an infringement of the present agreement, and shall therefore be punishable by the laws of war.

IV

That, if a Frenchman or a Dutchman being guilty of a criminal act or an infringement of this agreement, or of disobedience to the commands of his superiors, or shall move to the territory of the other nation, the contracting parties commit themselves to have such person arrested in their quarter, and to deliver him up to his Governor on the latter's first request.

V

That hunting, fisheries, salt-pans, rivers, ponds, fresh waters, dye-wood, mines or minerals, harbors and roadsteads, and other commodities of the said island shall be common and shall serve to provide for the needs of the inhabitants.

VI

That, French persons who are presently residing with the Dutch shall be allowed to join the French, if it so pleases them, and to take their movables, foodstuff and money, and other commodities with them provided they have settled their debts or given sufficient guarantee. The Dutch shall be able to do likewise and under the same conditions.

VII

That, if enemies should attack either quarter, the parties to this treaty shall be obliged to render each other aid and assistance.

VIII

That the delimitation and partition of the said island between the two nations shall be submitted to the General of the French and the Governor of Saint-Eustatius, and to the Nation representatives that shall be sent to visit the premises. Their report having been made, the two quarters shall be delimitated and the procedure shall be carried out as stipulated in the report.

IX

That any claims from either party shall be submitted to the King of France and the gentlemen of His Council, and to the Prince of Orange and the States General of Holland on either part. Meanwhile, the parties shall not be able to construct fortifications without contravening the present agreement and compensations with respect to the other party.

Drawn up on the above-mentioned year and day on the mount named Concordia of the said island, the contracting parties signed the present document in the presence of Bernard de la Fond, Knight, de l'Espérance, Lieutenant of a French company in St. Christopher. Thus signed de Lonvilliers, Martin Thomas, Henry de Lonvilliers, de Courpon, David Coppin, de l'Espérance, and Piter van Zeun-Hus.

APPENDIX 2
MAP OF SAINT-MARTIN/SINT-MAARTEN

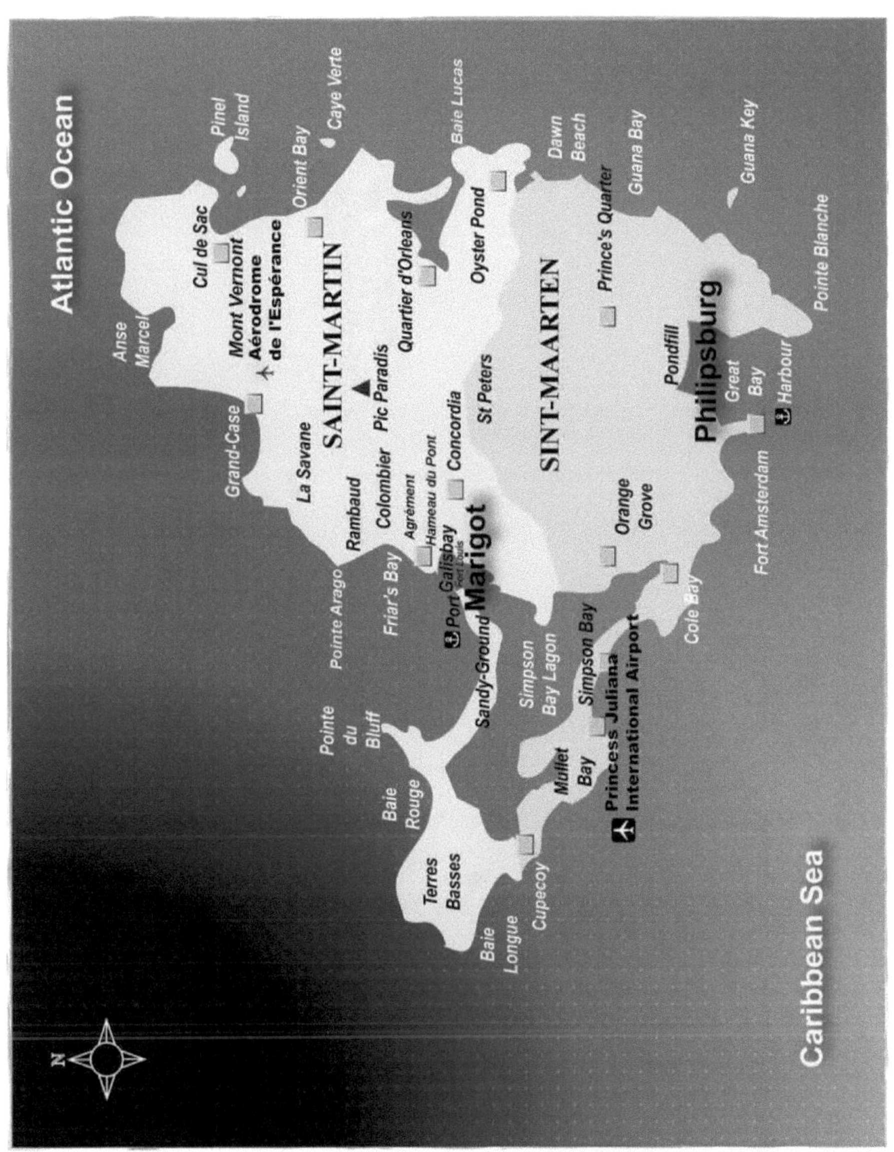

Map from Alain Paméole / Skoff

APPENDIX 3
JUNE 17, 1986

All of you will agree
And if I lie you could beat me
'Cause for sure
All of you know
That nobody on the island.
Ain't kill not a damn man
Nobody in the island
Never thief no PAF gun
Never thief no PAF cap
Never involved in no PAF corruption.
Never tasted no PAF drugs.
Never get in no PAF nastiness.
And for justice
They get licks.

That Day,
A Tuesday not like all days,
Early morning, they played their beat.
But we played our tempo.
PAF PAF PAF they knocked us down
PAF PAF PAF and we fall down.
They treated us like dogs
But they never see how dogs
Whether night or day
Are always ready to play.
They thought it would be a puppy show.
But there is one thing that they should know
Is that angry dogs
Got four feet
To jump higher,
To better cut their throat

There is one thing that they should know
Is that angry dogs
Never use their teeth
To eat no kind of blows.
There is one thing that they should know
Is that Haitian dogs,
'Spanish' dogs,
St. Martin dogs,
Are the same dogs.
They stand like a man
To fight for their dignity.

Christian Choucoutou
Published in NEWSDAY on Friday, June 20th, 1986
Written in St. Martin English

ABBREVIATIONS/LOGOS

ACASM: Association of Merchants and Craftsmen in Saint-Martin
ADICASM: Association for the Defense of the Interests of Saint-Martin Merchants and Craftsmen
AFPAG: Association for Vocational and Craftsmanship Training of Guadeloupe
AHSM: Association of Hoteliers in Saint-Martin
ANPE: National Employment Agency
AOM: Overseas Airline
APAIS: Association for Prevention and Assistance to Social Insertion
APLSM: Association of Professionals in Saint-Martin
ASMIS: Saint-Martin Association for Initiative and Solidarity
BDAF: Bank of the French Antilles
BEP: Vocational Diploma
BUMIDOM: Office of Migrations from Overseas Departments
CAP: Certificate of Vocational Proficiency
CARICOM: Caribbean Community
CCI: Chamber of Commerce and Industry
CGTG: General Labor Association of Guadeloupean Workers
CHRU: Regional University Medical Center
CRS: Republican Company of Security
CV: Curriculum Vitae - Résumé
DASD: Social Action Service in Guadeloupe
DDE: Public Works Headquarters in Guadeloupe
DDTE: Labor and Employment Headquarters in Guadeloupe
DOM-TOM: Overseas Departments and Territories
FISM: Inter-professional Federation in Saint-Martin
FIPCOM: Inter-professional Federation of the Overseas Collectivity
For' IDN: Training in the Northern Islands
HLM: Moderate Income Housing
IEDOM: Central Bank in the Overseas Departments
INSEE: National Institute of Statistics and Economic Studies
OMI: Office of International Migrations
OMS: World Health Organization
ONF: National Forest Service
PAF: Air Frontier Police
PAN AM: American Airline Company
POS: Zoning Plan

RMI: Minimum Revenue of Insertion
RPR: Gathering For the Republic
RSMA: Regiment of Adapted Military Service
SDF: Homeless people
SIG: Public Housing Company in Guadeloupe
SMIG: Guaranteed Minimum Salary of Insertion
SODEGA: Development Company of Guadeloupe
SPDEG: Company of Electric Production and Distribution of Guadeloupe
SRPJ: Regional Service of Judicial Police
TGI: County Court
UDTSM: Labor Union of Saint-Martin Workers
UGTG: General Union of Guadeloupe Workers
UMP: Union of Presidential Majority
ZAC: Zone of Concerted Action

NOTES

INTRODUCTION

1. Jacques Adélaïde-Merlande, *Historial Antillais,* Vol. III, Projets d'émancipation, p. 342
2. Victor Schœlcher, *Histoire de l'esclavage pendant les deux dernières* années, Tome I, p. 447
3. François-Auguste Perrinon, Former student at the Polytechnic School in Paris
4. *Le Moniteur Universel*, Official gazette of the Republic of France, Sunday, March 5, 1848
5. Daniella Jeffry, *1963:A Landmark Year in Saint-Martin*, pp. 1-2
6. Guy Lasserre, *La Guadeloupe*, Tome 2, p. 836
7. For a Saint-Martiner, a stranger does not refer to the nationality of the person, but to the fact that he is from elsewhere. It has no derogatory connotation; it is the general point of view of the islanders.
8. Daniella Jeffry, *The status scandal on the island of Saint-Martin*, pp. 184-185

FIRST PART
THE FRENCH CARIBBEAN SOCIETY AFTER 1946

1. Louis Boutrin & Raphaël Confiant, *Chronique d'un empoisonnement annoncé*, p. 25
2. Raphaël Confiant, Aimé Césaire: *Une Traversée Paradoxale du siècle*, p. 18
3. Albert Memmi, *Portrait d'un colonisé, Portrait d'un colonisateur*, pp. 139-140
4. Edouard Glissant, *Culture et Colonisation: l'équilibre antillais*, Revue Esprit, Avril 1962
5. Oruno D. Lara, *Guadeloupe : Faire face à l'histoire*, p. 63
6. *Historial Antillais*, Tome IV, p. 52
7. Lushena Books, *The Willie Lynch Letter & The Making Of a Slave,* pp. 7-9
8. Daniella Jeffry, *The status scandal on the island of Saint-Martin*, p. 16
9. *Ibid.,* p. 175
10. Françoise Vergès, *Abolir l'esclavage : une utopie coloniale, Les Ambiguïtés de la politique humanitaire*, p. 200
11. *Ibid.*, p. 199
12. *Ibid.*, p. 199
13. http://Guadeloupetraditions.free.fr/bumidom.htm, Le BUMIDOM, BIBIDOM en créole : Un exode volontaire ? p. 1
14. http://fr.wikipedia.org « Bumidom », p. 2 [Bureau pour le développement des Migrations intéressant les Départements d'Outre-mer]
15. http://www.evene.fr/cinema/actualite/interview... Entièrement à part, Propos recueillis par Mélanie Carpentier et Jean-Nicolas Berniche, 01 février 2007
16. http://arcH.I.V.esforum.zouker.com, Génocide par substitution : le cas de la Kanaky
17. http://www.humanite.presse.fr, Comment l'Etat colonial a dû reconnaître l'identité kanak ? par Jean Chatain, 25 mars 2006
18. *Ibid.,* Nouvelle-Calédonie : un pari sur l'avenir par Jean Chatain, 7 novembre 1998

19. *Sept Magazine,* N° 2056, 23 septembre 1999, p. 16
20. *Ibid.*

SECOND PART
THE SAINT-MARTIN SOCIETY 1977-2007

I. Beginnings of the Modern Period

1. Arrow-root is transformed into flour, used for infants as a porridge or pap, and also made as cassava bread. It is a very important activity in the village of Colombier to which the population is invited to participate at the end of February as *jollification*, traditional unpaid work done as a group.
2. Lou Peters, A History of Commerce in St. Maarten in *Windward Islands Newsday* Vol. 4 N° 348, March 12, 1980
3. J. Hartog, *History of St. Maarten/St. Martin*, 1981, p. 135
4. *Nouvelles des Iles du Nord*, Journal N° 17, Décembre 1974
5. *Ibid.,* Journal N° 19, Janvier 1975
6. *Ibid.*
7. *Ibid.*
8. *97_1 Hebdo* N° 6 (not dated[2])
9. *Nouvelles des Iles du Nord*, Journal N° 19, Janvier 1975

II. The Societal Impact of Development

1. See Appendix 1 : The 1648 Treaty of Concordia
2. *Vu*, Décembre 1976, Communiqué du Maire de Saint-Martin, p. 3
3. *Ibid.,* Révocation, p. 3
4. Remi de Haenen, born in London in 1916 and died in St. Barths on July 31, 2008; General Councilor for 21 years since 1953; Mayor of St. Barths from 1962 to 1977, the first to request a special status at the visit of General de Gaulle in St. Barths in 1964.
5. *Trait d'Union* N° 75026, March 1977
6. *Trait d'Union* N° 75030, July 1977
7. *Trait d'Union*, N° 75036, February 1978, p. 10
8. *Cogito,* Bilingual Quarterly Review 1st year N° 4, Dec. 78/Jan. Feb. 79, p. 9
9. Sandy Ground: a sandy stretch of land between the Simpsonbay Lagoon and the Caribbean Sea and between Marigot in the north and the Bluff in the west.
10. Sub-Prefect's speech.
11. Reference is made to Europeans.
12. *Windward Islands Newsday*, December 14, 1981, A distressed student in Guadeloupe.
13. *Ibid.,* August 15, 1980, Request for a Cultural Center, pp. 2 & 12
14. André-Louis Sanguin, *Saint-Martin, les mutations d'une île franco-néerlandaise des Antilles*, Cahiers d'Outre-mer, 35(138) avril-juin 1982, p. 132
15. *Windward Islands Newsday*, Vol. 8 N° 893, March 7, 1984, Interview of Mayor Elie Fleming with PJD2 Radio in Philipsburg, St. Maarten
16. André-Louis Sanguin, *ibid.,* p. 133
17. *97_1 Hebdo,* N° 18, not dated, « Expulsion des Haïtiens », J.J. Laplagne, p. 4
18. Felix Choisy (1915-1989), a politician and patriot; 1er Deputy Mayor (1959-1977) and General Councilor of Saint-Martin (1973-1979).
19. *97_1 Hebdo, Ibid.,* p. 4

20. Jollification: The tradition in Saint-Martin of unpaid work done as a group for solidarity purposes.
21. *97_1 Hebdo*, ibid., pp. 5-6
22. *Windward Islands Newsday*, Vol. 4 N° 369, April 24, 1980, Is St. Martin under a state of martial law?
23. *Ibid.*, p. 2
24. *Windward Islands Newsday*, Vol. 4 N° 363, April 14, 1980, Protest signs appear on French St. Martin, p. 1
25. *France-Antilles*, 21 avril 1980 et *Windward Islands Newsday*, April 18, 21 & 28, 1980
26. *97_1 Hebdo*, N° 25, Janvier 1981, Le Concorde à St. Martin, p. 3
27. *97_1 Hebdo*, Expulsion des Haïtiens, J.J. Laplagne, pp. 5-6
28. *97_1 Hebdo*, Editorial : Je ne comprends plus…
29. *Windward Islands Newsday*, Vol. 4 N° 348 March 12, 1980, A History of Commerce in St. Maarten by Lou Peters.
30. *France-Antilles*, 21 mars 1983
31. *Le Progrès Social*, 23 avril 1983
32. *Le Progrès Social*, N° 1360, 9 avril 1983, p. 2

III. Mirage of Tourism Development

1. *L'Expansion*, 16 mars/5avril 1984, p. 43
2. *… on condition:* Investments are however subject to three protective measures…
3. *Le Quotidien* de Paris, N° 1345, 21 mars 1984, p. 12
4. *St. Martin Eco Mag* N° 9, Rencontre, 1999, pp. 22-23
5. Fabian Badejo, *Claude : A portrait of power*, International Publishing House, St. Maarten, N.A., 1989, p. 77
6. *Windward Islands Newsday,* Vol. 10 N° 1122, July 25, 1986.
7. *Ibid.* N° 1125, July 30, 1986.
8. *Ibid.* Vol. 10 N° 1092, February 19, 1986, Letter from Sub-Prefect Hubert, p. 1
9. *Windward Islands Newsday*, Vol. 10 N° 1119, June 20, 1986
10. *France-Antilles*, 19 juin 1986, Incidents dans l'île de Saint-Martin.
11. *Ibid.,* Après les événements de Saint-Martin.
12. *Windward Islands Newsday,* June 25, 1986, Long live the determination of the people of Saint-Martin by Louis Hamlet.
13. *France-Antilles,* 1er Juillet 1986, A Saint-Martin : Manifestation silencieuse des parents d'élèves.
14. *Windward Islands Newsday*, Vol. 10 N° 1132, August 13, 1986, Saving St. Maarten/St. Martin from unhappiness and tension by Roland Richardson.
15. *Ibid.,* Vol. 11 N° 1179, January 23, 1987, SMECO: St. Martin needs a direction.
16. *Ibid.,* N° 1181, January 28, 1987, Will Marigot as trade port support Great Bay?
17. *Ibid.,* N° 1182, January 30, 1987, French have plans to build a casino in Cole Bay.
18. *Ibid.,* N° 1193, March 2, 1987, Interview, Fleming: We have no intentions of becoming a colony or department of France.
19. *Ibid.,* N° 1175, January 14, 1987, Wathey: St. Maarten's labor market saturated with cheap labor.
20. *Ibid.,* N° 1180, January 26, 1987, Immigration raids hurt local shopkeepers.
21. *Ibid.,* N° 1215, May 6, 1987, Happy Bay workers not paid.
22. *Ibid.,* N° 1174, January 12, 1987, Mayor Fleming: Locals must stop sitting back.
23. *Ibid.,* Vol. 10 N° 1150, October 22, 1986, New public housing development for St. Martin, by L. Stephen Emmanuel.
24. *Ibid.,* Vol. 11, April 24, 1987, Has Mayor Fleming lied to us about housing for St. Martiners? by SMECO, p. 5

25. *Ibid.*, N° 1186, February 11, 1987, St. Maarten/St. Martin's first Private ambulance service, pp. 1B & 11
26. *St. Martin's Week*, N° 320, 12 septembre 1991, p. 21
27. *Newsday* Vol. 11 N° 1191, February 25, 1987, Police and Gendarmes working together against Lowlands Outlaws, pp. 1, 2 & 11
28. *Newsday* Vol. 11 N° 1187, February 13, 1987, Are the Lowlands becoming St. Maarten/St. Martin's Badlands? pp. 1 & 4
29. *Newsday* Vol. 11 N° 1195, March 9, 1987, Italian, Dominicano, and Frenchman summoned to court on drugs.
30. *St. Martin's Week,* N° 147, 18 mai 1988, p. 14
31. *Ibid.*
32. *Letter of the General Councilor,* February 1989, Editorial: The last chance, p. 1
33. *Ibid.*, Saint-Martin : Multiracial Crossroads, p. 2
34. *St. Martin's Week,* N° 320, 12 septembre 1991, p.21
35. *Ibid.*, 17 octobre 1991, Les commentaires de l'architecte Frank Jespersen sur le lotissement des Terres Basses.
36. *The News*, N° 122, 12 septembre 1992
37. Law n° 86-2 of 03.01.1986 – Law n° 83-630 of 12.07.1983 – Law n° 92-3 of 03.01.1992 – Law n° 95-101 of 02.02.1995.
38. *St. Martin's Week,* 1988, Entretien avec M. le Sous-préfet, par Daniel Ducharme, p. 10
39. List of local businesses existing in the center-of-town: 1.A.O. Self-service 2. The Happy Shop 3. Oulito 4. Simportex 5. Christine 6. Caps 7. Mme Joseph Richardson 8. E. Barry Department Store 9. General Foods 10. Sosamag Self-service 11. Eddy's Grocery 12. Emile Tondu 13. Galisbay Cash & Carry 14. One Stop Superette 15. Ray's Super Shop 16. Chez Henri 17. Chez Cecile.
40. *St. Martin's Week*, N° 197, 4 mai 1989, Maison de St. Martin, Tourisme et communication.
41. *Newsday,* Vol. 13 N° 1523, November 10-11, 1989, p. 1B
42. *Newsday,* November 13-14, 1989, p. 3

IV. Demographic Excess

1. *Newsday,* August 27-28, 1990, p. 2
2. *The St. Maarten Guardian,* Vol. I N° 273, January 16, 1990, p. 6
3. *Ibid.*
4. Opposition party newly renamed *St. Maarten Patriotic Alliance.*
5. *Newsday*, January 24-25, 1990, p. 2
6. *St. Martin's Week,* N 261, 26 juillet 1990
7. *Ibid.,* Le Lycée Professionnel à l'heure des bilans, p. 11
8. *The News,* 6 août 1991, Forum de l'ASMIS, L'Echec scolaire à Saint-Martin, p. 4
9. Rapport de Mission, Octobre 1991, *Travail illégal et immigration irrégulière dans les départements d'Outre-mer, Le cas : Saint Martin* par Claude-Valentin Marie, p. 50
10. *Ibid.,* p. 49
11. Dossier *Saint-Martin/Sint Maarten, Le paradis des bonnes affaires*, par Lucienne Chénard, N° 88-89, p. 57-63
12. *St. Martin's Week*, 8 août 1991, p. 15
13. *Sept Mag,* N° 631, 25 juillet 1991, p. 25
14. *The News*, 23 juillet 1991, p. 4
15. *St. Martin's Week,* 7 janvier 1993, p. 13
16. *Eco Mag*, 1999 N° 9 Rencontre, pp. 22-23
17. *The News,* N° 90, 4 février 1992, pp. 4-5

18. *Ibid.*, N° 91, 11 février 1992, p. 6
19. *St. Martin's Week*, N° 342, 13 février 1992, pp. 22-23
20. *The News,* N° 90, 4 février 1992, p. 6
21. *The News,* 17 février 1992, p. 8
22. *St. Martin's Week,* N° 344, 28 février 1992, p. 22
23. *The New Age,* Vol. VII N° 32, September 15, 1977
24. *The News,* N° 134, 8 décembre 1992, p. 9
25. *Ibid.,* N° 129, 3 novembre 1992, p. 3
26. *Ibid.,* N° 125, 6 octobre 1992, p. 4
27. *Ibid.*, N° 128, 27 octobre 1992
28. *St. Martin's Week*, 12 mars 1992
29. *Ibid.,* 16 janvier 1992, p. 17
30. *The News,* 14 janvier 1992, p. 8
31. *Ibid.,* 21 avril 1992
32. *St. Martin's Week,* 28 mai 1992, p. 22
33. *The News*, N° 125, 6 octobre 1992
34. *Ibid.,* N° 149, 24 mars 1993
35. *St. Martin's Week*, 23 avril 1992
36. *The News,* 26 Mai 1992
37. *Ibid.,* N° 127, 20 octobre 1992, p. 6-7
38. *Ibid.,* N° 139, 12 janvier 1993
39. *L'Hebdo de St. Martin,* Octobre 1994, p. 4
40. *The News,* N°139, 12 janvier 1993, pp. 6-7
41. *Ibid.*, N° 146, 3 mars 1993, p. 23
42. *St. Martin's Week,* N° 385, 10 décembre 1992, p. 28
43. *The News* N° 149, 24 mars 1993
44. See Opening of the first senior-high class, p. 92
45. *The News*, 28 juillet 1992
46. *Ibid.,* N° 125, 6 octobre 1992, p. 9
47. Source : *St. Martin's Week,* 21 septembre 1999, p. 2
48. Rapport de mission du 2 au 12 décembre 1995, *En Guyane et à Saint-Martin, Des Etrangers sans droits dans une France Bananière*, mars 1996, pp. 9-10
49. *St. Martin's Week*, N° 626, 20 juillet 1997
50. *The News*, 4 octobre 1995, p. 4
51. *St. Martin's Week*, N° 625, 22 juillet 1997
52. *Ibid.,* N° 626, 29 juillet 1997
53. *Ibid.,* N° 629, 29 août 1997, Opinion: Coup de gueule.
54. *L'Hebdo Infos*, N° 7, 24 mars 1997, p. 1
55. *St. Martin's Week*, N° 627, 5 août 1997, p. 2
56. *The Daily Herald*, February 26, 1999
57. *St. Martin's Week*, N° 674, 30 juin 1998, p. 7
58. *Ibid.,* N° 622, 1er juillet 1997, p. 2
59. See Insecurity and Delinquency p. 182
60. *L'Hebdo de St. Martin*, 21 novembre 1998, pp. 3-4
61. *The News*, juin 1994, p. 12
62. *St. Martin's Week,* N° 679, 3 août 1998, p. 1
63. *Ibid.,* N° 676, 15 juillet 1998, p. 11. Soca: Caribbean rhythm.
64. *Ibid.,* N° 622, 1er juillet 1997
65. Chevènement Circular letter: Circular letter from the Interior Minister dated October 11, 1999 relative to the legalization of undocumented foreigners capable of proving a 10 year presence on French soil.

V. Societal Deception

1. Daniella Jeffry, *The status scandal on the island of Saint-Martin*, p. 184
2. CRC Reports: www.comptes.fr
3. François Seners, *Saint-Martin, Saint-Barthélemy : Quel avenir pour les îles du nord de la Guadeloupe ?* 1999, p. 36
4. *St. Martin's Week*, N° 462, 2 juin 1994
5. *Le Pélican*, 8 juillet 2004, p. 2
6. *L'Hebdo de St. Martin*, 5 juillet 1996, p. 3
7. *St. Martin's Week* N° 1045 bis, 12 août 2005, p. 3
8. *Le Pélican,* 11 février 2008, p. 7
9. *St. Martin's Week,* 3 janvier 2001
10. *The Daily Herald,* March 31, 2008, p. 40
11. *St.Maarten Business Week,* Vol. 1 N° 30, July 1-7, 2002, p. 16
12. *Sept Mag,* N° 1095, 29 juin 2000, Dossier : Spécial Saint-Martin, p. 8
13. *Today,* 23 mai 2001
14. *Le Pélican*, 10 mars 2008, p. 3
15. *St. Martin's Week* N° 986 bis, 25 juin 2004, p. 3
16. *Le Pélican,* 29 septembre 2009, p. 2
17. *Ibid.*, 8 décembre 2005
18. *St. Martin's Week* N° 919 bis, 14 mars 2003
19. *Our News*, N° 97, 13 mars 2003
20. *St. Martin's Week,* N° 920 bis, 21 mars 2003
21. *FaxInfo*, N° 2556, 25 mars 2003
22. *St. Martin's Week* N° 1197 ter, 11 juillet 2008
23. *FaxInfo*, N° 2247, 23 novembre 2001, p. 2
24. *Le Pélican*, 11 octobre 2007, p. 3
25. *St. Martin's Week,* N° 1185, 14 avril 2008, p. 1
26. *Le Pélican,* 2 juillet 2009, p. 4
27. *St. Martin's Week* N° 1230, 23 février 2009, p. 3
28. *L'Hebdo de St. Martin,* 22 février 1997, p. 6
29. In capital letters in the text. *St. Martin's Week* N° 1175 ter, 4 janvier 2008, p. 10
30. Vox, Non-exhaustive list of onomatopoeia, www.unige.ch/
31. *Smn-news.com,* May 21, 2008, French Quarter residents demand respect by rioting.
32. *Smn-news.com*, July 4, 2008, Fuentes must go ... says Collectif.
33. *Smn-news.com*, June 10, 2008, Open Letter to the Delegate Prefect, Dominique Lacroix
34. *St. Martin's Week* N° 1204 bis, 27 août 2008, p. 6
35. Diminutive for the name of the main island in the Federation of St. Christopher & Nevis.
36. *Today,* July 20, 2009, p. 3
37. See Naturalization diagram p. 238
38. *St. Martin's Week* 1264, 19 octobre 2009
39. *Le Pélican*, 20 octobre 2009, p. 5
40. *St. Martin's Week*, 16 avril 2002, p. 9
41. *Ibid.* N° 1261 ter, 2 octobre 2009, p. 2
42. *Ibid.* N° 1263 ter, 16 octobre 2009, p. 14

VI. The Awakening of 2009

43. *The Daily Herald*, September 24, 2009, Opinion: Our new friend on the Friendly Island, p. 39

BIBLIOGRAPHY

BADEJO Fabian, *Claude: A Portrait of Power*, Ife International Publishing House, St. Maarten, Netherlands Antilles, 1989

BANCEL Nicolas, BLANCHARD Pascal, VERGES Françoise, *La République coloniale*, Hachette Littératures, Collection Pluriel Histoire, Albin Michel, Paris, 2003

BILE Serge, *Noirs dans les camps nazis*, Editions du Rocher/Le Serpent à Plumes, Monaco, 2005

BLANCHARD Pascal, BANCEL Nicolas, *De l'indigène à l'immigré*, Découvertes Gallimard / Histoire, Paris, 2007

BOUTRIN Louis, CONFIANT Raphaël, *Chronique d'un empoisonnement annoncé, Le scandale du Chlordécone aux Antilles Françaises 1972-2002*, Editions l'Harmattan, Paris, 2007

BOUVET Laurent, *Le Communautarisme, Mythes et Réalités*, Editions Lignes de Repères, Paris, 2007

BRAFLAN-TROBO Patricia, *Conflits Sociaux en Guadeloupe, Histoire, identité culturelle dans les grèves en Guadeloupe,* L'Harmattan, Collection Sociétés et Economies Insulaires, Paris, 2007

BUCHANAN Patrick J., *State of Emergency*, Thomas Dunne Books, St. Martin's Press, New York, 2004

BULHAN Hussein Abdilahi, *Frantz Fanon and the Psychology of Oppression*, Boston University, Boston, Massachusetts, Plenum Press, New York, 1985

COMBES M., FELICITE Ch., MANLIUS J., etc., *La Traite Silencieuse : Les émigrés des départements d'outre-mer*, Librairie L'Harmattan, Paris, 1977

CONFIANT Raphaël, *Aimé Césaire : Une traversée paradoxale du siècle*, Ecriture, Paris, 2006

DE BALEINE Philippe, *Les danseuses de la France*, Librairie Plon, Paris 1979

DEGRAS Jean-Claude, *Félix Eboué, Le gouverneur nègre de la République (1936-1944)*, Editions Le Manuscrit, Paris, 2004

DIOP Boucabar Boris, TOBNER Odile, VERSCHAVE François-Xavier, *Négrophobie*, Editions des Arènes, Paris, 2005

FANON Frantz, *Les damnés de la terre*, François Maspéro, Paris, 1979

- *Peau noire, masques blancs*, Editions du Seuil, Paris, 1952

GERBEAU Hubert, CARTER Marina, *Etat et Communautarisme : Le cas de l'Ile Maurice,* dans *Cultures et Conflits* N° 15/16 – Automne-Hiver 1994, L'Harmattan, Paris, 1995

GIRARDET Raoul, *L'Idée coloniale en France de 1871 à 1962*, Hachette Littératures, Collection Pluriel, La Table Ronde, Paris, 1972, 2007

GLISSANT Edouard, CHAMOISEAU Patrick, *Quand les murs tombent : L'Identité nationale hors-la-loi ?* Editions Galaade, Institut du Tout-Monde, Paris, 2007

HELENON Véronique, *Races, statut juridique et colonisation, Antillais et Africains dans les cadres administratifs des colonies françaises d'Afrique*, dans *L'Esclavage, la colonisation, et après…*, Presses Universitaires de France, Paris, 2006, pp. 229-243
HUNT Gerard M., *Rambling on Saint-Martin, A Witnessing*, Trafford Publishing, Victoria, B.C., Canada, 2010
JEFFRY Daniella, *1963 : Année Charnière à Saint-Martin*, Edition bilingue, House of Nehesi Publishers, St. Martin, Caribbean, 2003
- *Le scandale statutaire sur l'île de Saint-Martin*, L'Harmattan, Paris, 2006
JOHNSON Charles, SMITH Patricia, the WGBH Series Research Team, *Africans in America : America's Journey through Slavery,* Harcourt Inc., A Harvest Book, New York, 1999
KABOU Axelle, *Et si l'Afrique refusait le développement*, Editions L'Harmattan, Paris, 2006
LAKE Joseph H. Jr., *Friendly Anger: The Rise of the Labor Movement in St. Martin*, House of Nehesi Publishers, St. Martin, Caribbean, 2004
LARA Oruno D., *Guadeloupe: Faire Face à l'Histoire*, L'Harmattan, Paris, 2009
LATIF Sultan A., LATIF Naimah, *Slavery: The African American Psychic Trauma*, Latif Communications Group, Inc. & Tankeo Inc., Chicago, 1994
LOZES Patrick, *Nous, les Noirs de France*, Editions Danger Public, Paris, 2007
LUSHENA Books Publisher, *The Willie Lynch Letter and The Making of a Slave*, Bensenville, Illinois, 1999
MARIE Claude-Valentin, *Travail Illégal et Immigration Irrégulière dans les Départements d'Outre-mer, Le cas : Saint-Martin*, Rapport de Mission, Mission Saint-Martin/Guyane, Octobre 1991
MAURIN Eric, *Le ghetto français, Enquête sur le séparatisme social*, Editions du Seuil et La République des Idées, Paris, 2004
MEMMI Albert, *Portrait du colonisé, Portrait du colonisateur*, Gallimard, Collection Folio/Actuel, Paris, 1985
Mission Saint-Martin/Guyane, *En Guyane et à Saint-Martin, Des Etrangers sans droits dans une France bananière*, Rapport de mission du 2 au 12 décembre 1995, Mars 1996
MORROW Alvin, *Breaking the curse of Willie Lynch : The Science of Slave Psychology, A Psychic Examination of Slavery's Haunting Effects on the Conscience of Black Men and Women*, Rising Sun Publications, St. Louis, Missouri, 2004
N'DIAYE Tidiane, *Le génocide voilé, Enquête historique*, Editions Gallimard, Collection Continents Noirs, Paris, 2008
OTHILY George, *J'assume tout!* Ibis Rouge Editions, Matoury, 2005
PERINA Michaëlla L., *Construire une identité politique à partir des vestiges de l'esclavage ? Les départements français d'Amérique entre héritage et choix*, dans *L'Esclavage, la colonisation et après …*, Presses Universitaires de France, Paris, 2005, pp. 509-531
RASPAIL Jean, 1. La Patrie Trahie par la République 2. HOFFMAN Michael, Réponse à Jean Raspail, Le Figaro Magazine n° 18619, Débats et Opinions, 17 juin 2004
RIBBE Claude, *Les Nègres de la République*, Editions Alphée, Collection Edit plus, Paris, 2007

SCHNAPPER Dominique, *Qu'est-ce que l'intégration* ?, Editions Gallimard, Collection Folio/Actuel, Paris, 2007

SENERS François, *Saint-Martin, Saint-Barthélemy : Quel avenir pour les iles du nord de la Guadeloupe ?* Rapport à Monsieur le Secrétaire d'Etat à l'Outre-mer, Décembre 1999

VALERIUS Robert, *La Guadeloupe d'en-France*, Editions Jasor, Pointe-à-Pitre, 2005

VERGES Françoise, *Abolir l'esclavage : une utopie coloniale, Les ambiguïtés de la politique humanitaire*, Bibliothèque Albin Michel, Idées, Paris, 2001

- *La Mémoire Enchaînée, Questions sur l'Esclavage*, Editions Albin Michel, Paris, 2006

VERSCHAVE François-Xavier, *Noir Silence, Qui arrêtera la Françafrique ?* Edition des Arènes, Paris, 2000

WILLIAMS Juan, *Enough, The Phony Leaders, Dead-End Movements, and Culture of Failure that are Undermining Black America – And What We Can Do About It*, Crown Publishers, New York, 2006

L'HARMATTAN, ITALIA
Via Degli Artisti 15; 10124 Torino

L'HARMATTAN HONGRIE
Könyvesbolt ; Kossuth L. u. 14-16
1053 Budapest

L'HARMATTAN BURKINA FASO
Rue 15.167 Route du Pô Patte d'oie
12 BP 226 Ouagadougou 12
(00226) 76 59 79 86

ESPACE L'HARMATTAN KINSHASA
Faculté des Sciences sociales,
politiques et administratives
BP243, KIN XI ; Université de Kinshasa

L'HARMATTAN GUINEE
Almamya Rue KA 028, en face du restaurant Le Cèdre
OKB agency BP 3470 Conakry
(00224) 60 20 85 08
harmattanguinee@yahoo.fr

L'HARMATTAN CÔTE D'IVOIRE
M. Etien N'dah Ahmon
Résidence Karl / cité des arts
Abidjan-Cocody 03 BP 1588 Abidjan 03
(00225) 05 77 87 31

L'HARMATTAN MAURITANIE
Espace El Kettab du livre francophone
N° 472 avenue du Palais des Congrès
BP 316 Nouakchott
(00222) 63 25 980

L'HARMATTAN CAMEROUN
BP 11486
Face à la SNI, immeuble Don Bosco
Yaoundé
(00237) 99 76 61 66
harmattancam@yahoo.fr

L'HARMATTAN SENEGAL
« Villa Rose », rue de Diourbel X G, Point E
BP 45034 Dakar FANN
(00221) 33 825 98 58 / 77 242 25 08
senharmattan@gmail.com

595166 - Janvier 2015
Achevé d'imprimer par